AF664456

# Education for Human Resource Development

# Education for Human Resource Development

*Edited by*

Vijaya Deshmukh

**ATLANTIC**

PUBLISHERS & DISTRIBUTORS (P) LTD

Published by
**ATLANTIC**
**PUBLISHERS & DISTRIBUTORS (P) LTD**
7/22, Ansari Road, Darya Ganj,
New Delhi-110002
Phones : +91-11-40775252, 23273880, 23275880, 23280451
Fax : +91-11-23285873
Web : www.atlanticbooks.com
E-mail : orders@atlanticbooks.com

Branch Office
5, Nallathambi Street, Wallajah Road,
Chennai-600002
Phones : +91-44-64611085, 32413319
E-mail : chennai@atlanticbooks.com

Copyright © 2012 Vijaya Deshmukh for selection and editorial matter; the contributors for individual chapters.

ISBN 978-81-269-1676-4

All rights reserved. No part of this publication may be reproduced, stored in a retrieval system, transmitted or utilized in any form or by any means, electronic, mechanical, photocopying, recording or otherwise, without the prior permission of the copyright owner. Application for such permission should be addressed to the publisher.

Printed in India at Nice Printing Press, A-33/3A, Site-IV, Industrial Area, Sahibabad, Ghaziabad, U.P.

# Preface

The education sector is generating a lot of interest. Foreign players and private equity funds are aggressively looking at education sector for investment opportunities. The driving force behind the 21st century economy is said to be education. The priority of policymakers today too is education and the concern about the employability and skills of the workforce. Long-term interests of the industry hinge on the quality of talent produced in the country. Industry must sponsor students and fund research in universities to increase their visibility. Education should not be de-linked from the needs of the industry. The concepts of creativity, collaboration, complex process of inquiry, critical thinking and communication need to be inculcated in the learning system. Investment in education and development of the human capital will ensure prosperity. Education should aim to produce responsible citizens embedded with humanism. The focus is on education for profitability, enrichment and generation of wealth, and rarely on humanism, imagination and critical faculties, which are crucial to the welfare of humankind. The concept of a link between education and an inclusive citizenship has a special urgency in today's time

A balance between liberal and instrumental education is necessary for a holistic social outcome. The basic purpose of education is to generate livelihood. Skills and knowledge relevant to employment must be central to the curriculum. The ability to think critically, the perspectives about society and scientific understanding of nature, are necessary and cannot be a luxury. Liberal education aims to foster and enable important abilities—the abilities to think analytically and critically, to synthesize, to reflect, to have curiosity to learn, etc. If we want to build a diverse society with deep commitment, we need to continuously discover and invent newer models of education that are adequately pragmatic.

### Inclusiveness and Equality

The government policies should lay emphasis on inclusive and equitable higher education. This will call for conscious efforts to ensure that the achievement in higher education does not suffer from disparities across regions, gender, social groups such as Scheduled Castes, Scheduled Tribes, Other Backward Classes, minorities, physically challenged and the economically deprived. The 11th Plan strategy for inclusion recognized three imbalances, namely inter-regional, inter-social and gender. The Plan proposed some measures to reduce these imbalances. It proposed support to universities and colleges located in districts having lower gross enrolment ratio (GER), opening of new colleges, with matching contribution from the states in 350 districts with lower enrolment.

Rural-based universities can play a critical role in raising the literacy rate and building social capital, which increases prospects of employability and self-employment, leading to high productivity and a higher GDP, higher standards of living and an improved quality of life and social well being. The rural university should function like a catalyst to bring about needed changes in rural India and should be re-organized to meet the requirement of the community. It needs a humane governance, organization of economic systems and a vigorous interface with the community for decisions, strategies and policies regarding education and allocation of resources.

Indian society consists of different religious groups, racial groups, cultural groups, linguistic groups, etc. All communities have their own way of life, occupation, moral, social and cultural system. All racial and cultural groups have their own pattern of lifestyle and behaviour. Protection of these unique cultures and patterns of life have become an important aspect of education. Education should protect, preserve and promote these unique cultures by introducing/implementing different plans and programmes and strategies. Education should have relevance to the social milieu, which changes over time.

## Human Resource Development (HRD)

Development of a nation is directly related to the development of human resources, and for adequate development of these resources, quality education is needed. HRD is the process of increasing the capacity of human resource through development. Skills and knowledge, technology and research and inquiry are required for advancement. Exploring into the unknown or unfamiliar comes naturally to all living beings. Creativity, innovation, capacity to know and use of latest technologies for aiding their learning process and to enhance their learning ability are necessary. The aptitude for entrepreneurship and taking calculated risk should be cultivated right from the beginning in the university environment. Leadership qualities in the students are also necessary so that they are able to guide others in future. Lifelong learning is necessary for wholesome and continuous development.

Economic progress and national development are directly related to knowledge growth since knowledge is power. Universities have to play a vital role in knowledge generation, information processing and knowledge management, which also require different types of expertise. Innovative approach essentially involves development of ideas and concepts, experimentation, interpreting the results and decisions. Tenacity, willingness to take risk, integrity, initiative, empathy and so on, are all shaped in a complex manner through life.

Skill enhancement is receiving a lot of attention. The Government has done well to launch a skill development programme that requires various departments, industry bodies, educational institutions and others to work together. The Prime Minister has recently appointed an advisor on skill development from the corporate world. The Finance Minister in his Budget speech of 2008-09 announced the formation of the National Skill Development Corporation, mandated to provide skills training to 50 crore people by the year 2022.

As the country continues to expand its share of youth population with an expected average age of 29 years by the year 2020, it becomes imperative that we create a conducive environment with productive jobs for the youth. Now, with the appointment of a person from the corporate world to oversee skills development, there is a great hope and enthusiasm in achieving this target. It is hoped that this will overcome the daunting unemployability challenge and provide productive jobs to millions of young people in the coming years.

### Technology in Learning Environments

Technology is another buzzword for the education sector. Digital content providers create content database using a wide range of topics to assist teachers or tailor-make lesson plans. Besides active teaching, additional skills such as personality development and value-based teaching are also being packaged. Use of e-readers and laptops by students has become more common as the educational institutions are becoming more computerised and automated with Enterprise Resource Planning (ERP) systems.

Knowledge-driven organizations are greatly affected by the rapid advances in Information and Communications Technology (ICT). Modern digital technologies such as computers, telecommunication, systems and networks are reshaping both our society and our social institutions. These technologies have vastly increased our capacity to know and to do things and to communicate and collaborate with others. Information Technology (IT) has the capacity to enhance and enrich teaching and scholarship; it also poses certain threats to our colleges and universities. We use powerful computers and networks to deliver educational services to anyone, at any place and any time, no longer being confined to the campus or the academic schedule. Technology is creating an open learning environment in which the student has evolved into an active learner and consumer of educational services, stimulating the growth of powerful market forces that could dramatically reshape the higher education enterprise.

The Open and Distance Learning (ODL) system has a history of about five decades in India and is the largest consumer of ICTs for delivery of content to a variety of learners. From correspondence courses to web-supported learning, all these modes are likely to remain in place for years to come. These modes aim at making out-of-classroom study more accessible to those learners who wish to pursue education/higher study for their professional growth as well as lifelong learning. In India, where a major section of the population belongs to the middle-level income groups and cannot afford high fees of regular colleges, various institutions are engaged in offering a variety of courses through the ODL system to cater to their needs.

The technological revolution of the country is being led by the young population and India can draw great economic leverage by developing this young human resource with the right kind of education and skills. The increased investment in creating technological infrastructure reflects the commitment of the country in exploiting the potential of ICTs for development.

Mobile learning (M-learning) aims at making the learning process more flexible, accessorised and personalised. M-learning is the acquisition of any knowledge and skill using mobile technology, anywhere, any time, that results in an alternation of behaviour. It can be defined as "learning that happens across locations or that takes advantage of learning opportunities offered by portable technologies." The term covers mobility of the learner, interacting with portable and fixed technology, learning in a mobile society, etc. M-learning improves access to information, so that people can update their knowledge continuously to satisfy the demands. The main technical challenges to the mobile learning are connectivity, battery life, interacting with small devices, displaying useful content on small screen devices, continuing expansion of broadband wireless networks, low resolution of displays, diversity of operating system, etc. The other challenges are to develop an appropriate theory of learning for the mobile age, design of technology to support a lifetime learning, tracking of results and proper use of this information, how to assess learning outside the classroom and how to support learning across many contexts.

The rapid evolution of digital technology will present many challenges and opportunities to higher education in general and research in particular, yet there is a sense that many of the most significant issues are neither well recognized nor understood by the Heads of our universities. Creative and visionary leaders can tap the energy created by threats such as the emerging for-profit marketplace and technology to engage their campuses, and to lead their institutions in new directions that will reinforce and enhance their most important roles and values.

## Blended Learning

Blended learning as a concept is on a sharp increase. It gets its name from constructing and blending learning with the active use of technology in different learning environments. Blended learning uses the interface of computer, cellular technology like smart phones, satellite televisions and video conferencing for enhancing learning.

Blended learning is learning that is facilitated by the effective combination of different modes of delivery, models of teaching and styles of learning, and founded on transparent communications amongst all parties involved with a course (Heinze, A. and Procter, C. (2004)). This is the process of incorporating many different learning styles that can be accomplished through the use of 'blended' virtual and physical resources. A combination of technology-based materials and face-to-face sessions are used together to present content. This method is a balanced blend of use of web-based technology and traditional methods in education.

## Conclusion

Merely sending children to schools will not do. Their ability to learn and be a part of the creative workforce later will depend on the development of cognitive skills, for which trained and quality teachers are required. The problem can be overcome only by bringing drastic reforms in governance and meeting performance challenges in government schools such as teacher attendance, learning outcomes, performance orientation, student employability, etc.

There is considerable discussion and debate on autonomy of educational institutions. But very little attention has been paid to governance in these institutions. Experts have called for sweeping changes in the higher education system and advocated shift towards adoption of a choice-based credit course along with semester system, promoting students' mobility within and outside the system, subjecting all faculty members to a review once every five years. A systematic system of assessment, accreditation and recognition for the institutions of higher education and the degrees awarded is necessary to avoid confusion among students and to provide seamless mobility of the graduates of Indian universities to international educational institutions.

The Prime Minister's advisory committee has favoured a specialist group of teachers to conduct examinations and evaluate students instead of the current practice of involving all teachers in setting question papers and checking answer sheets. Various measures for education reforms have been suggested by the advisory group to have a relook at the present examination system including the system of final examinations, entrance examinations, qualifying examinations, and selection examinations. The examination should not be a cause for harassment. All these are happy developments towards a hopeful bright future for education.

We have brought together a range of articles on higher education by grouping them into relevant contexts. We are thankful to all the authors for contributing their scholarly articles. It is only due to their efforts that the book could be prepared for the benefit of students and teachers of education in general and education in human resource development in particular as well as for those concerned with education in India.

**Vijaya Deshmukh**

# Contents

## The Technology Effects



## Total Quality Education

**Perspectives Across Disciplines**

# Education Policy and Governance

# 1

# Challenges in the Implementation of Right to Education Act, 2009

*Saroj Sobti Farwaha* and *Vandana Malik*

When a need gets articulated into the shape of a Bill, it emphasizes the immediacy and urgency of the need and compels commitment. The Right to Education Bill to ensure education to the young citizens of India falls in this category.

The demand for education is a felt need. How can education reach the last student? How can it be relevant to life? How can quality education be assured? Within these questions are contained issues of universal coverage, enrollment, retention, completion, future growth, costs, skill education and training. They are also pointers to future issues that may arise with better Primary Education.

Faced with the global challenges the need of the hour is to strengthen our education system to make it competitive. It is noteworthy that India after independence had undertaken commendable steps towards providing 'Education for All'. To large extent, we have been able to bring children to school, increase enrolment rates and to reduce dropouts.

For a democracy to be meaningful, it is necessary that people in India are able to read and write. Proper education is the basic pre condition for a democratic society. We have to change the mindset of the large cross-section of the decision-making population and initiate change, bring revolution in education and make India a knowledge economy.

In this background, Right to Education Act was passed in both the Houses of our Parliament on 4 August 2009. In this Act, elementary education in India aims to imbibe in all children, the qualities essential of the vibrant and dynamic democracy, including value of tolerance, morality and compassion as well as the basic abilities of reading, writing, comprehension and reasoning. The salient features of the Right to Education Act are as follows:

- Free and compulsory education to all children of India in the 6-14 age group.
- No child shall be held back, expelled, or required to pass a board examination until completion of elementary education.
- A child who completes elementary education (upto class VIII shall be awarded a certificate).
- Calls for a fixed student-teacher ratio.
- Will apply to all over India except Jammu and Kashmir.
- Provides for 25 per cent reservation for economically disadvantaged communities in addition to class I in all private schools.
- Mandates improvement in quality of education.
- School teacher will need adequate professional degree within five years or else will loose job.
- School infrastructure (where there is a problem) to be improved in three years else recognition cancelled.
- Financial burden will be shared between State and Central Government.

No doubt, many efforts have been continuously made by the government to achieve the goal for Right to Education for every child, but there are a lot of hurdles in the way of this noble target.

### Increasing Population

Right to Education has brought many challenges, which we will have to face and the greatest challenge is posed by the fast growing population and the other, of the comparatively slower growing economy, sandwitched between the twisted wrap of a large section of people who were left out by economic progress. In spite of the fact that there has been a continuous upsurge in the number of schools established at the primary level, thus increasing physical access to schools, large masses of population have remained outside the orbit of the benefits from the public education system in India.

### Illiteracy of Parents

Large number of population is still illiterate and is not aware of the importance of education for the upliftment of human life. They are reluctant to send their wards even to the neighbourhood school. Therefore, a large number of our population is missing the opportunity of right to education. Though the bill prohibits any person from preventing the child from going to school, it has ignored the reality of the majority of poor children who are employed in agricultural sector and who bear the burden of housework and siblings care. The bill needs to categorically state that all the forms of employment and engagement, which hinder the development of child, should be banned and made cognisible offence.

### Lack of Awareness

No doubt, our government has passed the bill quite enthusiastically, but most of the teachers, teacher educators, social activists and the common men are not aware of the salient features of this act. How they can be helpful in implementation and achievement of targets set in the Bill remains to be seen.

But to bring sustainable change in the education sector, the pressure has to be laid on creating awareness among the general masses and the intensive attitudinal transformation. Additionally, rational utilization of allotted resources and striving towards the goals with genuine commitment can only bring success to educational programmes.

### Educational Deprivation

Educational deprivation has two dimensions:

- lack of schools and poor infrastructure
- poor quality of teaching.

The latter is the combined effect of lack of school supplies, insufficient incentives for teachers and weak links between the school systems and society. There has been a greater policy emphasis on the provision of more schools (quantity) than on activities that actually take place inside classrooms (quality).

At the elementary level, universal access to quality, infrastructure and effectiveness of teaching are serious challenges!!!!

Poor quality of education can be attributed to a variety of factors including poor curriculum and syllabus, deficient pedagogy, negligent teachers and parents who are unconcerned. But the real reason is the gross under funding of school education in India. If the required magnitude of funding is available, many of the factors allegedly accountable for the poor quality of school education would disappear.

The most important means of ensuring quality is to establish minimum norms and standards relating to all relevant aspects of school education and ensure that they are applied uniformally to all schools. No doubt, some norms have been laid down in the schedule attached to the right to free and compulsory education act. But they are utterly inadequate.

### Lack of Resources

Teaching children anywhere requires not just passion for making sure that every child gets educated, but a certain level of acceptance in terms of equipping a student to read, write and speak with proficiency.

For this, we need a system that is graded in terms of teaching techniques and goals set. Therefore, there is urgent need of science lab, language labs, computer labs, libraries, teaching learning materials, teaching aids are badly needed. Some funding and aid assistance is provided at present, but it is not adequate.

### Lack of Financial Assistance

To create new infrastructure, new school buildings, laboratories—a huge amount will be required. To make any real impact on lives of children, the country needs to spend at least 10 per cent of GDP on school education and health.

Instead of investing in public resources, we as a country are opening up a core sector to private players—a move that goes against both the short- and the long-term interests of children.

### Children with Disabilities

In the right to education, all the children are supposed to be admitted in nearby schools. But there is no provision for children with disabilities in every school. Special facilities and specially trained teachers are required. Regular school teachers are not sufficiently aware of the concept of disability and education of these children. Therefore, the disabled children will be deprived of this opportunity.

### Physical Infrastructure

To fulfill the targets of the right to education Bill, a number of school buildings infrastructure, materials, classrooms, blackboards, laboratories, libraries and furniture is required.

No doubt, under DPEP, Operation Blackboard and Sarvashiksha Abhiyan, many plans to improve infrastructure were implemented but still there is huge drive needed for its implementation.

As reported by the Common School System Commission, Bihar, in order to universalize free and compulsory education for children, 25,000 additional primary schools, 15,500 middle schools and 19,100 secondary schools are required. The teacher requirement at the primary level was 2.55 lacs, 3.4 lacs at middle level and 4.29 lacs at secondary level.

Therefore, if we want to overcome these challenges then it would be necessary to transform the entire education system and the following suggestions can be helpful:

1. Quality of the foundations of all educational systems will remain weak until quality pre primary education is provided to children in the age group of 0-6. Therefore, the state shall endeavour to provide early childhood care and education for all children until they complete the age of six years. Teaching faculty should be strengthened with professional training and skills enhancement.

2. All the children, including child labour, should be motivated to learn.
3. Only qualified persons should be appointed for teaching in every part of the country. Hence, those who are practicing teaching without proper qualification will be sacked if they do not complete it in a stipulated time.
4. For equitable education, proper infrastructure should be provided to remove economical, social, cultural, linguistic, locational and disability related barriers.
5. Weak students must be part of a remedial syllabus that gets incorporated into the daily routine, without missing out the regular routine.
6. Children with disabilities should be provided extra facilities in neighbourhood schools and specially trained teachers should be recruited in every school to provide the right to education for all.
7. A performance based evaluation of teachers should be done and efficient and innovative teachers should be reawarded.
8. Teacher training should be school based and knowledge of the subject should be in greater detail. Regular training programmes and value-oriented workshops and training are absolutely essential.
9. Technology and teaching aids should be provided for different laboratories, libraries and workshops.
10. Additional schools as required should be established and made functional.
11. Adequate facilities for training of teachers and other personnel to meet the human resource requirement for the implementation of this act should be created.
12. Provision of financial assistance to local authorities for implementation of this act in accordance with such formula regarding sharing of costs of such implementation as the appropriate government may determine from time to time.

13. Perception and periodic revision by the competent academic authority of the curriculum for elementary education and courses of study for each grade should be followed.
14. To provide sufficient financial assistance to educational institutions, 10 per cent of development funds should be spent on the school education and health of the children.
15. For equitable quality education minimum infrastructure, administrative faculties, financial, curricular, pedagogic, linguistic and socio-cultural norms should be fulfilled.
16. Special assistance such as ramps, Braille readers, etc. for learning of disabled students should be provided in schools.
17. Parents should be educated about the need of education in present era and material should be provided to create awareness among rural masses.
18. Women are the basis of family education therefore, women or mothers should be educated through adult education.

## Conclusion

If India has to grow into a developed nation, it must put its 'House in order' in the form of high class education in primary, secondary, vocational and higher education.

'Right to Education is every Child Right'

Your support can make it happen!!

Every child is a dream- Hoping to be realized

Indian education is so uneven. Big picture and small picture to be tackled together.

In the end we can say that the problems are solvable and the ways of doing are scalable.

## REFERENCES

Agarwal, Yash (2000), *Public and Private Partnership in Primary Education in India: A Study of Unrecognized Schools in Haryana*, National Institute of Educational Planning and Administration, New Delhi.

Indicus Analytics (2005), *Private Primary Schooling in India*, draft report submitted to the University of New Castle by Indicus Analytics, Delhi.

NCERT (1993), *Sixth All India School Education Survey (1993)*, National Council of Educational Research and Training, Delhi.

# 2

# Prospects and Global Challenges of Higher Education in India

*Misri Lal Verma* and *Pratima Katiyar (Verma)*

The traditional roles of the university revolve around the core of teaching and scholarship: we educate the young, seek truth and create knowledge, propagate our culture and values from one generation to the next, sustain the academic disciplines and professions, and constructively criticize our societies. At the core, our activities are characterized by critical thinking, analysis, moral reasoning and judgment. But today, much more is asked of our universities. Around their peripheries, our universities are heavily involved in utilitarian roles such as technology transfer, healthcare, entertainment, national defense, and economic and international development.

The changing nature of higher education increasingly dependent upon knowledge and ever more inter-dependent. This paper is to focus challenges and future prospects of higher education in India in view of global economy, Clearly, we live in a time of very rapid and profound social transformation, a transition from a century in which the dominant human activity was transportation to one in which communications have become paramount, from economies based upon cars, planes, and trains to one dependent upon computers and networks. We are shifting from an emphasis on creating and transporting physical objects such as materials and energy to knowledge itself, from atoms to bits; from societies based upon the geopolitics of the nation-state to those based on diverse cultures and local traditions; and from a dependence on government policy to an increasing confidence in the marketplace to establish public priorities.

Today, we are evolving rapidly into a post-industrial, knowledge-based society, a shift in culture and technology as profound as the shift that took place a century ago when our agrarian societies evolved into industrial nations (Drucker, 1994). Industrial production is steadily shifting from material- and labor-intensive products and processes to knowledge-intensive products. A radically new system for creating wealth has evolved that depends upon the creation and application of new knowledge. In a very real sense, we are entering a new age; an age of knowledge, in which the key strategic resource necessary for prosperity has become knowledge itself—educated people and their ideas (Bloch, 1988). Unlike natural resources such as iron and oil, that have driven earlier economic transformations, knowledge is inexhaustible. The more it is used, the more it multiplies and expands, as knowledge can be created, absorbed, and applied only by the educated minds. Schools, in general, and universities in particular, will play increasingly important roles as our societies enter this new age. In a sense, knowledge is the medium of the university. Through the activities of discovery, shaping, achieving, transmitting, and applying knowledge, the university serves society in a myriad ways: educating the young, preserving our cultural heritage, providing the basic research so essential to our security and well-being, training our professionals and certifying their competence, challenging our society and stimulating social change. But the age of knowledge will substantially broaden the roles of higher education. Erich Bloch, former Director of the U.S. National Science Foundation, stated it well when he noted, "The solution of virtually all the problems with which government is concerned: health, education, environment, energy, urban development, international relationships, economic competitiveness, and defense and national security, all depend on creating new knowledge—and hence upon the health of our universities" (Bloch, 1988). Global economy to the university having the challenging factors for 'skills race', 'markets', 'technology', and 'global sustainability'.

**The Skills Race**

Ask any public leader today about priorities, and you are certain to hear concerns about education and the skills of the workforce. United States Governors' Association remark is notable that: "The driving force behind the 21st Century economy is knowledge, and developing human capital is the best way to ensure prosperity". Today, a college degree has become a necessity for most careers, and graduate education becomes desirable for an increasing number in India, a growing population will necessitate some growth in higher education to accommodate the projected increases in the number of traditional college age students (estimated at 14 per cent over the next decade). But even more growth and adaptation will be needed to respond to the educational needs of adults as they seek to adapt to the needs of the high performance workplace. Some estimate this adult need for lifelong learning at the university level will become far larger than that represented by traditional 18- to 22-year old students (Dolence and Norris, 1997). Our universities are facing more fundamental educational challenges than simply growth in the demand for higher education. Young, digital-media savvy students and adult learners will likely demand a major shift in educational methods, away from passive classroom lecture courses packaged into well-defined degree programs, and toward interactive, collaborative learning experiences, provided when and where the student needs the knowledge and skills. The increased blurring of the various stages of learning throughout one's lifetime—K-12, undergraduate, graduate, professional, job training, career shifting, lifelong enrichment—will require a far greater coordination and perhaps even a merger of various elements of our educational infrastructure.

There is an increasing tendency in the society to view the university as an engine for economic growth through the generation and application of new knowledge. There has been a shift in emphasis within the university away from simply distributing and analyzing knowledge, i.e. "teaching" and "scholarship" to creating and applying knowledge, to activities such as "innovation", "creativity" and "entrepreneurship". The growing and changing nature of the needs for higher education has triggered strong economic forces. Our societies ask us to do ever more, but they are not always increasingly generous in their support of these activities. In many nations, there is a declining priority for public support in the face of other social priorities such as the health care needed by an aging population in our country, traditional sources of public support for higher education such as state appropriations or federal support for student financial aid, have simply not kept pace with the growing demand. This imbalance between demand and available resources is aggravated by the increasing costs of higher education, driven as they are by the knowledge- and people-intensive nature of the enterprise as well as by the difficulty educational institutions have in containing costs and increasing productivity. In other words, the current paradigms for conducting, distributing, and financing higher education may not be able to adapt to the demands and realities of the times.

## Markets

Market forces also act on our colleges and universities. Even though we generally think of higher education as public enterprise, shaped by public policy and actions to serve a civic purpose, society seeks services such as education and research; academic institutions must compete for students, faculty, and resources. In the past, most colleges and universities served local or regional populations. While there was competition among institutions for students, faculty, and resources extent to which institutions controlled the awarding of degrees (credentialing), gave universities an effective monopoly over advanced education. Today, all of these market constraints are being challenged. The growth in the size and complexity of the post-secondary enterprise is creating an expanding array of students and educational providers. Rapidly evolving information and communication technologies are eroding relaxed geographical constraints. New competitive forces such as virtual universities and for-profit education providers enter the marketplace to challenge credentialing. The weakening influence of traditional regulations and the emergence of new competitive forces, driven by changing societal needs, economic realities, and technology, are likely to drive a massive restructuring of the higher education enterprise. From our experience with other restructured sectors of the economy such as health care, transportation, communication, and energy, we could expect to see a significant reorganization of higher education, complete with the mergers, acquisitions, new competitors, and new products and services that have characterized other economic transformations. More generally, we may well be seeing the early stages of the appearance of a global knowledge and learning industry, in which the activities of traditional academic institutions converge with other knowledge-intensive organizations such as telecommunications, entertainment, and information service companies (Peterson and Dill, 1997). It is important to remember that most of our institutions were the result of public policy and public investment through actions of governments at the national and regional level (Zemsky, 1997; Zemsky and Wegner, 1998). These policies, programs, and commitments were driven by strong social values and a sense of national and regional priorities. Yet today, in our country and many other nations, public leaders are increasingly discarding public policy in favour of market forces to determine priorities for social investment. Public higher education can no longer assume that public policies and investment will shield them from market competition. The market forces driven by increasing demand for higher education and unleashed by technology are very powerful. If allowed to dominate and reshape the higher education enterprise, we could well find ourselves facing a brave, new world in which some of the most important values and traditions of the university fall by the wayside. As we assess these market-driven emerging learning structures, we must bear in mind the importance of preserving the ability of the university to serve a broader public purpose.

### Technology

As knowledge-driven organizations, colleges and universities are greatly affected by the rapid advances in information and communications technology. Modern digital technologies such as computers, telecommunications, and networks are reshaping both our society and our social institutions. These technologies have vastly increased our capacity to know and to do things and to communicate and collaborate with others. They allow us to transmit information quickly, linking distant places and diverse areas of endeavour in productive new ways. They allow us to form and sustain communities for work, play, and learning in ways unimaginable just a decade ago. While information technology has the capacity to enhance and enrich teaching and scholarship, it also poses certain threats to our colleges and universities. We use powerful computers and networks to deliver educational services to anyone, at any place and any time, no longer confined to the campus or the academic schedule. Technology is creating an open learning environment in which the student has evolved into an active learner and consumer of educational services, stimulating the growth of powerful market forces that could dramatically reshape the higher education enterprise.

We the social scientist professionals in Kanpur have launched a project for better understanding and implications of information technology for the future of the research universities (www.professorguru.com). The rapid evolution of digital technology will present many challenges and opportunities to higher education in general and the research university in particular, yet there is a sense that many of the most significant issues are neither well recognized nor understood either by leaders of our universities or those who support and depend upon their activities. Three primary conclusions during the early phase of this study are as follows:

(i) The extraordinary evolutionary pace of information technology will not only continue for the foreseeable future, but could well accelerate on a super exponential slope. Digital technology is characterized by an exponential pace of evolution in which characteristics such as computing speed, memory, and network transmission speeds for a given price increase by a factor of 100 to 1000 every decade. For planning purposes, one can assume that by the end of the decade we will have available infinite bandwidth and infinite processing power (at least compared to current capabilities). The number of people linked together by digital technology will grow from millions to billions. We will evolve from "e-commerce", "e-government" and "e-learning" to "e-everything", since digital devices will increasingly become our primary interfaces not only with our environment but with other people, groups, and social institutions.

(ii) The impact of information technology on the university is likely be profound, rapid, and discontinuous—just as it has been and will continue to be for the economy, our society, and our social institutions (e.g. corporations, governments, and learning institutions). This is a disruptive technology (Christensen, 1997) that will affect all of the activities of the university (teaching, research, outreach), its organization (academic structure, faculty culture, financing and management), and the broader higher education enterprise. However, at least for the near term—meaning a decade or less—we believe the university will continue to exist in much its present form, although meeting the challenge of emerging competitors in the marketplace will demand significant changes in how we teach, how we conduct scholarship, and how our institutions are financed. Universities must anticipate these forces, develop appropriate strategies, and make adequate investments if they are to prosper during this period.

(iii) Universities should begin the development of their strategies for technology-driven change with a firm understanding of those key values, missions, and roles that should be protected and preserved during a time of transformation. Procrastination and inaction are the most dangerous courses for universities during a time of rapid technological change.

## Global Sustainability

Global sustainability seems a particularly appropriate topic in the wake of the India on Sustainable Development in Kanpur. As social scientists, we are convinced that there is compelling evidence that the growing population and invasive activities of humankind are now altering the fragile balance of our planet. The concerns are both multiplying in number and intensifying in severity: the destruction of forests, wetlands, and other natural habitats by human activities leading to the extinction of millions of biological species and the loss of biodiversity; the buildup of greenhouse gases such as carbon dioxide and their possible impact on global climates; the pollution of our air, water, and land. It could well be that coming to grips with the impact of our species on our planet, learning to live in a sustainable fashion on Spaceship Earth, will become the greatest challenge of all to our generation. We must find new ways to provide for a human society that presently has outstripped the limits of global sustainability. This will be particularly difficult for India, a nation that has difficulty in looking more than a generation ahead, encumbered by a political process that generally functions on an election-by-election basis, as the current debate over global change makes all too apparent. Ironically, the tragic events on everyday happening, create terror in between public might be viewed as a wake-up call, if we view these terrorist attacks not simply as a brief and brutal criminal attack but rather the consequence of more fundamental causes. India is rapidly changing with eyes of global competition, and we, along with everyone else, must do a better job. Sustainability science has a good deal to say about how we can logically approach the challenges that await us, but the social dimensions of our relationships are also of fundamental importance. Globalization appears to have become an irresistible force, but we must make it participatory and humane to alleviate the suffering of the world's poorest people and the effective disenfranchisement of many of its nations. As many have stated in the context of the current world situation, the best defense against terrorism is an educated people. Education, which promises to each individual the opportunity to express their individual talents fully, is fundamental to building a peaceful world. There are 30 million people in the world today who are fully qualified to enter a university but for whom no university place is available. Within a decade there will be 100 million university-ready people. Yet, as Sir John Daniels, former head of the British Open University notes, in most of the world, higher education is mired in a crisis of access, cost, and flexibility (Daniel, 1996). Billions of people in coming generations will be denied the education so necessary to compete in, and survive in, an age of knowledge. We must realize that the wealthy nations of the world have a particularly important role to play to assist developing nations in building the educational systems to meet their exploding needs. The university models characterizing most developed nations seem ill-suited to guide us out of this global education crisis. Our colleges and universities continue to be focused on high-cost, low-technology, residential education and on the outmoded idea that quality in education is linked to exclusivity of access and extravagance of resources. Our current concept of the campus-based university could well deny higher education to nearly all of the billions of young people who will require it in the decades ahead.

## Transforming the University to Serve a Global, Knowledge Society

These social, economic, technological, and market forces powerful than many within the higher education establishment realize. They are driving change at an unprecedented pace, perhaps even beyond the capacity of our colleges and universities to adapt. Our current paradigms for higher education, the nature of our academic programs, the organization of our colleges and universities, the way that we finance, conduct, and distribute the services of higher education, may not be able to adapt to the demands and realities of our times. So how might one approach the challenge of transforming the university to serve a 21st century world?

Typically, discussions of change in higher education begin with bread-and-butter issues such as the financing of higher education, technology transfer, or expanding the university's broad array of services to society. Some important factors are remarkable issues for the process of transformation in Indian institutions.

**Values**

It is important for any effort aimed at institutional transformation to always begin with the basics, to launch a careful reconsideration of the key roles and values of the university that should be protected and preserved during a period of change. For example, how would an institution prioritize among roles such as educating the young (undergraduate education), preserving and transmitting our culture (libraries, visual and performing arts), basic research and scholarship, and serving as a responsible critic of society? What are the most important values to protect? Clearly, academic freedom, openness to new ideas, a commitment to rigorous study, and an aspiration to the achievement of excellence would be on the list for most institutions. But what about values and practices such as shared governance and tenure? Should these be preserved? At what expense?

**Diversity**

Diversity will become an increasingly important theme in higher education, driven by the dramatic changes occurring in the populations served by our universities, and affecting all of the characteristics of our institutions: their academic programs, their broader roles in our society, and their aspirations for excellence. In many developed nations, demographic change is first thought of in terms of the aging of our populations. We are already feeling the consequences, as our national priorities increasingly focusing on the concerns of the elderly (e.g. health care) rather than the needs of the young (e.g. education). On a global basis, however, half of the world's population is under the age of twenty, with over two billion teenagers on planet Earth, most living in Asia, Africa, and Latin America. Their demand for education will be staggering. To sustain even current participation rates for higher education would require creating a major new university every week to serve this growing population of young people in parts of the world with severely limited resources and little experience in higher education (Daniel, 1996). An equally profound demographic phenomenon is the increasing diversity of many of our nations with respect to race, ethnicity, and nationality. Moreover, women have already become the predominant gender in many of our nations and are rapidly assuming leadership roles in both the public and private sectors. The full participation of currently underrepresented minorities and women is crucial to our commitment to equity and social justice, as well as to the future strength and prosperity of our societies. We cannot afford to waste the human talent, the cultural and social richness, represented by those currently underrepresented in our society, yet the challenge of increasing diversity is complicated by social and economic factors. As both a leader of society at large and a reflection of that society, the university has a unique responsibility to develop effective models of multicultural, pluralistic communities. We should strive to achieve new levels of understanding, tolerance, and mutual fulfillment for peoples of diverse racial and cultural backgrounds both on our campuses and beyond. Universities need to shift their attention from simply access to educational opportunity for underserved minority populations to success in achieving educational objectives. It has also become increasingly clear that they must do so within a political context that will require new policies and practices.

## Subsidiary and Autonomy

Although the governance of higher education varies greatly, shaped by traditions and culture, there are several general issues that need to be put on the table. Foremost among these are questions relating to whether our citizens and their governments view the university as a public good benefiting everyone, or instead view education as an individual benefit, benefiting the individuals, the students, that receive it. Do governments view universities as a public investment for the future, or simply expenditure such as spending money on roads or buildings? Is the university a government agency or is it a social institution? In all of our societies, government is under increasing pressure to demand accountability, but how they demand accountability, while perhaps appropriate for the Ministry of Transportation, may not work for universities. Although many of the policies and practices characterizing the governance of higher education in India are unique to our culture, one with broader relevance arises from the belief that universities must have the capacity to control their own destiny, particularly during times of change. It means not simply granting the faculty traditional perquisites such as academic freedom, but allowing universities more control over all aspects of their operations, including academic programs, budgets, student selection, and faculty hiring, etc.

## Alliances

The same market forces that drive our colleges and universities to focus on core competencies where they can be competitive also provide strong incentives to build alliances to address the broader, more diverse needs of society. Many of our research universities are under great pressure to expand enrollments to address the expanding populations of college age students or growing educational needs of adults, possibly at the expense of their research and service missions. It might be far more constructive for these institutions to form close alliances with regional colleges and universities to meet these growing demands for educational opportunity with research university faculty developing curriculum and pedagogy while other institutions provide the actual instruction. International alliances will become increasingly important, whether through student/faculty exchanges programs such as IT programs co-laboratories made possible by advances in information technology. More broadly, alliances should be explored not only among institutions of higher education but also between higher education and the private sector (information technology and telecommunication companies). Differentiation among institutions should be encouraged, relying upon market forces rather than regulations to discourage duplication.

**Experimentation**

Many of the forces driving change in higher education are disruptive in nature, leading to quite unpredictable futures. Planning in the face of such uncertainty requires a more experimental approach to university transformation. Change was occurring far more rapidly that we had anticipated. The future was becoming less certain as the range of possibilities expanded to include more radical options. We came to the conclusion that in a world of such rapid and profound change, as the future became less certain, the most effective near-term strategy was to explore possible futures of the university through experimentation and discovery. That is, rather than continue to contemplate possibilities for the future through abstract study and debate, it seemed a more productive course to build several prototypes of future learning institutions as working experiments. In this way, we could actively explore possible paths to the future. Several examples illustrate this approach: (i) During the 1990s, we explored the possible future of becoming a "privately supported but publicly chartered university". (ii) We played leadership roles first in the building and management of the Internet (with IBM and MCI as partners) and more recently Internet to explore the "cyberspace university" theme. Of course, not all of our experiments were successful. Some crashed in flames, in some cases spectacularly! Even in these cases, however, we learned something (if only our own ineffectiveness in dealing with cosmic forces such as college sports). All of these efforts were driven by the grassroots interests, abilities, and enthusiasm of faculty and students. While such an exploratory approach was disconcerting to some and frustrating to others, fortunately there were many who viewed this phase as an exciting adventure; all of these initiatives were important in understanding better the possible futures facing our university; all have influence on the evolution of our universities and colleges by national accreditation analysis council (NAAC). In regard to analysis for accreditation, self-financing colleges need to maintain the ethic of higher education in view of global perspectives.

**Turning Threats into Opportunities**

Importance of this issues and decisions concerning university transformation as opportunities rather than threats. The status quo is no longer an option, but once it is acceptable that change is inevitable, we can use it, as a strategic opportunity to control our destiny, while preserving the most important of our values and our traditions. Creative, visionary leaders can tap the energy created by threats such as the emerging for-profit marketplace and technology to engage their campuses and to lead their institutions in new directions that will reinforce and enhance their most important roles and values.

As sociologists and educators, some of the questions which come to our mind are: (i) How should we respond to the diverse educational and intellectual needs of a knowledge-driven, global economy, as human capital becomes more important than physical and financial capital? While the educational needs of the young will continue to be a priority, we will also be challenged to address the sophisticated learning needs of adults in the workplace while providing broader lifetime learning opportunities for all of our populations, (ii) Is higher education a public good, requiring public investment? (Or) Is it a private good, to be funded primarily by the commercial marketplace? The benefits of the university clearly flow to society as a whole, but it is also the case that our public leaders have instead stressed the benefits of education to the individual student. The issues of access and diversity have largely disappeared from the broader debate about the purpose of the university, (iii) How do we balance the roles of market forces and public purpose in determining the future of higher education? (iv) Can we control market forces through public policy and public investment so that the most valuable traditions and values of the university are preserved? Or will the competitive and commercial pressures of the marketplace sweep over our institutions, leaving behind a higher education enterprise characterized by mediocrity? (v) What should be the role of the research university within the broader context of the changes likely to occur in the higher education enterprise?

Should it be a leader in change? Or should it simply strive to protect the important traditions and values of the academy during this time of change? Finally, perhaps the most important question of all: (vi) Are we facing in the years ahead a period of evolution, of revolution, or of the possible extinction of the university as we know it today? These are some of the issues that should frame the debate about the future of the university in India in the 21st century. As social institutions, universities reflect the values, needs, and character of the society they serve. These issues of access and opportunity, equality and justice, private economic benefits and public purpose, freedom and accountability, are part of a broader public debate about the future of our societies and our world. They provide the context for any consideration of the future of the university in a knowledge-driven global economy.

**Conclusion**

In totality, our institutions are one of our civilization's most enduring legacies. Clearly, in an age of knowledge, higher education will flourish in the decades ahead. In a knowledge-intensive society, the need for advanced education and knowledge will become ever more pressing, both for individuals and for our societies more broadly. Yet it is also likely that the university today, or rather the current constellation of diverse institutions that comprise the higher education enterprise, will change in profound ways to serve a changing world. But, of course, this is just as the university has done so many times in the past. We have entered a period of significant change in higher education as our universities attempt to respond to the challenges, opportunities, and responsibilities before them, much of this change will be driven by market forces—by a limited resource base, changing societal needs, new technologies, and new competitors. But we also must remember that higher education has a public purpose and a public obligation (Zemsky and Wegner, 1998). It is possible to shape and form the markets that will in turn reshape our institutions with appropriate civic purpose. From this perspective, it is important to understand that the most critical challenge facing most institutions will be to develop the capacity for change. As noted earlier, universities must seek to remove the constraints that prevent them from responding to the needs of a rapidly changing society. They should strive to challenge, excite, and embolden all members of their academic communities to embark on what should be a great adventure for higher education. Only a concerted effort to understand the important traditions of the past, the challenges of the present, and the possibilities for the future can enable institutions to thrive during a time of such change.

## REFERENCES

Drucker, Peter F. (1993), *Post-Capitalist Society*. New York: Harper Collins.

Duderstadt, James J. (2000), *A University for the 21st Century*. Ann Arbor: University of Michigan Press.

Duderstadt, James J. and Wulf, William (ed.) (2002), *The Impact of Information Technology on the Future of the Research University*. Washington, DC: National Academy Press.

E. Osterbrock, Donald. And Raven, Peter H. (eds.) (1992), *Origins and Extinctions*. New Haven: Yale University Press.

Eric, Bloch (1988), *National Science Foundation, Testimony to Congress*.

F. Drucker, Peter (1994), "The Age of Social Transformation", *Atlantic Monthly*, 274(53-6), 53-80.

G. Dolence, Michael and M. Donald Norris (1997), *Transforming Higher Education: A Vision for Learning in the 21st Century*. Ann Arbor: Society for College and University Planning.

Kurzweil, Ray (1999), *The Age of Spiritual Machines: When Computers Exceed Human Intelligence*. New York: Viking.

Langenberg, D.N. (1994), "Taking Control of Change: Reinventing the Public University for the 21st Century" in Patel, Kumar (ed.), *Reinventing the Research University*. Los Angeles: University of California Press.

H. Raven, Peter (2002), "Science, Sustainability, and the Human Prospect, Science", 297, 954-58, in Shaw, Wilfred B. (ed.) *The University of Michigan, An Encyclopedic Survey*. Ann Arbor: University of Michigan Press.

National Governors Association (2001), *Policy Position H-R 44*, Postsecondary Education Policy.

M. Christensen, Clayton (1997), *The Innovator's Dilemma.* Cambridge: Harvard Business School Press.

Perelman, Lewis (1997), "Barnstorming with Lewis Perelman". *Edu Com Review,* 32:2, 18-36.

S. Daniel, John. (1996), *Mega-Universities and Knowledge Media.* London: Kogan Page.

Weber, Luc E. (2001), "Critical University Decisions and Their Appropriate Makers: Some Lessons from the Economic Theory of Federalism" in Hirsch, Werner Z. and Weber Luc E. (ed.), *Governance in Higher Education: The University in a State of Flux.* London: Economica, 79-93.

www.professorguru.com/org/net/us/

W. Peterson, Marvin and D. Dill, David (1997), "Understanding the Competitive Environment of the Postsecondary Knowledge Industry" in Marvin W. Peterson, David D. Dill, and Lisa A. Mets (eds.), *Planning and Management for a Changing Environment.* San Francisco: Jossey-Bass Publishers, 3-29.

Zemsky, Robert (1997), *Rumbling, Policy Perspectives, The Pew Higher Education Roundtable,* sponsored by the Pew Charitable Trusts Philadelphia: Institute for Research on Higher Education.

Zemsky, Robert and Wegner, Gregory (1998), *A Very Public Agenda, Policy Perspectives,* 8(2). Philadelphia: Knight Higher Education Collaborative.

# 3

# A Solution for 21st Century Higher Education: Re-engineering?

*A.P. Sudheer* and *G. Varaprasad*

India has been a major exporter of human resources of worldwide in the field of Engineering, Medical and Management area. This can be continued only through changing the old paradigm of students attending the classes to accumulate the required number of credits to obtain a degree to new paradigm in which students gain competencies through variety of learning experiences, design and research projects and off-campus internships including participation in international projects.

According to Peter Smith (1992), "External forces are dramatically changing the public aspirations and expectations from higher educational institutions. And the system's perceived inability to respond effectively is seriously eroding public confidence". Public expectations, parent's concerns, demographic changes in student's population, and cost of education all are reasons for major changes in educational process design in higher educational institutions. Now output of education system simply graduates who are not fit to do the job directly. That is, today the gap between education system and industry/business system is so wide that what one studies in the classroom hardly matches with the actual practice. As socio-economic and business environment keeps changing, the situation becomes more complex. So now is the time to revolutionize higher education. This can be achieved only through re-engineering.

Advancement of technology, cost of education, global competition and society's expectations are the four major factors in transformation of higher educational institution's operation to the re-engineered one. Wiliams F. Massay (1989) described that between 1975 and 1985, administration functions grew by 60 per cent while the number of faculty grew by six per cent. Now also growing rate is not much compared to administration. These have been less attention to the academic upgradation as compared to administrative operations. Re-engineering is fundamental rethinking and radical redesign of an entire higher education system. Re-engineering the higher education in educational institutions or universities is freedom of process design with input from everybody that will be affected by the processes. Re-engineering means not only a change, but dramatic change which includes (1) Re-engineering in Administrative and Support Operations and (2) Re-engineering in Academic Operations.

## Re-engineering in Administrative and Support Operations

Re-engineering in administration and support should happen before academic re-engineering. Figure 1 represents the change from a function-oriented (traditional) organization to a process oriented (re-engineering) organization.

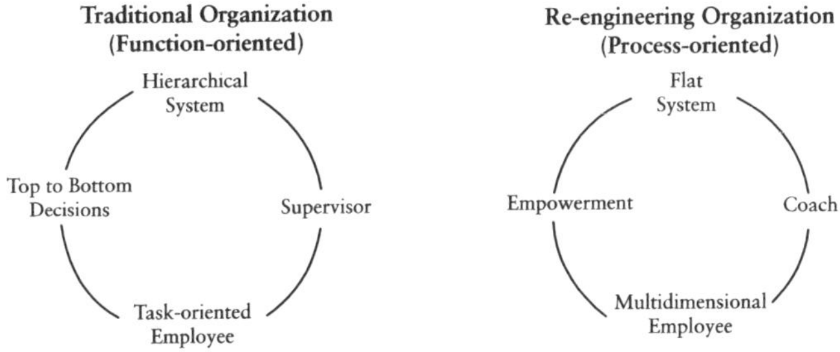


**Fig. 1:** Function- and Process-oriented Organization.

## Hierarchical to Flat Organization

The hierarchical system emphasized top-down and high control orientation, and employees are dependent on direction of leadership for survival, but in flat system the suggestion is from down-top with shared control orientation and there is encouragement for support of mission with freedom for independent action.

### Empowerment

Empowerment is the act of having authority, responsibility and accountability on the assignment. Today's process depends on the contribution from many different members. Leaders are no longer experts in everything related to the process and in most cases, a team member has greater skills and understanding in his or her individual positions than the leader. The main issue in the success of empowerment is the leader's eagerness to give up some power and responsibility to the team members.

### Task-oriented to Multidimensional Employee

In the traditional organization, team members are task-oriented (how to do the job). In the re-engineered organization, a team member has to have multidimensional talent and a basic knowledge about roles of other members in the team.

### Supervisor to Coach

In the traditional organization, supervisors like one way of decision-making and power practice. They believe in reactivity, which is a short-term solution, while a leader (coach) believes in proactively which is a power to choose with solutions based on the logic and principles.

### Re-engineering in Academic Operations

Now in India all engineering institutions, personal contact model of instruction have been dominant way of designing teaching and learning. In this model, the faculty's effectiveness and students' progress are measured by number of hours of lecture and availability of teachers to students. This has to be re-engineered by re-designing personal contact model to a digital-based model of teaching and learning in most of the subjects. This means not downsizing. In this new model, faculties have a new role as facilitators and directors, and students as researchers and participants. New model converts teacher-centered curriculum to teacher-student-centered or student-centered curriculum, it also changes process-oriented to outcome-oriented teaching and learning. In the new paradigm, computer technology has major role and contribution to the designing and implementation of the teacher-student-centered or student-centered models. Unfortunately, lack of attention to the human power (faculty) in the utilization of technology is the most important reason for failing most of the planning. Compared with all other resources, faculty is the only one that can direct and coordinate utilization of technology in the classroom. Figure 2 displays the process of re-engineering the higher education in institutions.

### Teaching and Learning

Today's teaching and learning is based on the educational computing technology. This educational computing refers not only to the hardware, instructional systems, and management systems, but also includes the software that embrace the curriculum and the intelligence and ideologies that guide the use of computers in educational environments.

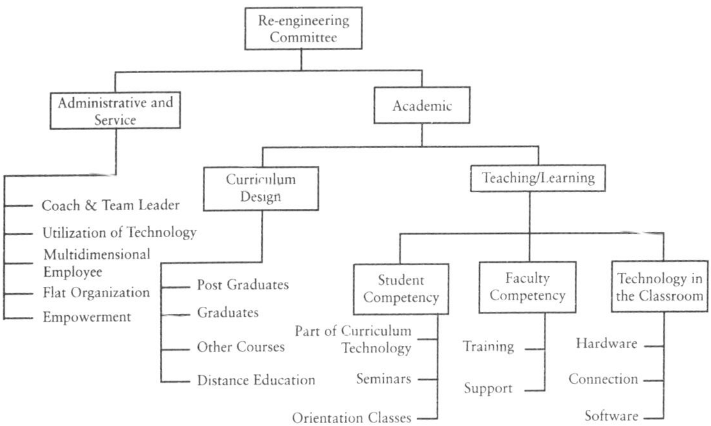


**Fig. 2:** Re-engineering in the Higher Education.

### Technology

Teaching by itself cannot satisfy institution's objectives and generate the desired outcome from teaching and learning. Higher education institutions should have adequate infrastructure for access and delivery in order to design and direct a technology-oriented curriculum.

### *Faculty Competency*

In most of the technical educational institutions, there is no revolutionized teaching and learning even though we have with all different forms of technology. Faculty development is the critical key for opening the new world of learning to the students. If institution's faculties are competent and comfortable with technology, that institutions will have remarkable success in using technology in curriculum. If faculty is not competent and comfortable, institutions should have to prepare faculty for this change. The first and last rule is to provide learning options and let faculty make decisions about learning.

### *Student Competency*

Faculty has a major role in the student's involvement with the computer technology. Student's development has direct relation with all teacher's assignments and expectations. In today's teaching and learning, most students use Internet application for access to educational resources and e-mail is a common part of communication with teacher and other students. Taking advantage of technology in the curriculum in the form of simulation, case study, intelligent system and problem solver are very important for the development of critical thinking and decision-making skills.

## Curriculum Design

In the curriculum design section, process-oriented activities should be converted to outcome-oriented activities with special attention to empowerment of students in learning process. There should be combined teaching and learning activities in all engineering curriculum like postgraduate, graduate, distance education, and other courses curriculum, etc. In order to realize our long-term vision of a curriculum driven by student projects three essential components must converge: (1) well-defined comprehensive, multi-disciplinary projects, (2) a flexible yet rigorous assessment tool in the form of a student learning portfolio, (3) a protocol for delivering technical information on needed basis (i.e. Just-In-Time Learning). Each of these components and their interrelation is shown in Fig. 3.

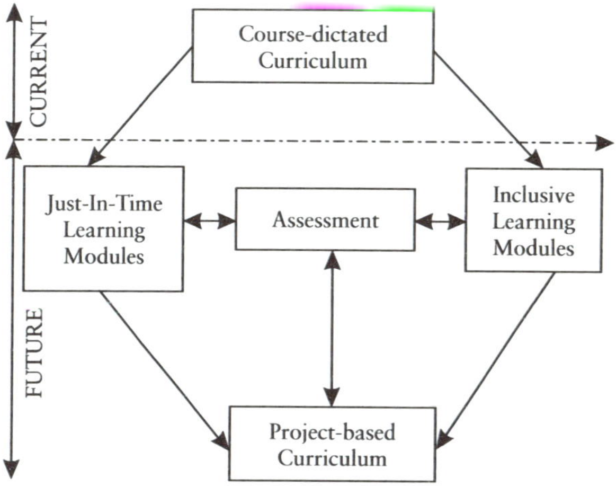


**Fig. 3:** Transition from Course-driven to a Project-based Curriculum.

The existing course-driven curriculum is shown at the top; the long-term goal of the project based curriculum is shown at the bottom. Our methodology to get from the current to future scenario is shown in the middle of the figure. That is, we will develop Just-In-Time learning modules, inclusive learning modules and assessment tools in parallel before merging them as a coherent curriculum.

## Suggestions for Re-engineering the Higher Education

Higher education system is not fully fit for moulding dynamic competent personalities of tomorrow. So re-engineering is the apt method for achieving this. The following are some important suggestions for re-engineering the higher education:

- Develop a Just-In-Time learning curriculum.
- Convert technology as a part of curriculum for accessing curriculum and computer-based education applications.
- Develop a process team—flat structure and quality culture.

- Provide world class infrastructure based on new technology.
- Provide relevant access for high level education research/projects, etc.
- Change present method/approach towards assignments/ tutorials/practical.
- Create a plan for continuous systematic investigation of faculty and student learning needs.
- Create a learning centre with multi-dimensional staff to help faculty to learn.
- Create ongoing workshops for department by department, based on the department's need assessments and evaluation.
- Create opportunities for one on one training, based on faculty's request.
- Provide free time for interested and committed faculty to develop computer-based curriculum.
- Strengthen our academic application development group.
- Design a faculty development grant program for using technology in the curriculum.
- Create reward system for innovative use of computers in the curriculum.
- Develop an industry institute culture.
- Develop a humanitarian culture among students and staff for fulfilling the responsibilities to the society.
- Government has to provide an open national policy separately for technical education.
- Form an effective placement department separately, headed by an officer for conducting various creative activities for students and staff.
- Develop the education grid between colleges, R&D organizations, resource institute etc in the state, national and world level.

- Recruitment of "academic entrepreneurs" as facilitators who can do things that impact industry and education.
- Acceptance of equality, access, quality, innovativeness and futuristic orientation as guiding principles in overall organization and administration of education.

### Proposed Education Grid

The proposed education grid is depicted in Fig. 4. The approach taken in the education grid of establishing and maintaining the course knowledge and collaboration space (CKCS) practically defines a new IT enabled approach for the formal higher education sector. Education grid integrates holistically the different components and requirements of applications and services intended in the several projects that are being initiated by MHRD, UGC and AICTE. What is needed is that the education grid services are duly recognized by the university and higher education system. The way the diverse component activities are proposed to be maintained across geographically distributed institutions is to establish and maintain a CKCS for each course.

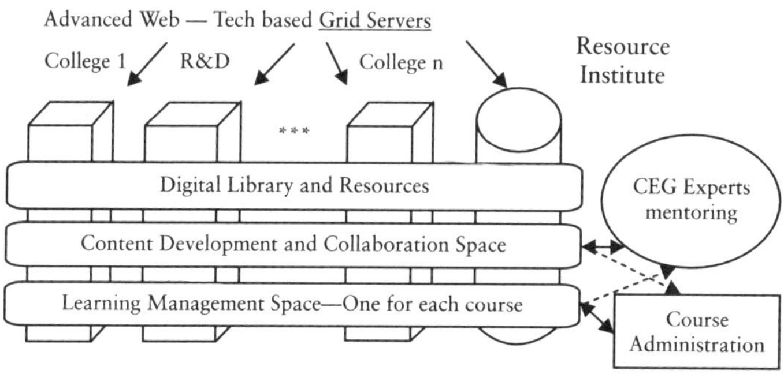


**Fig. 4:** Course Knowledge and Collaboration Spaces over Educational Trust.

A major challenge of the education grid project is to establish and maintain this CKCS consistently in the respective education servers of the participating colleges. This space is shown in Fig. 5.

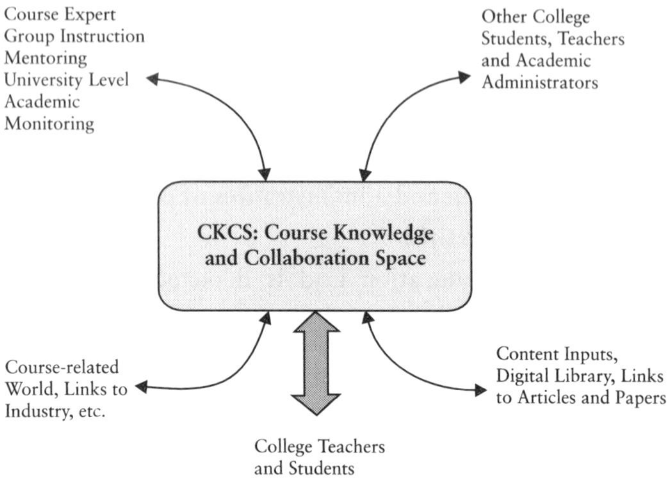


**Fig. 5:** Course Space as the Meeting Ground of Different Stakeholders.

## Conclusion

Re-engineering is a commitment from whole organization with practical and common sense strategic planning. This planning is based on the result of precise systematic investigations and inputs from everybody involved in the process. In the 21st century, survivors are those higher education institutions with extraordinary commitment to the proper utilization of technology in the process of teaching and learning. The intelligence and ideology that guide strategic planning are the most important tools for failure or success in this exciting journey.

## REFERENCES

Nick Obolensky (1996), *Practical Business Reengineering,* Kogan Page Ltd. Paperback Edn.

Micheal Covert (1996), *A Visible Solution Paper—Successfully Performing BPR,* Visible Systems Corporation, Copyright.

Herbert F.W., Stahlke and James M. Nyce (1996), "Re-engineering Higher Education: Reinventing, Teaching and Learning", *CAUSE/EFFECT*' Vol. 19, pp. 44-51.

V. Mariappan (March 2002), "Total Quality Education a Model for India", *Productivity*, Vol. 42, pp. 597-603.

R.R. Mohanty (December 1997), "What Do We Need to Know about BPR", *I.E. Journal*, Vol. XXVI, No. 12, pp. 20-29.

Buy L. Dee Fink R.L. Kolar, K.K. Muralidharan, R.W. Nairn, David A. Sabatini and Ronald L. (2000), "Reengineering Sooner Civil Engineering Education", *30th ASEE/IEEE Frontiers in Education Conference*, Kansas City, pp. 3-7.

K.R. Srivathsan, Director, IITM, (December 2002), Management of Referred Content Generation and Utilization for Formal Higher Education—Kerala Education Grid.

# 4

# For-Profit Provision of Higher Education

*Mahendra Sodha* and *Mohd Muzammil*

The debate at the global level is related with the justification of providing higher education on profit basis, although what is profit and how the profit is used are the issues that are defined differently. If an institution imparting higher education which is charitable earns profit that is some money remains after all the expenses are met and the profit (remaining money) is used again for the expansion and improvement in quality, it should never be called profiteering in higher education. Thus, even non-profit organizations may earn profit and reinvest the money in education. Purely, profit-oriented organizations are those that earn profit for being distributed among employees and among the owners. This may give an opportunity to the government to tax these organizations. The money accruing to the government through taxes may in turn be spent for higher education through public institutions. Viewed thus, even profiteering institutions will do some good though indirectly.

The recent controversy on reservation and the government's move to significantly increase the number of seats in central institutions of higher education, has once again highlighted (and this time with apparent urgency) the meagerness of our capacity for higher education of acceptable (if not world class) standards. A study of financing of 29 universities in India has revealed reduction in government grants to universities from about 65 per cent of the total expenditure 1996-97 to about 57 per cent in 2001-02 (Narula, 2004). It is well known that in recent times, along with the rightful emphasis on primary education, higher education has been given a low priority by the government (central and state, alike). The State Governments in particular are feeling greater resource crunch when it comes to financing higher education (for details of UP experience vide: Muzammil and Tabassum Khatoon, 2004).

This is the background in which the government has gradually been taking its hands off from financing of higher education, the present generosity of the Central Government in promising to invest a colossal amount of money for increasing the seats in central institutions, to contain the present anti-reservation agitation is too good to last in the long run. This aspect, along with the present acute shortage of quality faculty and the lower merit of entrants after the implementation of the new reservation quota, is bound to result in lower standards and loss of quality. The resulting adverse impact on quality and brand name can surely be minimized by good management, but by no means eliminated. Hence, there will be an inevitable erosion of standards in the presently elite institutions and in the best scenario the opportunities for the meritorious students will remain at the present level.

At a time, when the brand image and achievements of Indians (abroad) in science, engineering, medicine and management is at an all time high, the present gloomy situation at home should be a cause of concern, to all of us, including the decision makers. The basic concern of meritorious students that it is the caste and not the merit, which is important, has not yet been addressed; this has been detrimental to quality of higher education. If seats are limited and the number of aspirants large, some discrimination will have to be made to admit students in limited seats. This discrimination should be based only on merit and on other consideration (Muzammil, 1995).

The present dismal scenario can however be a blessing in disguise, if it sets our mind free from stereotyped thinking, to explore alternate and possibly better and more sustainable avenues for the creation of the required opportunities (with associated high quality) for meritorious students. It is rightly said that any adversity is also an opportunity. The solution so evolved can be feasible only if it can be implemented without putting any additional burden on the public exchequer. This paper presents some thoughts in this context.

## The Preferred Option

Until recently higher education was supposed to be provided only by the government (public sector) but now the scenario is changing. Private provision is coming up fast. This is true not only in India but globally also. Traditional systems and traditional beliefs are giving way to new order.

But as of now even the private universities and colleges that do not receive government grants are run and managed by the so-called trusts or societies registered as non-government organizations claiming that their purpose is not to earn profit but to promote the cause of higher education. It is another matter how far do they really adhere to what they claim. In fact, time has now come when even for earning pure profit universities and institutions of higher learning are being set up and they are still beneficial for the society. Like other private provisions, quality is maintained due to market competition. Similarly, in education also there may hardly be any risk involved in quality. There are winning experiences of this type of experiment in the USA and in some other countries as well like Japan and Germany.

In India, it is often debated as to what can be the alternative. For a way out one can get inspiration from the success story of industry and business in India. Until about 1990, the government had shown confidence in an inefficient public sector and put the private sector in a regime of permits and controls with a lollipop of protectionism. The government soon woke up and empowered the private sector by a programme of increasing liberalization and globalization. The global competition and the unshackling of the bonds of controls and permits released tremendous initiative, energy and creativity in the newly empowered business and industry; it is a tribute to their thinking and efforts, that now India is recognized as an economic superpower.

But, in the sector of education, there is the mess still writ large in the present Indian scenario. Many state universities in India (due to mismanagement) are sick institutions very much like the sick public sector undertakings which are increasingly being considered for disinvestment. "The comparison suggests that in view of the present national policy to disinvest the sick public sector units, disinvestment of sick universities may also be considered as a viable option, with a view to raise the quality of service and have an opportunity for the government to invest consequent savings and revenue on a selective basis" (Srivastava and Sodha, 2004, p. 161).

India is now known for its quality personnel. The excellence of Indian professionals (scientists, engineers, medical doctors and managers) at personal level has long been recognized internationally but their role as entrepreneurs and leaders in their respective professions has only recently come to the light. This has also highlighted the excellence of their alma mater. The IITs and IIMs are good examples of this process. The success of these professionals has also glorified (probably unjustified) our school education. We should, however, consciously remember that it is only the best products of our educational system, who have distinguished themselves abroad. These bright students, constituting a very small fraction of the extremely large number of students in the system are still large enough in number to cause the observed impact. If their number grows and they work effectively, they can create miracles.

Social sector (including education as the major constituent) in India has generally lagged behind the economic segment. Accordingly, higher education has not been able to keep pace, with the growth of business and industry on account of increasing (rather than decreasing) impediments in the way of liberalization and globalization, put up by an enthusiastic ministry, backed by more enthusiastic bureaucrats (including educationists) in the regulatory (like AICTE) bodies. It is a sad commentary that the post reform period of increasing liberalization and globalization in business and industry coincides with that of increasing controls and protection from foreign and to some extent private national universities in the education sector.

Thus, we have an ironic situation, while many engineering/medicine/management/science jobs of a demanding nature go a-begging, there are, at the same time, many unemployed or unemployable degree holders in these areas. The shortage of competent and skilled manpower in critical sectors also adversely affects our ability to exploit growing demand for such people, internationally. Thus, we are unable to play the role of an international talent reservoir for science, engineering, management and medicine. It is not the total number of professionals but the number of competent ones, which will determine our place under the sun. It calls for quality improvement and effective use of it. The for-profit education has tested itself to be more powerful in this regard.

In the present Indian context, the proposed increase in the number of seats in elite institutions (state or private aided) is not going to change the situation because merit based input to such institutions will remain the same. Further recent experience has shown that mere renaming and substantial financial input does not change the character, culture and ethos of an institution. Availability of adequate finance may be a necessary condition but it is not the sufficient condition for qualitative higher educational development (for details of arguments and the Indian experience vide, Muzammil, 1995b and 1998). What is needed is the required motivation in the faculty to produce competitive students. It has been awfully lacking in public institutions of higher education in general.

For-profit higher education may provide an answer. There appears to be an urgent demand for new elite institutions which can finance themselves and will meet the national and international requirement of highly competent manpower in critical areas and develop a unique culture of their own, which would be conducive to excellence. The investment and initiative cannot come from the government on account of financial constraints and different priorities. The private sector, however, if enabled and empowered (not only by words but more by deeds) can rise to the occasion. All is not glittering in the private sector either and there are issues that come up again and again when we try to entrust the role of providing high quality education to the private sector. In what follows we discuss the obstacles and the approach to private initiatives in higher education, to achieve the cherished objectives of higher education.

## Issues and the Approaches

During the planning period in India, the dependence for higher education was largely on government institutions or government-aided institutions of higher learning. But public universities and colleges left much to be desired so far as quality and competitiveness is concerned. Quality institutions have been lacking. The absence of private elite institutions of higher learning, at par with the best (like IITs, IIMs, AIIMS, etc.) shows that the present policy of the government is not conducive to attract private investment, commensurate with world class elite institutions. Of course, there has been a splurge of run of mill institutions (no worse than corresponding government institutions), which has gone a long way in meeting the aspirations of students for professional education.

However, unemployment/underemployment of graduates from many such institutions (despite unsatisfied demand for competent professionals) and the large number of vacant seats in these institutions points to the saturation of the present system and beginning of frustration, amongst the students and their parents. This is the reason that they are looking for such education which may be expensive but useful for them. The education that can open up for them, opportunities of decent work.

An alternative, therefore, the private sector may be encouraged, enabled and empowered by the government to put up the necessary investment and corresponding managerial skills for the establishment and successful running of private elite institutions by making provisions for legitimate profit and freedom of academic/administrative/financial management. The concept of earning profit from educational activity may at first instance shock and stir the classic educationists, traditional bureaucrats, politicians and the public, fed on old socialist myths, which are no longer in vogue even in the former socialist countries.

"Russia is among many countries where education law not only insists on non-profit status but also disallows tuition and fees that lead to profit—though enforcement is another issue" (Kinser and Levy, 2006, p. 110). In many countries, for-profit higher education is not eligible for government subsidy. Australia on the other hand illustrates dramatic attempt to create elite private higher education associated with for-profit initiative. Some countries do not explicitly use the term for-profit education but give full freedom to private entrepreneurs.

Quality is not necessarily a product of public sector. It has in fact been closer to private provision of goods and services. Why then it is often feared that in private universities likely to be set up by corporate bodies or private trusts etc. (which are known to seek maximum returns on their investment), the quality of education may become a casualty, defeating the very purpose for which private participation is being encouraged. This line of argument sounds unconvincing since no institute can survive for long on poor quality product and that too in the age of global competition. Education seems to be no exception to this universal truth. It is worth recalling institutions (like Gokhale Institute of Politics and Economics at Pune which celebrated its Platinum Jubilee in 2005), that were set up by private trusts are known for their values and concern for quality education. Institutes like Manipal Academy of Education, ICFAI University, etc. are known for maintaining standards in their chosen fields of education (Murty and Rajshekar, 2004).

In many countries abroad, private initiative in higher education for profit is gaining ground. Japan has made legal provision for for-profit higher education. Two for-profit universities have already been established. The Gulf countries in general welcome and support for-profit provision. Germany has already planned its first for-profit university. USA is most outstanding in this regard. Of the roughly 9,000 post secondary institutions in the US, nearly one half are for-profit (Kinser and Levy, 2006, p. 107).

There can be no across the board remark about the efficacy of institutions in the public and private sectors. We, in general, are apparently not disturbed by the fact that the managements of many private professional institutions (including the government-aided ones) are profiteering by dubious means, while there are many cases of honest management being constrained by rules, regulations, controls and lack of incentives in their efforts to improve quality and move well beyond the syllabus. The fixation of fees in professional colleges has little correlation with quality and is oblivious to efforts for excellence. A new, initiative is, therefore, needed to break this impasse and make a new and bold beginning.

The word profit is associated with stigma in Indian society. It appears to be a tainted word vis-à-vis charity despite the fact that many institutions in the name of charity are earning huge profits for personal use. The biggest mental block against the concept of profit in education is the age old legend that education is the noblest pursuit in life and it should not be contaminated with wealth. Accordingly, it is believed that education of all varieties and at all levels should be provided free or at throw away fee rates; there has been little or no concern about quality.

The high fees for the highly rampant coaching institutions have not been of much concern; similarly fees for employment-oriented short-term courses have also not raised eye brows. However, people get highly agitated by even moderate increase in fees for the degree and higher courses of learning. The concern for quality, employability and corresponding inevitable higher fee has yet to take roots in the society. A new approach will have to be adopted for making the system work better and in a sustainable manner.

Hymns are sung in honour of education. A great deal of lip service has been given to the concept of linkage of development with education [in fact even the Kothari Commission (1964-66) Report is titled as: Education and National Development]; however this concept is hardly reflected in the formulation and implementation of educational strategy at national or state level. As a result, higher education has not been able to keep pace with the demand for quality professionals, created by the progress of liberalization and globalization in business and industry. Thus, the advantage of improved quality in education at commensurate fees (which would have been reasonable on account of competition) has been denied to the providers and consumers of education. Economic compulsions of the government caused the reluctant acceptance of the principle of enhanced state—private partnership in higher education but the government has emphasized by words and deeds that the partnership has to be on its own terms and complete control has to rest with the government. Ground realities and incentives for quality and experimentation were not considered relevant to the partnership.

The emphasis on a formally recognized degree in Indian ethos and the conglomeration of legislations, rules, regulations, regulatory bodies and threats have enabled the Central and State Governments to ensure that all providers of education fall in line and none moves ahead and away from the groove, set by the government. But now the question is government versus market. In many areas of development, even in environmental issues which were supposed to be the responsibility of the government only, market has come to rescue.

Again, the main argument for strict controls is the professed dedication of the government to its perception of public interest. For political convenience, the public interest has been equated with making education available to maximum number of students at the lowest price, irrespective of quality (for full details of the politics of low priced education along with its iniquitous effects, see Kingdon and Muzammil, 2003). As an example, an undergraduate engineering institution is allowed to charge an additional fee of ₹ 500/- to ₹ 1000/- p.a. after getting the course, accredited by the appropriate body set up by the government. In real terms, it works out to be a negative incentive, because the additional costs, associated with accreditation far exceed the additional fee, allowed by the government. In addition, private institutions bear the brunt of the vagaries of Inspector Raj of the regulatory agencies (AICTE, etc.), government departments and the affiliating university.

A major fallacy, which is the philosophical basis for the apparatus of massive government and university intervention, is the false perception that the prospective students and their parents are gullible and the government should save them from their own actions. Nothing can be farther from truth. Much before the admission season begins and during the admission process, the students and parents visit the prospective institutions, see the laboratories, classrooms, library, workshop and other facilities, get details of the number and qualifications of the faculty, interact with present and former students and look at the record of placement. The institutes, in their own interest, facilitate such visits and attend to associated queries of students and impatient rather worrisome parents alike. An indication of the maturity of the students and parents is the fact that a large number of seats in professional colleges remains unfilled, while there is big rush for admission to good colleges. The amount of fees is a minor consideration in most cases.

### The Proposal: Special Education Zones

If one considers profit as the motivating factor of market driven system of development and look for opportunities, one finds this reality at work in all types of institutions and management. Let us first take up the opportunities in government and government-aided institutions. The experience of the universities in running self-financed academic programmes has been highly encouraging. The revenue generated by need based academic programmes has been used in the development of infrastructure, augmentation of the faculty and entry in emerging areas (Sodha and Muzammil, 1994). The threat to this approach has been the regulation of fees and thwarting the motivation of the institution by deducting (or the threat to deduct) the notional profit from the university grant. This process needs further liberalization to be made effective.

Next, one may consider the institutions, run by trusts or societies. In this case, there should also be the freedom to use a part of the revenue in other activities of the institution and the trust/society and partial payback of the investment. In all these cases, the institute should be able to fix the fee. Grading (one more aspect of accreditation) by the government and competition will ensure that the fee is indeed commensurate with quality and the students do not get overcharged; an analogy with coaching, where high quality and high fees co-exist, reinforces this view. This financial freedom should accompany academic liberty as well. As far as possible such institutions should have the status of "autonomous college" or "deemed to be university", so that maximum gain in quality for a given investment is ensured.

Maximum utilization of the infrastructure and offering additional need based programmes (even of different universities) should be the norms to keep the costs down, to enable the maintenance of high quality. Networking with business, industry and other institutions is another highly desirable option.

A crucial step will be to encourage, enable and empower corporate houses to establish and run normal or deemed universities, with world class infrastructure and world class faculty (with remuneration, perks facilities and environment, which is competitive with business and industry). The academic, administrative and financial (with room for profit and dividends) management should reflect the best of academic and management practices. This will be achieved when government liberalizes the procedures and conditions laid down for establishing private universities and institutes. Government should act like a facilitator and not like autocratic controller.

The case in point is the prolonged delay and the politicization involved in the clearance of the setting up of Maulana Mohammad Ali Jauhar University in Rampur from the Governor of Uttar Pradesh. The Governor gave his assent with the order that the conditions laid down by the Supreme Court of India be observed. These are (a) the condition to deposit Rupees two crores as endowment fees of the university, (b) the condition of 250 acres of land for the purpose, and (c) the condition of 24,000 square meters of constructed area "Jauhar University to be Functional in 2 years", *Indian Express* Lucknow, 20 June 2006). With economic liberalization that has led the country on a high economic growth trajectory, there is the need of academic liberalization to achieve a breakthrough in educational expansion and quality improvement.

Reputed foreign universities should be invited and encouraged to establish campus/campuses in India and run their activities, either alone or in collaboration with an Indian and/or a foreign corporation/university. The degrees could be awarded by the parent university, its Indian *avatar* or jointly.

It is evident that the needed increase in our capacity for world class higher education cannot take place without a change of mindset of all stakeholders, enabling legislation, supportive controlling bodies and good procedures. Taking a cue from business management, the functioning of the government and the controlling authorities should be supportive, expeditious and transparent. The hackneyed argument that poor meritorious students will not be able to afford the high fees in the elite institutions is countered by the experience, that even in the present system, students, admitted to an elite institution are also able to secure soft loans on easy terms to complete the course of study; the government can make it easier. The government can also ensure land on a preferential basis and soft loans for the establishment of such elite institutions; higher fees for foreigners and NRIs can subsidize the fees for Indian students. For providing several types of services to students in one cluster of institutions, we propose the idea of establishing special education zones.

A pioneering initiative for quality education can be taken by the Central Government or the government jointly with the corporate sector (and also by State Governments in India alone or in joint sector) by establishing Special Education Zones (SEZs) on the lines of Special Economic Zones in the country. The zones will be primarily dedicated to the development of higher professional educational institutions, R&D centres, state-of-the-art laboratory/workshop/training facilities/convention centres, etc. with all supportive infrastructure. These will attract investment in new establishments and new campuses of existing institutions. The SEZs should function with the modern *mantra* of networking. Advanced design, fabrication, laboratory, workshop, library and information and other academic facilities should be available to all on payment basis. Facilities for preparatory education (before regular admission) should also be available to all those who need it including foreigners.

The suggested scheme for setting up of Special Education Zones (SEZs) in the country will not only facilitate in the development of quality education and professional learning for the students of the country, it will also help export higher education as the SEZs will attract foreign students who will pay in foreign currency to receive the domestically generated service of education in India. These earnings may in turn be ploughed back into educational investment for further improvement in quality and expansion of facilities. The proposed SEZs will provide internationally competitive environment in the cluster of education service providers with hassle free procedures of admission, teaching and interaction, practical classes and examination. Efficiency and transparency will be the hallmark of academic administration in the proposed SEZs.

To begin with the following SEZs will be very feasible and efficient for various reasons: Delhi-Gurgaon-Ghaziabad, Ahmedabad-Baroda, Hyderabad-Warangal, Bangalore-Mangalore, Chennai-Pondicherry, Kolkata-Kharagpur-Burdwan, and Lucknow-Kanpur-Allahabad-Varanasi. Once successful experience is gathered from these, more such zones may be created in various parts of the country.

The most distinctive features of the SEZs will be that these zones be treated as foreign territory for free operation of universities and colleges and institutes without government intervention in the regulation of fees and other authoritarian conditions, etc. Instead government may assist them in establishment and see that they get free and competitive environment to work and start getting profit from producing the service of quality higher education. These zones should also be treated as duty (and tax) free zones for producing and trading educational commodities and services.

Nobody will disagree that there are risks in opening up higher education for profit. However, healthy competition and alert students/parents tend to minimize it. In view of meritorious students having stagnant or shrinking opportunities for good quality professional education and the trusts/societies or the government, not being able to help out, the private corporate sector and foreign investors have to be engaged in providing quality higher education. This will enable India to exploit the opportunities in the present knowledge age and prepare high quality manpower for further development of the country.

There are two overwhelming reasons why for-profit higher education appears to be inevitable in not too distant future. One, the sharp increase in the higher education age group population and the increased enrollment ratio of this age-cohort propelled by the fast economic development of the country; and second, the obvious failure of the traditional higher education system in India which is now dragging amidst the otherwise rapidly growing sectors of the Indian economy and society.

## REFERENCES

Forest, J.J.F. and Altbach, P.G. (eds.) (2006), "International Handbook of Higher Education", Part I *Global Themes and Contemporary Challenges*, Springer, Netherlands.

Kingdon, Geeta and Muzammil, M. (2003), *Political Economy of Education in India*, Oxford University Press, New Delhi.

Kinser, Kevin and Levy, Daniel C. (2006), "For-Profit Higher Education: US Tendencies, International Ethos", in J.J.F. Forest and Daniel C. Altbach (eds.).

Murty, G.R.K. and Rajshekar, N. "Globalizations and Challenges to Higher Education", *University News*, Vol. 42, No. 52, December 27, 2004-January 02, 2005.

Muzammil, M. (1995a), "Flout the Rule and Pay the Price", *The Education Supplement of The Guardian*, London, 28 February.

Muzammil, M. (1995b), Report on Higher Education in India, SAVSP, Queen Elizabeth House, Oxford, April.

Muzammil M. (1998), "Leading Issues in Economics of Higher Education", *University News* (special number on higher education as merit good), Vol. 36, No. 4, 15 June.

Muzammil, M. and Tabassum Khatoon (2004), "Resource Constraints to Higher Education: Evidences from Uttar Pradesh", *University News*, Vol. 42, No. 52, December 27, 2004-January 02, 2005.

Narula, Manju (2004), Universities Finances, An Analytical Study. NIEPA, New Delhi.

Sodha, M.S. and Muzammil, M. (1994), "Financial Crisis in Higher Education—Diagnosis and Reform", in M.V. Mathur, R.K. Arora and M. Sogani (eds.) *Indian University System—Revitalization and Reform*, Wiley Easter Publishers, New Delhi.

Srivastava, R. and Sodha, M.S. (2004), "Private Universities: Challenges and Opportunities" in K.B. Powar and K.L. Johar (eds.) *Private Initiatives in Higher Education*, Sneh Prakashan and Amity Foundation for Higher Learning, New Delhi.

# 5

# Managing Higher Education: Need for Multidisciplinary Private Universities

*P.V. Gupta* and *S. Chaturvedi*

## Prelude

In the existing policy framework of higher education only universities are authorised to award degrees. Education being in "Concurrent List" of Indian Constitution, universities can be established by the Central as well as State Governments. Traditionally, universities have been extending the privilege of awarding degrees to the institutions/colleges through the mechanism of affiliation. This still remains the basic structure of providing higher education in India. Institutions of excellence such as IITs, IIMs, IISc, and IIITs, etc. were created through special acts of Central Government. Governments—Central and States—continue to control higher education through the above policy framework.

This framework was handed down through the British legacy to India and pursued vigorously by the governments in the socialist economy. This framework could serve the purpose to the limited extent. When the demand for the access to higher education increased and budgetary support from the governments started shrinking, this framework came under strain. As patchwork mechanism, structural changes led to expansion of private affiliated institutions and deemed-to-be universities. But the governments' control in creating the universities remains firm. The exception to this was the misadventure by the Chhattisgarh Government. It gave a big jolt to the votaries of private universities. Governments across India further tightened their grip on the creation and expansion of private universities.

With the liberalisation of economy and globalisation, Indian economy acquired buoyancy. India today is at a juncture where we find that we have shortage of skilled quality manpower in every discipline. This shortage of skilled quality manpower is being realised to be the biggest constraint in sustaining the growth of economy and acquiring desired position in the comity of nations. Dispersion of knowledge through the verifiable and acceptable means (read degrees), inter alia, universities has emerged an area that needs to be given boost.

It is time to check our assumptions. It is time to check our hypotheses. It is time, for the political leadership, administrators and educationists, to check as to how much and to what level we wish to extend the reach of higher education. What budgetary support governments can provide to achieve the desired level? How to fill the budgetary gap to achieve the desired level? What should be the guiding principles for designing a structure for higher education? What is the role of private entrepreneurs in that structure?

## Existing System in India

Existing system of awarding degrees through the universities has evolved over the time and it has acquired many nomenclatures, viz.

(a) Central Universities

(b) State Universities

(c) Deemed to be Universities

(d) De-Novo Universities

(e) Private Universities.

Universities and institutes can be classified as general, technical, medical, agriculture, etc. Most universities in the country are affiliating type and remain occupied in conducting examinations. Some of these are teaching as well as affiliating type. Very few are engaged in research. The status of deemed-to-be universities has been conferred on outstanding institutions. The De-Novo university status has been conferred on some newly established institutions in specialised subjects with promise of their being developed as universities. Some of the private universities have also been setup under the State Legislative Acts.

As far as the institutions of higher learning are concerned these may be classified as national institutions (such as IITs, IIMs, AIIMS, IISc), government and government-aided institutions and self-financed institutions.

### Scope and Role of Higher Education

Higher Education covers education beyond 10+2 at graduation, postgraduation, doctoral, diploma and post-graduate diploma level, etc. It covers education in different disciplines such as Arts, Commerce, Science, Technology, Engineering, Design, Medical, Law, Management, Education, etc.

It has to prepare educated and skilled manpower for government, public and private organisations, business and industry, R&D labs, banks, offices, utilities, etc. It has to produce leaders and nation-builders, judges, lawyers, engineers, technocrats, business leaders, entrepreneurs, doctors, planners, teachers, etc.

Institutions of higher learning and universities perform a critical role in socio-economic and technological development of a country. They create knowledge. They impart and disseminate knowledge. Nations having large number of knowledgeable people in diversified fields can preserve their sovereignty and achieve strategic depth. Else, dependence especially in critical areas of knowledge leads to arms twisting. India has experienced such deprivation of knowledge in critical areas.

### Accessibility to Higher Education

A comparative analysis of population, number of universities and accessibility (the proportion of population in the relevant age group 18-24 years that enters the graduate education) to higher education is presented in the table below:

| Country | Population in Million | Number of Universities* | Accessibility |
|---|---|---|---|
| India | 1130 | 350 | 8% |
| USA | 303 | 711 | 89% |
| Australia | 21 | 37 | 80% |
| France | 64 | 84 | 50% |
| UK | 60 | 126 | 63% |
| Singapore | 4 | 5 | 21% |

* Source of data is Internet

Besides other factors, the shortage of talent pool is related with the accessibility to higher education to its population and the number of universities. The data presented above shows the large gap that India needs to bridge. The problem of accessibility in India typically appears in the form either large number of students do not get admission or not getting admission in the courses of their choice. Those who could afford and desire to achieve quality education join foreign universities for higher education. As per the estimates, there are about 1,60,000 students from India studying abroad.

The National Knowledge Commission (NKC) has projected that India needs 1500 universities to attain a gross enrolment ratio of at least 15 per cent by 2015. Though enhanced provisions have been made for this purpose in national budget of 2008-09, yet it alone would not be sufficient. It requires harnessing resources from all the quarters. So has been the recommendation of the NKC that public and private sources should be tapped for funding. The Knowledge Commission has also recommended that we need not only a much large number of universities but also smaller universities which are responsive to change and easier to mange. For comparison sake, it is worth noting that China has created 1250 universities in the last three years.

We need large participation from private entrepreneurs and international collaboration to achieve quality in this national endeavour. We need to create an enabling environment where large private funding is possible in higher education.

**Quality Concerns**

The quality of most Indian universities is much poor in comparison to international standards. The gap between Indian and foreign universities has been widening. None of our universities rank among the best, say the top 100 in the world. According to a recent survey, Delhi University ranks 254, IIT-Mumbai 269, IIT-Delhi 307, IIT-Kanpur 431, IIT-Madras 432, IIT-Roorkee 433, University of Calcutta 410, University of Mumbai 456, and University of Pune 469 in the world. Some of the common reasons, identified by the Knowledge Commission, for this poor showing are:

(a) Curricula have remained almost unchanged for decades; have not kept pace with the time let alone with extending frontiers of knowledge.

(b) Creativity is at a discount in the system of assessment, which places premium on rote learning rather than understanding.

(c) Boundaries between disciplines have become dividing wall that constitute barriers to entry for new disciplines or new courses, while the knowledge is developing most rapidly at the intersection of disciplines.

(d) Importance attached to research has eroded steadily over time.

In a recent article "What Makes a World Class University", Prof. Alison Richard, the Vice-Chancellor of the University of Cambridge, has listed the following four factors:

(a) The world class university must show a commitment to breadth and excellence in all fields of human inquiry, not simply in a particular area.

(b) It must engage in cutting edge research whilst at the same time teaching the next generation, their students. Teaching and research are intrinsically bound together with top researchers inspiring and mentoring their students. In turn, students themselves inspire and/or challenge teachers.

(c) The university must allow its researchers the freedom to experiment, succeed and sometimes fail.

(d) The university should have permeable boundaries. This means encouraging inter-disciplinary research and teaching. It means working with private sector, e.g. fostering and encouraging partnership with industry and it means encouraging international collaboration. World class university should look outward and think beyond conventional boundaries.

The current status of higher education in India is heavily slanted towards cognitive and uni-disciplinary subjects. While it should be retained in many cases, it is also necessary that multidisciplinary endeavours for inter-disciplinary understanding of the problems, which affect the society, should be brought in. For example, poverty, natural resource bases like energy, water and environment issues do require multidisciplinary effort. The problem of poverty must be a programme of studies, which can be dissected, analysed, understood and can lead to solutions for poverty reduction by the science, technology and social sciences education. Similarly, the issues of natural resources like water and energy require the same approach.

**Need of Multidisciplinary Universities**

In the development of knowledge, two things are happening simultaneously, one, micro specialisations; second, integration and interrelationship between different disciplines. Such a scenario demands creation of institutions and universities focusing not only on specialised fields but also providing programmes in multidisciplinary fields. As stated above knowledge is developing most rapidly at the intersection of disciplines, thus, India needs multidisciplinary universities. Such universities should:

(a) be moderate in size.
(b) offer job-oriented, industry need-based, interdisciplinary courses in engineering, technology such as computer science, IT, electronics engineering, fashion technology, product design, management, international business, business and entrepreneurship, law, medicine, etc.
(c) lay emphasis on innovation, entrepreneurship, research and development and creativity.
(d) ensure quality and excellence in teaching and learning.
(e) attract international students for admission.
(f) give introduction of new subjects with application orientation.
(g) vocationalisation of subjects from the point of view of the learner, region and tradition (including familiar ones).
(h) offer provision of field and hands on experience to students.
(i) search for new areas of linkages between the worlds of education and organizations.
(j) increase establishment of intersection between the worlds of education and organisations.

## Degree of Autonomy

For creating enabling environment, the critical issue is the 'degree of autonomy' given for establishing and managing the institutions of higher education. Many critical aspects for sustaining the structure of higher education revolves around 'autonomy'. Large-scale private investment in higher education depends on this single most important issue. The issue of 'autonomy' has been aptly dealt by the University Education Commission appointed by the Government of India on 4 November 1948 having Dr. S. Radhakrishnan as its Chairman and nine other renowned educationists as its members. In the report submitted by this Commission, in Paras 29 and 31 stated the following about the autonomy.

> Freedom of individual development is the basis of democracy. Exclusive control of education by the State has

> been an important factor in facilitating in the maintenance of totalitarian-tyrannies. In such States institutions of higher learning controlled and managed by governmental agencies act like mercenaries, promote the political purpose of the State, make them acceptable to an increasing number of their populations and supply them weapons they need. We must resist, in the interest of our democracy, the trend towards the governmental domination of the educational process.

The Commission further stated:

> Higher education is, undoubtedly, an obligation of the State but State aid is not to be confused with the State control over academic policies and practices. Intellectual process demands the maintenance of the spirit of free inquiry. The pursuit and practice of truth regardless of consequences has been the ambition of universities.

An eleven-judge bench of Hon'ble Supreme Court of India, in the case of T.M.A. Pai and others versus State of Karnataka and others, in Para 52 of the judgment delivered on 31 October 2002, made following comments on the above stipulations of the Commission's findings:

> There cannot be better exposition than what has been observed by these renowned educationists with regard to autonomy in education. Governmental domination of the educational process must be resisted. Another pity observation of the Commission was that the State aid was not to be confused with State control over academic policies and practices. The observations (of the Commission) clearly contemplate educational institutions soaring to great heights in pursuit of intellectual excellence and being free from unnecessary governmental controls.

The views of Knowledge Commission on this aspect are:

> The present regulatory system in higher education is flawed in some important respects. The barriers to entry are too high. The system of authorising entry is cumbersome. There is a multiplicity of regulatory agencies where mandates are both confusing and

overlapping. The system, as a whole, is overregulated but under-governed. NKC perceives a clear need to establish an Independent Regulatory Authority for Higher Education (IRAHE). The IRAHE must be at an arm's length from the Government and independent of all stakeholders including the concerned Ministries of the Government.

If we wish to expand the network of universities and enhance the accessibility to higher education, we need to liberalise the policy framework to create new universities and ensure their long-term sustenance. Strategy of one-time capital investment without ensuring the policy framework for its long-term sustenance will be a recipe for disaster and failure. Autonomy is required not only for the privately managed institutions but for the state-managed institutions also. Procedures and rules for granting approval for setting private universities need change in the mindsets, rather a different mindset. We must get rid of controls, which breed nepotism and corruption. The more the controls, the greater is the corruption. We need to come out of perceived threats and allow NRIs and foreign funding to enhance the network of universities.

It is futile to find a 'symmetric' solution to 'asymmetric' problem. There is asymmetry in the requirements of expertise. There is asymmetry in the availability at the input level. There is asymmetry in affordability. We need people with different abilities at different levels. Trying to develop uniform education system is a wild goose chase. Such a step will be retrogressive and is bound to bring mediocrity and not excellence. Government should cater to the strategic needs of the country and look after talented people with limited economic means. Let private sector play the role as allowed in the developed countries. Regulation is needed but not the controls. The issue of 'Control' versus 'Regulation' needs to be resolved for posterity. We need to re-examine the role of our regulatory bodies such as AICTE, UGC, etc.

# 6

# University Education in the Era of Globalization: Some Challenges

*R.B.S. Verma*

## University Education

Universities are the institutions of higher education and learning. They are established for imparting individuals with advanced knowledge and skills to discharge responsibility in government, business and profession. They provide advice and consultancy to government and business. These institutions are expected to produce new knowledge by undertaking research relevant to local needs and by serving as conduits for the transfer, adaptation and dissemination of knowledge generated elsewhere in the world (World Bank, 1994: 4). Being centres of higher education and public funded, they are accountable to the people and ought to respond to the overall national educational plans. They not only improve individual lives but also enrich wider society in different ways such as by helping to increase wages and productivity that directly enrich individuals and society, by allowing people to enjoy an enhanced life of mind which offers wider society both cultural and political benefits and by promoting independence and initiative, both of which are valuable intellectual resources for the generation and dissemination of knowledge in society (World Bank Task Force on Higher Education and Society, 2000:37). Commenting on the role of Professor and Head, Department of Social Work, University of Lucknow, India, higher education in the promotion of democratic values, this

Task Force Report (2000) mentioned two ways in which universities could earn the right of moral leadership. Firstly, by research and interpretations, social sciences encourage debate on ways to build/maintain a pluralistic, accountable democracy. On the other hand, research in humanities brings forth ethical and moral values appropriate to a specific society through careful reasoning. Secondly, higher education helps enlightened citizens grow by speaking of the superiority of reasoned discourse over partisanship, of tolerance over discrimination, and of free/open search over secrecy and deception. The education process is based on tolerance, pluralism, merit, reasoned argument, etc. and the existence of these values is critical to building/maintenance of democracy (World Bank, Task Force on Higher Education and Society, 2000:44-45). Emphasizing the role of universities in upholding democratic traditions, Dr. S. Radhakrishnan, noted Indian philosopher, also said that the function of the universities is not merely to send out technically skilled and professionally competent men, but it is their duty to produce in them the quality of compassion, the quality which enables the individuals to treat one another in a truly democratic spirit. (Convocation Address at Karnataka University on 26 October, 1953).

### Aims of University Education

There are certain goals of university education which are universal in nature. These are:

(a) The pursuit of knowledge of self, society and nature.

(b) Enriching the mind and promoting creativity among people.

(c) Improving the efficiency and productivity of the social production system (Shukla, 1999:64).

(d) Empowering people through development of knowledge, skills and values.

(e) Providing means for upward economic and social mobility.

In the era of globalization, there are major goals of universities in case of developing countries:

(a) Making the economy globally competitive by training students for employment in knowledge, economy and transforming knowledge to private business.

(b) Promoting social inclusion by enhancing opportunities for a wider section of society to obtain higher education in some form whenever they require it with a focus on science and technology.

(c) Changing social structure in response to the needs of time.

(d) Assisting in the process of economic development, particularly of countryside where vast majority of people live in the state of resourcelessness and powerlessness.

(e) Establishing close links with their culture and traditions.

## Globalization in University Education

Universities and colleges are not immune to the globalization of production, distribution and consumption. The technological revolutions in transport and communication have affected university education. From the positive and instrumental perspective, the implications of globalization for university education should include maximizing the relevance of university education to global development and pooling up the best intellectual resources, support and initiatives from different parts of the world for learning, teaching and research (Daun, 1997:19 and Holmes, 1999:10).

Before presenting an analysis of globalization of university education, the process of globalization should be discussed.

## Importance of Globalization Prccess

Rapid globalization is one of the most controlled, crucial, critical, consequential and indispensable aspects of the new millennium, mainly due to increase in the flow of trade and capital as well as transfer of information and communication technologies among nations day by day. In this era, every nation, irrespective of its liking or disliking of the process of globalization, has to make efforts for accelerating its economic and modernizing its societies through integrating itself with world economy. Since globalization refers to the accelerated international flow of goods, capital, labour, services and information which have occurred in response to improved transport, the seemingly limitless revolution in communication technologies, and the deregulatory policies/restructuring adopted in many countries during the past two decades. The process of restructuring has made the nations to liberalize and then privatize and globalize and these structural reforms are mainly related to trade, industry, and financial, fiscal and agricultural sectors. Consequently, in the new millennium, there should be multiple globalizations including technological globalization, economic globalization, social globalization, political globalization, cultural globalization and learning globalization.

## Origin and Growth of Globalization

Historically, globalization has existed since the development of international trade. However, its origin can be seen dated back to sixteenth century which was a period of colonization. Collapse of communism and eclipse of socialist pattern has made possible the return of classical capitalism with free market economy leading to liberalization, deregulation and privatization. This system has been capable of delivering economic good as well as supply of various consumer goods in abundant resulting into self-legitimizing of capitalism. But the process of global economic integration gained momentum in the 1970s with the development of capital markets at international level. The process of globalization got momentum with the establishment of International Monetary Fund (IMF), the World Bank and World Trade Organization (WTO). The process of trade liberalization was started with the GATT (General Agreement and Trade and Tariff) in 1947. As a result of the Uruguay Rounds of Trade negotiations, World Trade Organization (WTO) was established in 1955 for settling trade disputes among nations. This has given a rapid boost to trade among nations leading to the process of globalization. The rise in the international trade has benefited many countries who have been participating in this trade. This has led to raise the influence of international financial markets as well as short-

and long-term capital flows leading to internationalization of financial markets through financial flows at global level, i.e. Official Development Assistance (ODA) and Foreign Direct Investment (FDI). The establishment of MNC (Multinational Corporations) having trans-border production networks is another development in the process of globalization. This process has been further accelerated due to the rapid advancement in the fields of science and technology, information and communication, biotechnology, trade, commercial practices, banking, insurance, etc. (Kishore, 2003:9).

Thus, in a nutshell, it can be concluded that though globalization is not a new phenomenon, yet it has different and distinctive features in the present era. These features are: creation of new markets have globally linked foreign exchange and capital markets, use of new tools, i.e. Internet, the web, e-mail, media networks, etc., new actors such as WTO, World Bank, IMF, MNCs, TNCs, etc., new rules, i.e. multilateral agreements on trade and commerce, international treaties, intellectual property, etc., new approaches, i.e. international cooperation and collaboration, international alliances and competition, use of international standards and benchmarks, etc.

## The Concept of Globalization

The concept of globalization is frequently used but clear-cut meaning of this concept is rarely available. However, some writers have explained this concept—such as according to Cheng (2000:156), it may refer to the transfer, adaptation and development of values, knowledge, technology and behavioral norms across countries and societies in different parts of world. Knight and de-Wit defined globalization as "The flow of technology, economy, knowledge, people, values, ideas across borders. Globalization affects each country in a different way due to a nation's individual history, traditions, culture and priorities" (1997:10). The United Nations Development Programme (UNDP) in its Human Development Report (1999) states that globalization implies much more than the flow of money and commodities across the globe. Globalization refers first and foremost to the growing interdependence of world's people. It is a process of integration involving not only the economy but also technology and governance.

Summarizing multiplicity of meanings of globalization available in the literature, Asie Kacwicz (1999:3) concluded that globalization is (i) the intensification of economic, political, social and cultural relations across border; (ii) the historical period (or historical epoch) launched since the end of the cold war; (iii) the transformation of world economy epitomized by anarchy (literally defined) of financial markets, (iv) the triumph of US values, through the combined agenda of neo-liberalism in economic and political democracy; (v) an ideology and an orthodoxy about the logical and inevitable culmination of the powerful tendencies of the market at work; (vi) a technological revolution, with social implications; and (vii) the inability of the nation-states to cope with global problems that require global solutions such as demography, ecology, human rights, and nuclear proliferation. Operationally, globalization refers to:

(a) international flow of goods, capital, labour, services and information;

(b) globalized production, marketing technological as well as information networks;

(c) economic interdependence through mutual cooperation and collaboration between countries specially in the areas of trade, technology, labour and internal capital flows;

(d) multi-cultural integration and use of international standards and benchmarks leading to universal homogenization of ideas, cultures, values and even life styles; and

(e) deteriorilization and villagization of the world.

To conclude, it can be maintained that globalization is a process by which the economies of the world get increasingly integrated leading to the consciousness of the globe as one world through intensification of economic, political, social and cultural relations across international boundaries.

## Meaning of Globalization in University Education

Globalization of university education means growing interdependence and interconnectedness of the globe through increased movement of students and academics over national boundaries due to lowering of barriers for their movements and better international communication. This process is further strengthened by international agreements that facilitate the movement of professionals between the countries. In this way, university education is being treated as commercial product with dealings in it being governed essentially by market forces and the principles of marketplace.

## Globalization in University Education under WTO Policy Regime

Education, particularly university education, in developing countries falls within the ambit of WTO and GATS. Trade in services was not covered under GATT into the conclusion of Uruguay Round in 1994, but keeping in view the fast growth of trade in services during the pre-Uruguay Round period, shifting composition of GDP in favour of service sector in most of the countries and competitive advantage to develop countries in this sector, it got included in the final act of Uruguay Round.

The General Agreement on Trade in Services (GATS) provides an international as well as multilaterally accepted legal framework for the promotion of liberalization of trade in services. Trade in services has been defined under GATS in terms of four modes of supply, viz.:

(a) Cross-border supply mainly related to courses provided through distance education, Internet, etc.; any type of educational testing service and any educational material that can be sent across national boundaries.

(b) Consumption abroad referring to education of foreign students and is the most common form of trade in educational services.

(c) Commercial presence referring to actual presence of foreign investors in a host country. This would also include foreign universities providing for courses or setting up of institutions in another country.

(d) Movement of natural persons which means the movement of people across countries to provide educational services.

Basic principles of GATS have been:

(a) Most favoured nation treatment, i.e. no discrimination amongst other members of the agreement in terms of treatment accorded to their service suppliers.

(b) National treatment, i.e. foreign services and service suppliers to be treated no less favourably than nationals.

(c) Progressive liberalization, i.e. the process of liberalization is irreversible because of binding commitments on the negotiated levels market access.

(d) Transparency, i.e. all policies related to barriers to market access and discriminatory restrictions by the members are to be notified.

Falling within the ambit of the WTO and GATS, university education of particular country is supposed to open its university campuses for another country and admit its students to the institutions of that country. Similarly, this particular country can open its campuses on the land of other country and admit the students of that country.

Thus, to conclude it can be said that in the context of university education, globalization is a process of integrating science, education, technology, culture and governance. It is going through following four modes:

(a) Operation of educational institutions on foreign land by granting franchise or agreement/arrangement with the educational institutions of the host countries.

(b) Establishment of campuses/centres of foreign universities in host countries.

(c) Establishment of centres by governments of the countries abroad for promoting education and programmes offered by other universities/institutions with multiple objectives to enrol more and more international students.

(d) Operation of virtual campuses by using satellite and information super highway. Very recently a new trend of utilising cyber space has started for marketing education.

## Impact of Globalization on University Education

There has been multidimensional impact of globalization process on university education. This process has benefited the university education system on the one hand and on the other hand, there are some apprehensions also.

It has been said that the process of globalization has benefited university education system in the following manners:

- Improvement in the overall quality of university education due to competition generated due to global sharing of knowledge, skills and intellectual assets.
- Large numbers of organizations are providing university education within and outside country.
- Use of information and communication technologies inside the country as well as outside the country for delivering educational services.
- Greater access to students for wider range of educational opportunities both at home and abroad.
- Reduction in knowledge gap in developing countries and increase in access to university education.
- Promotion of understanding of at least one other culture.
- Increase in understanding of global systems and enhancing mutual support, supplementation and benefit to produce synergy for various developments of countries, communities and individual.
- Generation of additional resources in the field of university education, particularly in developing countries, where state funding of university education is being curtailed.
- Motivating universities to revamp curricula to reflect the need for international understanding.

- Broadening the opportunity to study abroad and internship opportunities for all students.
- The regional and international cooperation among developing countries can help in the capacity building of those areas.
- Promotion of faculty development and reward.
- Providing opportunities to examine the organizational needs of international education.
- Bringing universities together to build consortia to enhance capabilities.
- Promotion of cooperation with institutions of other countries.
- Establishment of national regulatory framework for controlling the operation of foreign providers and protecting students from bogus institutions.
- Helping in developing benchmarks to test the international character of the knowledge base.
- Strengthening the existing system to meet the challenge by facilitating multi-way communications and interactions and encouraging multi-cultural contributions at different levels among countries.
- Innovations through new providers and delivery modes.
- Creation of values and enhancement of efficiency through the global sharing of knowledge and giving mutual support in the distribution of knowledge for the purpose of meeting local needs and ensuring growth.

To conclude, it can be maintained that globalization in university education has benefited countries, specially developing countries, who are participating in the process, generally, in three ways:

(a) Academically, it has created better understanding in relation to national phenomena, i.e. laws, principles and processes in nature resulting into the better use of machines and greater output and extension of information and knowledge from one country to another in the context of intellectual culture.

(b) Professionally, it has produced qualified employees for economic development to benefit society, particulary large number of information technology specialists and other technologies.

(c) Socially, it has created better understanding of impact of advancement on society, broadened general education to prepare students, lifelong learning making students better learners, better thinkers, better communicators and better performers.

**Some Challenges**

The advancement in the field of information technology has given birth to globalization which totally revolutionized the process of trade, exchange and communication resulting into producing such a global scenario in which structure, functioning and role of universities have to be redefined. Now, universities are no longer centres of learning established in isolation from mainstream of social happening. They will have to function under all pervading influence of the communication technology revolution which has underwritten world economy globalized knowledge, accelerated innovation and facilitated the individual's access to information and skills (Patted, 2003:743). The universities have to globalize in terms of curricula and quality. In this era of globalization, the university education will increasingly be privately supported but publicly accountable and socially committed, accordingly independent and constructively partnered; knowledge based but students oriented; research driven but learning focussed; technologically sophisticated but community dependent; quality obsessed but procedurally efficient and professionally attuned but humanly informed (Rhodes, 1999:17). This state of affairs has given various forms of university education such as:

- Virtual universities offering programmes through Internet and other means.

- Distance education programmes delivered through satellite, computers, correspondence or other information technology means across national boundaries.
- Sale of proprietary materials such as books, courseware or testing together with associated services.
- Franchised operations, using a third party to give degree.
- Twinning arrangements in which a degree is gained through study in more than one country as a result of agreements between institutions in different countries to offer joint programmes.
- Study abroad semester or credit earning arrangements similar to the twinning arrangement.
- Branch or satellite campuses set up by an institution in another country to provide its educational programmes to foreign students.
- Free standing programmes operating outside the country of the provider with or without a combination of the above-mentioned arrangements (Stella, 2002:8).

The new developments in the area of university education have been posing innumerable challenges such as:

- Meeting the increase in costs and tuition fees to be realised from the students of public as well as private institutions.
- Gradual privatization of public institutions due to curtailment in state funding as well as seeking alternative sources of funding.
- As per GATS rules, public funding is equaled to unfair subsidy, consequently, foreign institutions willing to provide education insist the governments to decrease funding resulting into jeopardizing of the public funded domestic institutions.
- Academic centres, located in English speaking countries, will become stronger due to the dominance of English language.

- Fast movement of professionals, teachers and researchers to these countries which are able to provide lucrative pay packages resulting into shortage of capable and competent staff.
- Potential danger for poorer nations as inequalities are likely to be accentuated with developed countries more dominant and the developing countries getting marginalised in the process as well as enhancement of inequalities among developing countries also.
- Commercialization of university education and dominance of values of marketplace among university campuses leading to the establishment of profit-motivated private universities making university education a profitable business.
- Mushrooming growth of sub-standard universities/ institutions of higher learning posing a challenge to establish a clear and compatible regulatory mechanism for monitoring, controlling and restraining the private and foreign universities providing sub-standard education.
- Erosion of indigenous art and culture of developing countries by developed countries through export of their degree programmes affecting social and cultural fabric of the recipient country.
- Erosion of autonomy of universities, particularly in developing world due to the interference of WTO because advanced education and research would become just another product subject to international treaties and bureaucratic regulations (Altbach, 2001:23).
- Challenge will be faced for the recognition of qualifications and transfer of academic credits due to new types of education providers, new delivery modes, new cross-border education institutions and new levels of students mobility.
- Dominance of information technology companies in the new international commerce in knowledge and knowledge-based products.

- Imbibing of new norms, values, languages, scientific innovations and knowledge products into existing heterogeneous educational system of countries will pose another challenge.
- Maintaining 'public good' aspect to universities for the socio-cultural development of the nation in the era of marketization of education.
- Challenges also involved in restructuring of academic courses, introduction of modern teaching and learning methods, curricular design and updation for meeting needs of fast changes.
- Introduction of uniform credit-based system with international compatibility, since many countries have their national policies for credit system.
- Modernization of teaching methods in order to minimize traditional chalk and talk method of instruction and use of digital presentation of lecture notes for making contact teaching more effective.
- Preparation of course materials of modules, getting feedback through student evaluation of courses, employees' opinion and pear suggestion are also the challenges of operational system of the university education.
- Continuous training and development of faculty service conditions of faculty members as well as their retention and participation in the overall development of institution.
- Conducting research relevant to local needs having global significance and interacting as well as providing valuable services to the community by making use of resources available through advice and consultancy (Madhsudanan and Manjunath, 2003:1).

Thus, to conclude, it can be maintained that in this era of globalisation, the basic challenge emanates from the great demand for paradigm shift from the traditional paradigm of site-bounded education towards the new paradigm of triplisation including globalization, localization and individualization in education with support of information technology and various types of local as well as global networking (Chong: 2003:60).

## REFERENCES

Altbach, Philip G. (2001), "Higher Education and the WTO: Globalisation Run Amok", *University News*, Vol. 39, No. 37, Sept. 10-16.

Cheng, Yin Chong. "ACMI—Tripalisation Paradigm for Reforming Education in the New Millennium", *International Journal of Educational Management*, 14(4), 156-74.

Chong, Yin Cheong (2003), "Local Knowledge and Human Development in Globalization of Education", NIEPA, *Globalization and Challenges for Education*, Shipra.

Daun, H. "National Forces, Globalization and Education Restructuring: Some European Response Patterns", *Compare*, 27(1), 19-41.

Holmes, W. "The Transforming Power of Information Technology", *Community College Journal*, 70(2), pp. 10-15.

Kishore, S. "Globalization, Skill-development and Distance Learning", *University News*, Vol. 41, No. 15, April 14-20.

Knight J. and De Wit, H. (1997), "Internationalization of Higher Education" in *Asia Pecific Countries*, European Association of International Education, Amsterdam.

Madhusudanan, K.N. and Manjunath, B.R. (2003), "Internationalization of Higher Education: Indian Scenario", *University News*, Vol. 41, No. 39, Sept.-Oct.

Natarajan, R. (1999), "Emerging Trends in Education, Teaching and Learning and Knowledge Management", *University News*, 37(28), July.

Patted, L.B. (2003), "Globalization and Impact on Human Development", *Challenges for Education*, Shipra.

Rhodes, F.H.I. (1999), "The New University" in Hirsch, W.B. and Weber (Editors), *Challenges Facing at the Millennium*, Pergamon and IAU Press, Paris.

Shukla, S.P. "Globalisation and Higher Education", *New Frontiers in Education*, 29(1).

Stella, Antony (2002), "Quality Assurance of New Forms of Education", *University News*, Vol. 40, No. 7.

World Bank, Higher Education in Developing Countries: Perils and Promises, Task Force on Higher Education and Society, Washington DC.

World Bank, Higher Education: The Lessons of Experience, Washington D.C.

# 7

# Management Challenges of North East Education

*Tapan Kumar Basantia*

The challenges, needs, problems, prospects and paths of education of the North East part of the country is different from the challenges, needs, problems, prospects and paths of education of many other parts of the country due to the unique characteristics of North East society and unique demands of the North East region. The states of Mizoram, Manipur, Meghalaya, Assam, Tripura, Nagaland and Arunachal Pradesh constitute the North East India and more lovingly they are called seven sisters (now, they consider the state of Sikkim as one of their sisters for many purposes, and they themselves including Sikkim are sometimes called as eight sister states). The state of Assam is generally considered as the elder sister state of all other north eastern states and it guides the other north eastern states in many cases politically, judicially, commercially, educationally and the like. Except Assam, almost all the north eastern states are relatively young states and just are entering into mainstream of development. Barring a few parts, almost all other parts of North East India are filled with hills and mountains of varied type and the ranges of these hills and mountains vary from too high to too low in altitude. The plain areas of North East mainly constitute the people of different cultural and religious groups whereas the hill and mountain areas of North East are being constituted by hundreds and thousands of tribal groups having their own way cultural dialects, dwelling system, occupation and psychology.

Education has become a challenge for North East society. Because North East society urgently needs to develop itself economically, socially, culturally, psychologically, politically and intellectually; and for the development of all these aspects, the role of education is more vital. After independence, the Government of India has taken a lot of initiatives to provide better education to the North East region of the country. The Government of India has opened a lot of central level institutes/universities in the North East region in order to facilitate its education. Some such institutes/universities are Mizoram University, North Eastern Hill University, Assam University, Tezpur University, Manipur University, Indian Institute of Technology (Guwahati), North East Regional Institute of Science and Technology (Itanagar), National Institute of Technology (Silchar), North East Regional Institute of Education (Shillong), etc. Government of India is also now taking initiation/has taken initiation to open/make at least one central university in each of the North Eastern state. Besides the higher education, the school education system of north east region is being facilitated by Government of India in many ways. A lot of Kendriya Vidyalayas, Navodaya Vidyalayas, etc. are being opened in different parts of North East region for enhancing school education. In addition to the direct intervention the Government of India, also indirectly providing a lots of grants/aids to the State Governments as well as non-governmental organizations through its different plans and programmes in order to revamp the schools as well as higher education in North East region. The different states of North East are launching different plans, programmes, either personally or in collaboration with different external bodies in order to achieve their targets relating to education.

Due to the intervention of the Government of India, State Governments and non-governmental bodies, the education system of North East has expanded a lot and also is expanding lot, but now it requires proper management. Because a well-managed educational system can easily achieve its objectives than an ill-managed system. Since North East society is unique, geographical location is unique, style of life is unique, economical base is unique, so, the management of North East education also seeks the unique directions/paths by which it can face all the needs, demands and challenges of the society.

## Management Challenges of North East Education

*Challenge of Liberalization, Privatization and Globalization (LPG) and Management of North East Education*: Starting from 1990s, the whole world has been tilted towards the plans, programmes, policies and agendas of three recurring challenges/ values, i.e. liberalization, privatization and globalization (LPG); and each and every country of the world now is trying their best to taste the realities of LPG in all their aspects of life, i.e. social aspect, economic aspect, educational aspect, etc. Due to the practice of liberalization policy, now one country is able to share with the other countries in terms of economy, education, politics, business strategy, culture, defence, law, etc. for its own benefit. The policy of privatization of a country provides a lot of flexibility and freedom to its citizens to use their talents and resources in maximum extent for the maximal development of themselves and the country at a time. Similarly, globalization policy of a country leads its members to achieve the values of multi-culturalism, internationalism and global understanding by sharing ideas, values, work ethics, business, commerce, technology, art and morals, laws, etc. with many other countries. Though India has followed the policies of LPG for its greater benefits, yet the impact of this LPG on North East India is found in a lesser scale. On one side, the people of North East India are hardly ready to accept the principles of LPG, and on the other side, it is also difficult to implement the principles of LPG in North East India due to many geographical, physical and other such barriers. The geography of North East India is too unique. The North East India is separated from other parts of the country as well as other parts of the world due to the geographical isolation, communication problem and the problems of its physical features like difficult hills and mountains, different types of forests and jungles, etc. So, education has to play a vital role in order to help the North

East India to taste the values of LPG and to achieve the targets of LPG. In this regard, there is need for re-designing, re-orienting and re-fitting the management system of North East education from the perspectives of LPG, so that the wider objectives of LPG can easily be achieved by the society.

*Management Challenges of Science, Technical and Mathematics Education in North East*: It is a true and not debatable fact that the standard of science, technical and mathematics education in most parts of North East India is very weak except few parts of Manipur, Tripura and Assam. In the states of Arunachal Pradesh, Nagaland, Meghalaya and Mizoram, the standard of Science, Technical and Mathematics education is not at all encouraging. While discussing about the standard of Science and Mathematics education in the state of Mizoram, Hluna (1992, p. 230) remarked that "Not only the Mizos, but the average tribal students are well trained in literacy and verbal articulation and more discipline, but they don't have solid ground in Mathematics and Science which are the hallmark of modern outlook. On the part of the government, no serious attempts have been made to right the wrong till recently. This seems to be a basic common problem of education not only in Mizoram, but also in the southern hill areas of North East India." It is a surprising fact that the number of Science related departments are too scanty in comparison to humanity and Arts related departments in most of the North Eastern universities. The scope of Science, Technical and Mathematics education is very poor in North East India due to two main reasons, i.e. (i) the students are not mentally so much active to accept the abstract principles of Science, Mathematics and Technology, and (ii) facilities for Science, Mathematics and Technical education are not adequate in this region. So management of Science and Technical education has been a challenge in this region today. Therefore, on one hand there is a need for developing positive attitude among the students of North East towards Science, Technical and Mathematics education, and on another hand, there is a need for providing all types of facilities for Science, Technical and Mathematics education in North East schools, colleges, universities and other educational institutions. To meet these challenges, all the aspects of education system of North East need to be redesigned starting from aims and objectives till to the training of teachers, from the point of view of Science, Technology and Mathematics.

Prospects of multi-culturalism and inclusiveness in North East and management of North East education inclusiveness and multi-culturalism is a recurring challenge for the present-day North East India. Since education acts as an instrument for all types of change and developments, so, for achieving the values of inclusiveness and multi-culturalism in North East society, education can be used as the best means. Therefore, all contents and processes of North East education need to be managed in such a way that those can easily achieve the multi-culturalism and inclusiveness in North East society. Delor's International Commission on Education (1996) viewed that learning to live together should be the motto of our education and this can be achieved through multi-cultural education. North East India as a part of this international society should pay respect to the idea/practice of living together by providing proper multi-cultural education to its individuals.

*Demand for Peace and Harmony in North East and Management of North East Education*: In North East region of the country, peace has been disturbed in many ways. Many times, we can find religious fight, racial fight, cultural fight, linguistic fight, etc. in this region. The people of North East India are demanding peace in many ways. A lot of promising talks between the Government of India and different states of North East are going on from time to time for creating peace in different regions of North East India. This lure for peace in North East region can best be attained through motivational approach than forced approach. And education is one of the best instruments through which the peace can be attained and people can be motivated towards peace. Therefore, the whole process of education in North East region should be directed towards creation of peace and harmony in that region.

*Challenge for Quality Management of North East Education and Quality Demand of External World*: The external world is a world of competition, a world of innovation and a world of comparison. Quality is more demanded in this external world than the quantity. If the education system of North East India wants to compete with the education system of external world, then education system of North East India must enhance its quality and competency. The quality issues like lack of proper teachers' training especially at the school stage, low students' participation in teaching learning process, use of less qualitative/effective teaching, learning materials and textbooks, lack of proper infrastructure, lack of proper professional growth and development of teachers, etc. are found in North East education system. Therefore, quality management of North East education has become a challenge today. This quality needs to be maintained starting from its aims and objectives, curriculum, teaching learning strategy to evaluation procedure. Starting from the administrators, teachers and students to community people and guardians should be much careful about maintenance of quality education.

*Level Specific and Area Specific Management Challenges of North East Education*: Now, both the external world and the North East society itself are demanding a lot from North East education. This demand is very broad and comprehensive, which touches all the levels of North East education starting from pre-primary to higher education, and all the areas of North East education starting from general/liberal education to Science, Vocational, Technical and Computer education. Many new and innovative areas of education like Micro-Biology, Bio-Technology, Biochemistry, Genetic Engineering, Space Technology, Mountaineering, Marine Technology, Forestry, Environmental Sciences, etc. also need to be given due importance. North East education needs to be designed and managed in such a way that it can meet all its level specific and area specific issues and challenges.

*Need for Information and Communication Base in North East and Management of North East Education*: North East society is moving towards the peak of progress and development in a snail's speed due to the severe problems of transport and communication. Due to the rough geography of North East region, transport and communication has become very poor; and due to poor transport and communication, the people of North East fail to get the updated information about the world of work and activities. The modern means of communication like e-mail, Internet and other types of computer generated communication techniques are not widely and easily facilitated there, due to many other reasons. Education has to face the challenges of transport and communication of North East. So, the education system of North East is needed to be managed in such a way that it would facilitate the technological knowledge for removing the existing barriers of transport and communication in North East. Introduction and implementation of information communication technology (ICT) based education in North East would be much helpful in this regard.

*Challenge for Socio-Economic Sustainability in North East and Management of North East Education:* Development of economic condition of the North East has become a challenge today. Except Assam, in all parts of the North East, agricultural fields are rarely found due to the irregular terrain of hills and mountains. Most of the North East states are not economically sustainable. Except few jungle products, they do not have any other sources of income. Trades and industries are rarely found in north eastern states. Only the state of Assam is rich in rice, tea and petroleum product. The scope of Technology and Science is very low in North East. In this juncture, education has to play a vital role for making the north eastern states economically self-sufficient and sustainable. A well-managed education system is necessary in the North East region which can facilitate more productivity in agriculture, trade, industry, business, etc. by which the region can be self-dependent region in economy.

*Protection of Unique Culture of North East and Management of North East Education*: The culture of North East is very much unique. The North East India is consisted of different religious groups, racial groups, cultural groups, linguistic groups, etc. Hundreds and hundreds of tribal groups like Nagas, Kukis, Mizos, Garos, Khasis, Jantias, Misings,

Bodos, etc. are found in North East and each of these tribes have so many categories of sub-tribes. All of these tribes and their sub-tribes have their own way of life, occupation, morale and social and cultural systems. Like these tribes, all other racial and cultural groups have their own pattern of lifestyle and behaviour. Protection of these unique cultures and patterns of life have become an important aspect of North East education. North East education should protect, preserve and promote these unique cultures of North East by introducing/implementing different plans and programmes and strategies. The study of North East culture and tradition should be an important part of North East education and the education system of North East should be directed towards protection of North East culture.

### Management Strategies for North East Education

In order to face the challenges of North East education, the following plans/programmes/techniques/strategies of management may be much helpful:

- Securing co-operation from National University of Educational Planning and Administration (NUEPA).
- Re-designing the roles and functions of Departments of Education, Directors of Education, Boards of Education and all other administrative departments and administrators of education.
- Securing co-operation from both private bodies (NGOs) and government bodies.
- Securing co-operation from national, state as well as local level bodies.
- Coordinating among different levels of management.
- Development of special packages, plans and programmes about the management of North East education.
- Separating narrow politics from the management of North East education.

- Developing supervisory relationship among different personnel involved in management of North East education.
- Professional development of the administrators.
- Providing a democratic climate for the management of North East education.
- Emphasizing grassroot level management by involving teachers and pupils in management process.
- Achieving participatory management in management process.
- Emphasizing on different levels, areas and aspects of management of education of North East.

| | |
|---|---|
| | Pre-primary level |
| | Primary level |
| Levels of Management | Secondary level |
| | Higher secondary level |
| | Higher level, etc. Management of Liberal/general education |
| | Management of Science and Technical education |
| Areas of Management | Management of Medical education |
| | Management of Environmental education, etc. |
| | Management of Human Resources |
| | Management of Finance Resources |
| Aspects of Management | Management of Material Resources |
| | Management of Time Resources |
| | Management of Activity Resources, etc. |

- Emphasizing different aspects of education in management of North East education:

  Aims and objectives

Curriculum

Methods/techniques of teaching

Discipline

Teacher training/education

Textbook

Evaluation procedure, etc.

- Restructuring and remanaging the educational institutions.
- Giving special place to management of North East education in policies and programmes of the governments.
- Special emphasis on management of Science, Technological and Mathematics education.
- Emphasis on peace and multi-culturalism in management of North East education.
- Making educational administrators, supervisors and inspectors responsible for their duties and securing both external and internal accountability in them.
- Making the management system more stronger by achieving/promoting educational complex.
- Discussing the management issues of North East education by organizing meeting, workshops, seminars, symposium, orientation courses, etc.
- Formulating advisory committee for providing necessary suggestions/directions for the management of North East education.
- Decentralizing the North East education management system.
- Frequent monitoring and evaluation of existing planning and management system of North East education.
- Expansion of educational facilities on the basis of demographic, geographic and other related factors.
- Effective use and implementation of existing government and any other bodies sponsor programmes of educational planning and management.

- Formulating a set of code of guidelines for effective management of North East education.
- Establishing liason department in order to maintain relationship between different agencies working for planning and management of North East education.
- Developing appropriate teaching learning materials, slides, aids, programmes, etc. for giving appropriate training to the administrators and supervisors for better planning and management of North East education. Such programmes need to be broadcasted through audio-video means.
- Introducing the periodic evaluation or periodic self-evaluation of management and administration of North East education.
- Suggesting the educational institutions of North East to prepare their activity profile and suggesting the competent agency to give grant to the educational institutions of North East on the basis of their activity profile.
- Facilitating research in management of North East education.

## REFERENCES

Barpujari, H.K. (1986), The American Missionaries and north-east India (1836-1900 A.D.). Guwahati: Spectrum Publications.

Behera, L. and Basantia, T.K. (2006), Evaluation of pre-service teacher educatioin syllabus in Orissa, Indian Educational Review.

Basantia, T.K. (2006), Quality Management of Elementary Education in the State of Mizoram: Some Strategies. A paper presented in the NEIES Conference-cum-Seminar on Planning and Management of Education in North East; Problem and Prospects, Deptt. of Education, Mizoram University, Aizwal, 26th and 27th October.

Hluna, J.V. (1992), *Education and Missionaries in Mizoram*, Guwahati: Spectrum Publications.

NIEPA (1994), Educational Administration in Mizoram, New Delhi: NIEPA.

Singh, A.K. (1994), Approaches to Tribal Development, New Delhi: Sarup & Sons.

Yogi, A.K. (1991), *Development of North East Region—Problems and Prospects*, Guwahati: Spectrum Publications.

# 8

# Indian Universities: Miles to Go Yet!

*M.S. Kurhade*

Education means knowledge refined, reshaped and then imparted in simple easy steps so as to enable the learner to absorb it, ruminate upon and digest. Education would then be instrumental in bringing about emancipation and sure progress in an individual. Thus, all the centres of learning right from schools and colleges to universities should be so equipped to facilitate quick and effective learning. The teaching and the non-teaching staff engaged by these centres of learning as well as the authorities who run them, are thus entrusted with the monumental responsibility of shaping the youth of today and consequentially the destiny of the nation tomorrow.

Basic education moulds the common man, whereas higher education hones him to balance and manage key positions in society. In this regard, the role of higher education needs to be thought upon, deliberated upon with due care and consideration. The centre of higher education is the university, the pivot of a nation. The need to study every aspect of university education cannot be highlighted enough. Keen observation of every minute detail about university functioning and university operations and making the necessary amendments and adjustments to suit the need of the time is largely the responsibility of the government and the university authorities.

And it is an established fact that a majority of Indian universities are hampered and controlled by men who do not understand the objectives of higher education. Therefore, the universities are unable to respond to the changing needs of the society. At the global level, the universities are becoming more technology driven and highly informative. But here, the fact is that most universities are without commitment or proper infrastructural facilities, as a result of which maximum number of unproductive students are produced. The onus on any university is to impart the right kind of education resulting in the provision of a suitable culture where the stakeholders can successfully achieve their expected goals. The most important elements which constitute any university are:

- The governance system of the university
- Visionary leadership
- Educational programmes, offerings and services
- Teaching standards
- Educational level of the university workforce
- Social responsibility
- Focus on the future
- Curricular revisions
- Examination system
- Research
- Student teacher ratio
- Recruitment and retention of faculty
- Options in courses and careers
- Physical facilities and
- Work culture of the university campus.

The quality of education in the Indian universities can be judged on the basis of each of the above cited fifteen criteria. Many universities rely on the old governance system. Therefore, there is less accountability on the part of the university and that is the main reason for poor performance. At present, we do not find transparency in the operations of governance. Hence, there is no internal control on the various departments/sections of the university. It is expected that the various departments/units work in close coordination with each other. But the major hurdle in Indian universities is an organized anarchy. A major cause of inefficiency in governance in Indian universities is the indiscipline, protest, politicization and disruptive activities of the teachers, students and non-teaching staff. Moreover, the vested interest of the politicians in the elections of the senate, the academic council, the students' council, the board of studies and the executive council have added to the problems in the day-to-day functioning of the university.

The working culture refers to university administration. The freedom to work, flexibility in the system and an accountable workforce are the basic factors which are required to run the university for the betterment of tomorrow. The Vice-Chancellor is the main decision-maker. The Vice-Chancellor of the university is the chief of university governance. He is expected to set the highest standards of conduct and performance by personal example and deal firmly with illegal practices. It has been observed that most of the Vice-Chancellors' personal actions do not reflect commitment to the university. Also that, the Vice-Chancellors and other university authorities are not interested in promoting a healthy environment that would foster harmony and ethical behaviour. Although the university authorities are aware that there is a need to create a healthy culture for improvement of the overall performance, they have failed to create a sustainable university. Many universities do not have visionary Vice-Chancellors. Leadership without a clear vision or commitment would do nothing for the progress of the university. It would also explain the unreasonable, inexplicable malfunctioning of the various departments of the university. There is so much power and authority with the Vice-Chancellor but if he is unaware of the strength of his post or complacent by nature, no change can be brought in the university either gradual or radical. It is not easy to change the system but a determined and committed Vice-Chancellor can work wonders and move mountains. The Kothari Commission Report says: "Generally the Vice-Chancellor should be a distinguished educationist or an eminent scholar in any of the disciplines or professions, with a high standard in his field and adequate administrative experience. We are not generally in favour of appointment of persons who have retired from other fields. An exception to this general recommendation should be made only in the case of outstanding persons whose association with the universities would be desirable from every point of view and should not be made an excuse for 'accommodating' or 'rewarding' individuals who do not fulfill the conditions laid down", this is how a Vice-Chancellor is expected to be. The Vice-Chancellor as the principal academic and executive officer of the university should exercise overall supervision and control over the affairs of the university and give effect to the decisions of all the authorities of the university.

Many universities as they function today are ill-equipped to perform their duties or execute their responsibilities effectively. There is no coordination of design and the delivery process. Representatives of most units are neither dedicated nor involved in working harmoniously and in sync with other departments. Policy implementation, staff training, public disclosure of information and monitoring systems are rarely found. There is no mechanism to evaluate the programmes. So, we find the plan only on paper without any concrete contribution towards university development. Use of modern technology and the allotted funds is only a matter of talk. In reality, legal and regulatory requirements are seldom followed. Therefore, a planned strategy is much needed. Technological and organizational innovation for effective functioning of work-systems may help to accomplish the university objectives. It has been observed that despite considerable efforts by the UGC, AICTE, NCTE and the government, the universities of India are lagging far behind compared to the universities abroad. University authorities and the university workforce have become lethargic and pessimistic. Any proposed change is strongly opposed and criticized. The philosophy of ethical behaviour has become a thing of the past. The bureaucratic working system of governance is completely outdated. The mechanical way of working, lack of understanding about the aims and objectives of a university often results in disorientation and chaos. The goal remains unidentified and elusive. Hierarchy in the university workforce and operations is a chain of ongoing conflict and jealousy. So, implementing the decisions taken by the higher authorities becomes very difficult. Our universities are influenced by rigid traditions of administration and so change in the system has become a gargantuan task. In the light of the above cited conditions, there is an urgent need therefore to ponder over the culture of the university. The present scenario indicates that the process of planning and implementation has hampered progress and development. A comprehensive programme for university improvement has to be designed. Also the entire planning at the university level should be directed towards the pursuit of quality. Planning for short- and long-term is a must for any university. Any university should conduct self-assessment on the basis of the following three questions:

(a) Is there a planned strategy for each new academic year?

(b) Is there provision for sustaining quality over a long-term?

(c) How many educational reforms are actually implemented each year?

All these questions have to be answered to fulfill the university objectives. Introducing innovative educational programmes, services and operations is the only solution to meet future challenges. The major hurdle is that universities are not equipped to envision the future. The redirection of resources, grants, endowments, research, new partnerships, modifications in instructional design need to be worked out, deliberated upon and put into practice.

The role of universities in this regard is multifaceted. Therefore, it is expected that quality education be imparted to develop competent and capable individuals who can hold their own in the competitive dynamic environment of tomorrow. In order to ensure high quality of education and to meet the needs of the students' community in the ever changing academic, social, and economic scenario, and to enable the students to take on the world, serious revamp and reformation is required. The need for thinking afresh upon issues like the university campus, university facilities, student-centric learning, interdisciplinary approach, use of modern technology, well-equipped laboratories, flexible admission policy, funding, fully qualified and committed faculty and effective governance cannot be highlighted enough.

A student-centered education is the key to success. Yet students' needs and expectations are not given the necessary priority. We do not find a concrete action plan to achieve the outlined goals. Insufficient financial resources and an inept staff are major hurdles in the accomplishment of the university plan. It is also important to take into account the students' dissatisfaction with the quality and variety of courses offered by the universities. A comprehensive plan to attract, satisfy, and retain students also needs to be evolved. In many universities, there are no access mechanisms which enable students to seek information. Moreover, the complaints of students are not attended to and resolved effectively. The universities are unable to provide sufficient research opportunities to the students. As a result, there is low demand for our students in the world market. The "voice of the students" is nowhere found in Indian universities. If at all, it is in the form of politics. Students are often instigated by political parties and teachers to strike and protest. The students are of an impressionable age and easily influenced. Hence, rational thinking and decision-making has to be inculcated in them to help them excel in their chosen walk of life.

University examinations have been the subject of many a discussion right from the beginning. Delay in declaring the examination results and malpractices followed during the examination is the major set back to university education. Appointments of the examiners and paper setters are not reviewed and evaluated. The feedback from the examiners is not given due importance. Ethical standards for paper setters and examiners are only on paper. In reality, accepting commissions or any other valuable consideration in return for awarding marks is a common phenomenon. Self-assessment at university level which is much required especially in examination work is totally overlooked in most Indian universities. The core values which are required for a strong foundation and for class performance in the examination section are sadly missing. Favouritism and corruption have laced the examination system at all levels. The Vice-Chancellor, the Pro-Vice-Chancellor and the Controller of Examinations together can superimpose and bring about radical changes in this regard.

The teachers' knowledge of the subject and an understanding of the cognitive, social, emotional, and ethical development of the student is not up to the mark. How then, would the teachers contribute towards student development? The main flaw lies in sticking to a teacher-centric paradigm, which largely focuses on the supply side of knowledge and ignores the curiosity of students. A rigid set-up and the narrow minded outlook of the teachers have spoiled the university environment. The academic and research work is so poor that there are no takers. Groupism, unionism, political motivation on the part of the teachers as also their prejudice towards sex, caste, creed, race and class have damaged the image of university system. It is a matter of fact that teachers are not able to inspire students with a sense of social responsibility or with a need to discover intellectual delights. According to Bertrand Russell, a Nobel Prize winner, "The teacher, like the artist, the philosopher, and the man of letters, can only perform his work adequately if he feels himself to be an individual directed by an inner creative impulse, not dominated and fettered by an outside authority." Yes, it is true that the process of recruitment of teachers is not foolproof. Without warm affection towards the students and a genuine desire to impart knowledge, no man can be good teacher. But the modern-day teachers are mere teachers and not guardians. In return of the salaries that they get, they supply rather than impart knowledge, they teach rather than preach, they inform rather than inculcate. They play a very impersonal role when what is required on their part is dedication of mind, body and soul.

The workforce of the university is the backbone of all work systems. The most important part is workforce commitment, both emotional and intellectual, for accomplishing the tasks at hand. The university workforce is expected to be engaged in high performing work environments in which people are motivated to do their utmost for the benefit of the students. But in reality, workforce problems are deeply rooted in discontent, jealousy, hierarchy and incompetence. Therefore, their impact on the university is an enormous malfunction and underperformance. The ability of the university workforce to accomplish its academic and administrative responsibilities is unimaginably poor. The knowledge, skill, and competency of the staff is much below par. It is a fact that there is no encouragement to the university staff to better their credentials neither does a two-way communication system between the staff and the university authorities. So, how do the university authorities communicate key decisions to their entire staff? The conventional procedure of administration is outdated. There is no recognition and reward programme to reinforce high performance among the staff. Moreover, no university observes a performance measure for regular review of the staff. Most universities have become virtual battlefields, in which political and other factions, backed by teachers and aided by other staff, often fight for supremacy and the stakeholders suffer all the more.

Education is a dynamic and a continuously evolving process. The university is not merely an institution for instruction. Rather, the university campus is a huge playground where the student-players try to excel each other to be an integral part of the global environment. In order to achieve this, the major thrust of the university education should be on:

- Improvement of quality, and standards of higher education through renewal of curriculum, provision of appropriate physical facilities and use of modern technology.
- Mobilisation of resources for the improvement of existing circumstances and for future development.
- Effective governance for better results and reforms in the examination system.
- Establishing links between the university and the industry keeping in mind the socio-economic goals of the community as well as introduction of credit system.

- A multi-disciplinary and an inter-disciplinary approach and increased research.
- An environment conducive for effective teaching and learning.
- A faculty with the requisite credentials for quality education and an all round development of the student.
- Induction of knowledge and its application.

To sum up in the words of great teacher, Dr. S. Radhakrishnan, "There is need for change in the perception and attitude of universities realizing that their field is wider, task is greater and goal is higher in building a strong and happy India. The universities are not merely places of conferring degrees and distinctions. They, besides being places of learning are also centres of service and wholesome development of human personality; of men and women, turning them into fine human beings. The universities can't stand isolated; they should be active participants in developmental activities, which are benevolent and beneficial for people. It is unfortunate that the hopes, aspirations and expectations of students are not fulfilled to the extent expected. Therefore, it is time to mend and amend the systems, which have a negative effect on the society. The universities have a great role to play in instilling and encouraging the spirit of secularism and patriotism. The universities besides being venues of learning should be service centres in letter and spirit".

# 9

# Co-Relation between Education and Globalization

*Dinesh Kumar Paliwal*

Relaxation in the political barriers across the globe to facilitate the trade and effective interaction in various spheres among nations may be called as globalization. The phenomenon of globalization was started in the last century at the initiative of developed nations, under the leadership of United States of America (USA), at a time when they were going through a period of economic recession. In order to give a boost to their economy and support their domestic industry, developed nations supported the idea for free trade across the boundaries of the nations with the intention to target the market of some of the developing countries, having potential for vibrant economy, for their domestic industry and other business houses. With this intention, in the year 1995 a body in the name of World Trade Organization (WTO) was established with its headquarters at Geneva, Switzerland.

The objective of WTO was to promote free trade among the nations, who are its members by lifting or relaxing legal provisions, that were impediments to free trade, and within a framework of rules, regulations and guidelines prepared by WTO. The policies of WTO were primarily influenced by the developed nations. A significant number of nations were motivated or guided, through various diplomatic and other channels and negotiations, to join WTO. Consequent to the establishment of WTO and operationalization of various clauses of its charter, desirable boost in the trade, in favour of developed nations was observed and the economy of these nations had started thriving.

Inspired from the success of WTO and liberalization of trade in commodities and its benefits, a move was initiated to extend the cover of WTO to the trade in services. Accordingly, a General Agreement for Trade in Services (GATS) was drafted in the year 1998. In this agreement, education was included as one of the services. GATS provides for trade in education through following four modes:

(a) Operation of educational institutes on the foreign land by granting franchise or agreement/arrangement with the educational institutes of the host countries.

(b) Establishment of the campuses/centers of the foreign universities in host countries.

(c) Establishment of centers by the governments of the countries abroad for promoting the education/programmes offered by their universities/institutes with multiple objectives to enroll more and more international students.

(d) Operation of virtual campuses by using satellite and information super highway.

Nations have become the signatory of GATS for one or the other level of education in one or the other way of trade. Thus, the day is not too far, when trade in education shall be in full swing and the commercialization of education shall become a reality, at least at international level. Being a member of international community, India has also to live with this bitter truth and has to make its position clear after considering all pro and cons. Therefore, an in-depth study of this aspect could be interesting and may help in formulating a policy to safeguard the national interest in the future era of international trade in education.

Since long, the countries having relaxed laws with adequate availability of skilled and semi-skilled manpower at low cost have been the preferred locations for multinational companies (MNCs) to locate their manufacturing units. Therefore, the countries of East Asia, South America and even China could attract the investment from MNCs in past. India, which is one of the largest producers of skilled manpower (technocrats) become a point of attractions for foreign investors in various sectors with the onset of liberalization and opening of economy in nineties of twentieth century. This was the time, when developed countries of the West have started reaping the benefits of the globalization under WTO's regime.

In the aftermath of the unfortunate event of 9/11 (September 11, 2001), when World Trade towers in the city of New York were attacked by terrorists, the flourishing economy of United States received a strong jerk, which also sent shock waves among the economy of other nations that were having effective trade and dealings with United States. As a result, some developed nations have seen closure of companies even after the best efforts by their respective governments to provide diplomatic, economic and other supports. For the sake of their survival, certain companies have started looking for different solutions to cut down their expenditure for maintaining the level of their profit at optimal level for their survival. This attempt has given rise to a new concept of outsourcing the operations (other than manufacturing) in the countries with low wage structure and cost of operations. These companies have made best use of the Information Communication Technology (ICT) in this process.

At this juncture, India, which was having a significant pool of English speaking educated manpower, enjoyed an edge over other developing countries. This factor supported by natural factor of the time difference and the policies of liberalization of the government have proved a boom for Indian economy. This attributed to the boom in economy of India through establishment of Business Process Outsourcing (BPO) units in the form of call centers of quite a significant number of foreign-based companies. Since ICT is the backbone of BPOs, the software and ICT sectors have also witnessed an upward swing, which in turn benefited the IT segment of Indian industry.

Needless to mention here that prior to 9/11, India had made its presence felt, globally, as a main hub for the IT manpower. It may not be inappropriate to say that the above two factors had fueled the Indian economy and resulted into the growth of its various sectors, be it the infrastructure sector, service sector, travel and tourism sector or finance sector. Inspired from the economic benefits of the process of outsourcing, the multinational companies started working on the outsourcing of Knowledge Process Operations (KPO), i.e. outsourcing the research to the countries having significant pool of talented scientists and engineers.

Inadequacy of English Language courses in the curriculum of the Chinese education system has left trained technocrat manpower of China at disadvantage vis-à-vis Indian technocrats, who are fluent in English, in international market. China, at this stage effectively realized the weakness of its education system and has given a flip to its education policy with greater emphasis on English language in the curriculum in order to maintain an economic edge over its contemporary economic rival, India, for attracting foreign investment in BPO and KPO sectors too and maintaining the level of inflow of foreign funds. This move of China, in due course, could place Indian technocrats in stiff competition with their Chinese counterparts.

Indian economy, in the sectors stated above, had witnessed an average growth of around 9-10 per cent during last few years and the corporate sector felt the heat of the shortage of trained manpower and therefore started recruitment of manpower from abroad. Certain sectors where the manpower is being hired from abroad are Aviation; Finance; top management positions; Investment Banking; high-end technological industry and even the education sector. This indicates that India's higher education system was not ready to support this pace of the economic growth of the nation. It may be considered as a cause of concern, specially, with regard to the fact that the nation has a large pool of manpower, which is still unemployed. This suggests that our education system, at present, is generating unemployable manpower.

In support of the contention in the preceding paragraph, attention is be drawn to a report published in the *Economic Times*, New Delhi Edition, 17 November 2007 issue, citing India Labour Report 2007, states that unemployability is a bigger crisis than unemployment. The news item has quoted from the above said Labour Report 2007 that while 53 per cent of employed youth suffer some degree of skill deprivation, while only eight per cent of youth are fit for employment. According to the report, 57 per cent of country's youth suffer from some degree of unemployability and 90 per cent of our colleges/ schools' output is with bookish knowledge. The report goes on saying that the skill deficiency hurts more than infrastructure deficiency because of equality while poor infrastructure maintains inequality.

It is indicative from the contents of preceding paragraph that the country's education system was not prepared to face the challenges of globalization and support the growth of the economy. In order to support the growth of economy, the education system specially the post-secondary system of education needs to be oriented suitably and geared up. A detailed study of the process of globalization, its present status and the future direction it might take, may be helpful in investigating co-relation of globalization with education and to arrive at certain conclusions that may give a new dimension to the system of higher education and training, make it relevant to the needs of growing economy.

At this juncture, it is important to have a better understanding of the words education and training, which have distinctly different meaning. Education empowers a person to think logically, do the analysis and innovations, and contribute to the world of knowledge. Thus, education develops the human resources as scientists, philosophers, strategists and policymakers, etc. Whereas training empowers a person to act as a professional and work in a given situation to deliver the desired results as per well laid down process. Even though, it is difficult to draw a sharp line of distinction between education and training, the better understanding of the term education and training and their appropriate use in developing the human resources could be useful in the overall growth of the country.

The strong education systems of the developed economies may be cited as an example and in support of the hypothesis that strong economics needs and survives only if, they are supported by stronger Higher Education System that adapt itself to the need of economy and provide education and training of relevance. Moreover, a need of development of an integrated system to assess the discipline and profession-wise need of trained manpower at present and in near future and the projections for future as per the rate of growth and direction of economy may be felt as a necessity.

Given consideration to the above, it may be concluded that there is a standing need to keep an eye on the economic trends through regular studies for developing such a system of education and training that supports the growth of economy. An in-depth study to assess the impact of possible global trade in educational services on Indian education system is equally important, in present time, to reap the benefit of possible global education market.

# 10

# Redefining College Administration

*M.S. Kurhade*

The word 'Administration' is such a broad term that to comprehend it, one needs to take stock of all those things which are directly or indirectly implied by it. To administer is to give, to carry out, to ensure, to inculcate, to inject, to deliver, to manage, to dispense so on and so forth.

Good administration is a prime requisite for the smooth conduct of any institute be it corporate, government or educational. Corporate administration is easier as compared to the other two since the power to execute and the power to reform rests with the top few. But the administration of a government office or an educational institute is much difficult especially in the Indian context because lethargy and inactiveness has pervaded into almost every department. People working in government offices and educational institutes feel no threat to their jobs and take their bread and butter for granted unlike people working for corporates. And hence the resultant complacency.

What is needed, is a severe jolt to shake them out of this inertness. It could be in the form of reorganisation, re-scheduling, revamp, reform and rejuvenation enlisting the whole-hearted support of all the employees concerned, motivating here, goading there so as to make every government office, every university, every college and school a living, breathing entity.

In colleges, the day-to-day administration is carried out by the officers headed by the principal, vice-principal/s, heads of the department/s, professors, readers and lecturers. The principal is both the administrative and academic head. The vice-principal/s and heads of the various departments assist him in both academic and administrative functions.

Under the Society's Registration Act, the Public Trust Act and the Maharashtra Universities Act, the executive committee of the college includes the President and the Trustees of the Education Society or the College Governing Council. It acts in the name of the Education Trust in conformity with rules of business allocation and conduct of the college constitution. The management of the college may entrust either conditionally or unconditionally, to its Principal, the executive power in relation to any matter of the college.

In modern times, administration in colleges has several complex functions. The following administrative authorities exist in a college:

1. The Management of the College
2. The Principal
3. The Vice-Principal/s
4. Head of the Department/s
5. Estate Manager
6. Campus Director
7. Librarian
8. Finance Officer/Cashier
9. Sports Director
10. Chief of the Health Centre
11. Chairman of the Examination/s
12. In-charge of National Service Scheme
13. Co-coordinator of Department of Adult and Continuing Education and Extension
14. Convener of Women's Development Cell

15. Officer of Right to Information
16. Public Relation Officer
17. Convener of Grievances cell
18. Local Managing Committee
19. Students' Council
20. Rector
21. Registrar
22. Office Superintendent.

The efficient administration of a college will ensure smooth conduct of the various activities of the college. The goal of the entire administration is to impart quality service so as to ensure students' and parents' satisfaction. Students' satisfaction will be seen from the students' assessment of the services provided by the colleges. Administration would surely improve if students feel more secure about where they are headed and how the college is taking them there. The colleges should provide better services to the students to help them gain confidence to face the challenges in this highly competitive and ever changing world. College administration should put in place a system where man and machine should work in tandem towards fulfillment of the objectives. The responsibility of providing the right information with a student focus, creating a congenial atmosphere for student development and providing all the campus facilities rests wholly with the college administration.

The main objective of college administration is to render an efficient service to those whom the office serves. In the case of an office attached to a college, it serves mainly—

(i) Students
(ii) Parents
(iii) Teachers
(iv) Community
(v) University
(vi) Government
(vii) University Grants Commission

(viii) National Assessment and Accreditation Council
(ix) National Council of Teachers Education
(x) All India Council of Technical Education.

Actually, the real need is action in college administration which is missing. The aim and purpose of the college is to impart education which can bring about a change in response to economic and social changes. Such changes are bound to demand the best administration for new objectives to be achieved in education. In view of the social, economic and technological changes at the global level, the process of teaching and learning is becoming more and more varied and complex than it has ever been before. College administration connotes an environment in itself. The old fashioned self-enclosed administration has to eventually give way to a more flexible and functional space. In view of the rapid development in the field of higher education, it is essential that the whole system of administration be reoriented.

In view of the fast changing globally competitive environment, our colleges must focus on an effective and responsive administrative system, which can successfully take up the challenges. The colleges are required to make continual adjustments in their internal factors to move towards developing a healthy future for the students. The task will involve an overall change in the approach of the governance of a college. A large number of colleges are still dependent on the traditional approach of governance and bureaucracy. This needs an overall re-engineering by application of new strategy and techniques. At present, college administration is not very encouraging and therefore calls for initiatives for reform and improvement. The practice of the college units within the system to work in isolation creates a serious obstacle in college development. Reforms are therefore required at different stages to enhance the performance of the administrative system.

There is, therefore, a need for each of the existing colleges to be re-examined with the aims of bringing them up to an acceptable standard. The kinds of questions which need to be asked are:

1. Is there decentralization in the college administration?
2. Is there timely and efficient communication with students and parents?
3. Are the functions of different departments and units stated in clear terms?
4. Is college information updated and made easily available?
5. Is there a harmonious inter-personal relationship among the staff?
6. Is there an efficient grievance redressal and conflict resolution mechanism?
7. Is there a proper employment of technology for total e-governance?
8. Is there missionary zeal among the staff?
9. Is the developmental plan and detailed information about the college made available to the general public?
10. Are there IT centres developed in the college campus?
11. Is the course curriculum and facilities provided by the college printed in English and local languages?
12. Is there a constant monitoring mechanism in administration?
13. Is the college "web-enabled"?
14. Is there a "working culture" in the college?
15. Does the administrative staff respond quickly to the queries?

Since the idea of college administration envisages the formulation, implementation, monitoring and evaluation of a plan not by the principal of the college alone, but by the management, teachers, students, parents and the non-teaching staff, it is expected that all contribute towards it willingly and welcome the changes with an open mind. It is necessary to call meetings of all concerned at regular intervals to identify the needs and assess the resources to meet the identified needs. Smooth functioning of the college depends upon the working culture. If there is a congenial and transparent culture then it can inspire the students towards perfection. An effective information system can help the college to grow in a healthy manner. Good communication can help a lot many students to save on their time and effort. To create an atmosphere of love, trust and security in the college is of utmost importance. The college should understand its own problems, assess its own needs through planned efforts, find alternative solutions to those problems and develop appropriate programmes and projects to meet the assessed needs by itself.

Vital insights and best practices are essential that will help to understand, implement and maintain a complete network of administration. A superset of performance excellence methodologies that are built on a balanced combination of leadership, participation and effective service would work wonders for the students' community. Since activities are better managed by the individuals who perform them, decentralisation becomes essential. It is necessary to allow the exercise of initiative by principal and teachers with a view to enhance the quality of college administration.

No college can become the best overnight. It is a long, tedious process and takes years of perseverance and focus. If the college lives up to its image, makes good all its promises, people would slowly but steadily start believing in it. Faith and goodwill builds up the reputation of a college. Persuading students to dream big and helping them to realise these dreams would definitely help the college to build a niche for itself. Sharing of experiences and facilities and observance of the norms of conduct by the principal, management, teachers, students, parents and the non-teaching staff would help the college serve the society better. The significant fact to be noted is that the control of the powers of administration and the redress against its improper use can be obtained under the Indian legal system by the following ways:

1. By seeking relief under Article 32 of the Constitution of India when one can claim that his fundamental rights have been violated.
2. Under Articles 226 and 227 of the Constitution of India, the aggrieved party may approach the

Honorable Court on the ground that there has been a substantial injury on account of the administrative action.

3. Under the Right to Information Act, the aggrieved person can file a suit if the college authority exercises such power for any purpose other than the one for which power was conferred.

The real problem starts with the nature of college bureaucracy. In most colleges, the bureaucracy is hyper sensitive to its controlling character and there is a large governance problem. The result is distrust and disrepute to the administrative system of colleges and the students connected with it. Despite aid from the UGC, NAAC, NCTE, AICTE, etc., we could not achieve much success because of the administrative system which has not been able to respond to the global educational needs. Taking into serious consideration the above scenario, we realise that the magnitude of the changes required is so great that if we do not start the process of introducing significant changes with immediate effect, we, who are already behind the times, would become lame and invalid. Therefore, an effective and a modern administrative set up alone can make for the rapid progress of the colleges.

The modern concept of college administration is work simplification. A programme of work simplification would consist of the following steps:

1. Find out what work is now being done.
2. Ascertain the purpose of each kind of work.
3. Ask "Is this work necessary? If so, why?"
4. Eliminate unnecessary work.
5. Use the computer and modernize facilities.
6. Eliminate the duplication of work.
7. Review all factors periodically.
8. Standardise the methods to be used.
9. Establish necessary controls.

10. Co-ordinate the activities of various units.
11. Provide a proper guidance.
12. Prepare a tight schedule and time-table and execute it.

The college authorities now need to take in the developing situation. There has to be a radical change to enable the students to gain quick access to knowledge in every field. But today, the higher education system at college level has become dysfunctional. This outdated system has to inevitably give way to modern reforms. To make the best use of the resources available and to achieve rapid overall progress of the colleges, it is essential that the basic concepts and techniques of good administration with suitable modifications be introduced in toto. Today's colleges should prepare a potential staff with this objective and march ahead. A cooperative staff, a broad outlook, hardwork, emphasis on prompt service, avoidance of extremist attitudes, a good understanding of the students' psychology and the college environment is required for the able administration of any college.

To sum up, college administration should encompass office administration which looks after payment of salaries, receipt of fees, maintenance of documents and records, etc., academic administration which takes care of organised conduct of lectures, exams and assessment and general administration which would categorically supervise and superimpose on the former two. When this happens, there's no stopping the college from being the 'Numero Uno'.

# The Technology Effects

# 11

# Acceleration of ICT and ODL Interaction due to Globalisation

*Bucherla Murahari* and *V. Vijaya Kumar*

Enrolment in higher education in India accounts for only 8 per cent of the eligible age group whereas in a country like Canada it is 100 per cent. We have, therefore, much to do in terms of expansion capacity so as to cover the left out 92 per cent of the eligible group from access to higher education and to make them fit to the active partners in the progress of be country. Apart from this young group, there are others who missed higher education due to various reasons and would like to improve their qualifications and/or upgrade their skills who may be working or otherwise. The low percentage of higher education enrolment compelled the nation to increase it at par with the developed nations. That is why the matter is highlighted in the 11th Plan to enhance enrolment at least upto 25 per cent and lion's share being earmarked to ODL. Quality, equity, access and excellence are the main pillars of higher education. Review and modernization are the periodical interventions needed for its enrichment. Cost effectiveness is a major factor that needs focus. The world and inevitably India are in the throes of major economic and technological changes. The process will affect not only the market economy of the nation, but also the whole system of higher education which has to prepare its graduates for participation in the social and economic development of the country and the type of cultural environment and ethos it will need to foster. Moreover, education is itself being internationalized and universities are losing their territorial boundaries. Information and Communication Technology is further contributing to this change and will have a major impact on the structure, management and mode of delivery of the educational system.

### Effect of Globalisation on Higher Education

We are living through a period of social, economic and information revolution which cannot leave our educational system untouched. Like many aspects of life, education is undergoing constant changes under the effect of globalization. Globalization and a shift to a market-led knowledge based economy demands education to become the corner stone of development. The introduction of information and communication technologies (ICTs) are changing the forms of education and the process to impart it. Changes are taking place in consonance with the students and teachers and producing a shift in the society from industrialization towards an information based society. The teachers and the institutions are ready to face this organizational and cultural change. For example, the teaching staff today are using the web to find resources to incorporate into their teaching. Teachers are guiding the students to use resources on the web directly and students are finding resources themselves. Learning has become student centric and the teacher has become a facilitator (Barr and Tagg, 1995) and teachers and students are working in collaboration in constructing knowledge castles together. The changes in education are taking place and as a result the structure of education is being altered to enable it to cooperate in the global open market. This is often termed as the co-modification of education. However, one should think of the impact of globalization in a positive mind. Globalization allows students to go overseas for studies and overseas students coming to India as in the ancient Nalanda and Takshasila University times. This can improve their studies by placing them closer to their field in which they are interested as well as allowing them to study at universities that specialize in the area concerned. Apart from that, the rise of global society evolving by technological and communication developments are shaping the children—the future citizens of the world into global citizens with a broad range of skills and knowledge. Children cannot be effective in tomorrow's world if they are trained in yesterday's skills. Nor should teachers be denied the tools that other professionals take for granted (Blair, 1988).

It is obvious that globalization has opened many new doors in the world of education. In the developed world, it improved the level of education now available and many developing countries now have a vastly improved education system that previously would not have existed at such a level. Usage of ICTs in ODL is multiplied. The use of computer-aided assessment is increasing much of it delivered online and course management systems are supporting registration and course administration as well as providing feedback on assessments and other performance data. Globalization has improved and diversified the curriculum in a varied way and thus globally and unequivocally improved the education. As a result, educational institutions have reacted accordingly by becoming more market-oriented, focusing their energy more on creating funds than on providing quality education for students which contradict the Indian philosophy for education. However, education has created unprecedented new opportunities for sustainable development and for eradicating poverty. ODL mediated learning for development as advocated in UN Millennium Development Goals (2006) form a blue print agreed to by all the countries of the world. Catalytic activity of globalization is accelerating the ICT and ODL interaction and internationalization of education should be welcomed and sustained.

## Open and Distance Learning

Distance education, an ugly duckling a few decades back, is an elegant swan today. It has come to stay and is no more a step sister of formal education. It provides open access to higher education to all those disadvantaged groups who could not or did not join the formal stream for various reasons. It aims to train people in various arts and crafts leading to the growth and development of the individual for the betterment of the society as a whole. The quality of distance education is now widely recognized in educational, commercial and political circles of the world. As many educational authorities and planning stalwarts could foresee the distance education which is cost effective has provided a viable alternative to labour intensive and expensive conventional education. The study carried out by Gubarnick and Ebeling (1997) revealed a big difference in cost. It costs University of Phoenix $ 237 to provide one credit hour of open and distance education against $ 486 per hour for Arizona State University (Conventional education). Open and distance learning offers a viable solution encompassing all the above requirements. This cost effectiveness might be called the Big Bang Theory of distance education (Hawkridge, 1995). It has great potential for pluralistic approaches and unprejudiced learning, however. It is up to the distance educators to avail themselves of these possibilities by presenting in as unbiased a way as possible alternative approaches and interpretations, inspiring search and discussion free from dogmatic shackles (Holmberg Borje, 2003).

The increasing demand for distance education is due to highly effective and personalized mode of teaching, making use of the new information processing technologies. Just as companies are customer-oriented, the distance education institutions are learner-oriented. They provide programmes which are designed to meet the needs, interests and aspirations of the learners. It is free from constraints of classroom learning which is time and place bound. The programmes are accessible for all learners irrespective of their location, age and formal qualifications. Flexibility is an inherent character of the system. Learners choose their own combination of subjects and complete the courses at their own pace and places. In the developing country like India, the vast majority of the people live in rural areas and are largely pre-occupied with the struggle for survival—including the need for basic skills, vocational skills, health, social and civic education. The distance education empowered by multimedia could make this group of citizens more functional and productive in their work as housewives, cooks, farmers, traders, teachers, technicians, nurses, etc. All of these could help us build a healthier, happier, more stable and informed, better cultured and self-reliant citizenry (Anjanappa, 1988). The requirement for a workforce with up-to-date skills and the need for continuing professional updating and training means that the educational and training process needs to be viewed as ongoing. There is also considerable interest now being addressed in older learners, those who have perhaps finished in full-time employment and have the time to pursue educational activities for personal fulfillment. It is the system that emphasis on lifelong learning. From this perspective, education is not something that only happens during childhood and early adulthood but rather is a continuing process throughout an individual's life. Never before has distance education been accepted to such a great extent as a regular form of learning (Peters, 2002). The Information Age is upon us and that the education must prepare the students for the ever changing workplace in the future.

### Multimedia in ODL

One of the reasons for the growing acceptability of distance education by teleconferencing is that this family of media allows groups of distant learners to be taught in real-time by a classroom teacher (Moore, 1995). Constraints of time and space together with the rapid obsolescence of knowledge in some areas of science and technology have created a huge demand for different courses from different institutions in the distance mode. Open universities have been the leaders in technological innovations and making the best use of them for better results. Perhaps Garrison (1987) did not exaggerate when he stated, "Distance education is inexorable to the technology delivery. Without the use of technology, distance education would not exist." Dhanarajan (2003) also emphasized the value of technology in education, saying "the opportunity is to utilize every technology that is appropriate, to deliver those educational services at an acceptable cost, with convenient access and, most importantly, without losing the desirable good traditions of the teaching and learning environment." Technology Enhanced Learning is a solution. It attempts to exploit the rapid developments in Information and Communication Technologies. As the communications bandwidth continues to increase and the cost of computer power continues to drop, Technology Enhanced Learning will become an economically viable solution. Visionaries of the Information Age have predicted and anticipated these developments four decades ago. Bush (1945), Pask and Curran (1982), Nelson (1990) and several others of recent times have considered how global networks will impact our lives.

The credibility enjoyed by distance education today is mainly because of its multimedia approach. Media eliminates the problem of distance and carries education to the door-steps of the learners. Different media tend to support self-directed, individualized, as well as collaborative learning, and add new dimensions to the transaction of course curriculum (Horgan, 1998). Distance education has evolved from print-based media to web-enabled media in a very short period—a feature characteristic of dynamic organic entity. Furthermore, new distributed learning committees have evolved over this time. Daniel (1999) and Bates (2000) have suggested that a new instructional paradigm is likely to result, given the way the concerns of online teaching and learning are being addressed by open universities the world over. Services of a few experts are made available for the whole nation. Media not only compliment the face-to-face method, but also off-set the disadvantages of the face-to-face teaching. Blend of media gives maximum benefit to the students. The multimedia approach not only multiply classrooms and teachers but also creates enthusiastic environment to the learners in distance teaching. While print still tends to be the core medium of distance education, there are examples of highly sophisticated multimedia systems in use throughout many parts of the world. The first and best use of multimedia in India has been videoconferencing which was introduced to impart knowledge by the UGC-CEC network with the help of ISRO and Doordarshan in the year 1992. In distance education, we seek to shift focus from teacher to learner and classroom teaching to self-learning. This is done by the use of multiple media instructional package where print is supplemented by technology.

The role of multimedia in distance education is detailed and discussed else where (Murahari, 2007).

**Option of ICTs and Their Impact on ODL**

National policymakers have chosen to explore the use of ICTs for education along side educational broadcasting three decades back. Post-economic liberalization and large-scale privatization over education there has been an increased effort to use ICTs in Open and Distance learning. The year 1971 marked the beginning of the concerted efforts for use of electronic media for improving the quality and reach of education. However, use of electronic media remained sporadic without any clear direction or policy. A situation analysis of children's television echoed those basic issues in the use of educational broadcast (Agarwal and Aghi, 1987; Agarwal et al., 1999). It is only of the creation of distance teaching and learning systems that educational broadcast has come centre-stage. There has been dramatic shift from the 1980s to present-day in the use of technology in the delivery of education in general and ODL in particular. The ICTs are the key to interactive learning and shall determine future prospects of distance education. Some of the global trends in ICTs include convergence, miniaturization, increased mobility, enhanced processing power and reduced cost (Khan, 2000). The single most important innovation is the convergence whereby multimedia is becoming uni-media (Inglis et al., 1999).

New learning technologies can transform the way the knowledge packaged, delivered, accessed, acquired, and measured altering higher education's core productions and delivery processes. Relying on technology rather than bricks and motor, non-traditional competitions will give colleges and universities a run for their money. While many equate information and communication technologies primarily with mobile and more advanced technologies, a more useful definition of information and communication technologies includes all technologies that enable the handling of information and facilitate different forms of communication. A new kind of educational instruction using a mix of technologies and face-to-face teaching to reach students wherever they are—at home, in the workplace, in the remote classrooms or in campus classrooms. By expanding the notion of information and communication technologies to include both older and newer technologies, from newspapers, radio and television to camcorders, computers and cell phones, the full impact of information and communication technologies on the community development and youth in particular can be better understood. The distinction between old and new technologies may become outdated as radio, television, satellite technologies and the Internet are combined in an innovative ways to reach a wide range of target audiences.

The ICTs are being used in India for various purposes not only for gathering information but also for imparting skills as well as enhancing knowledge by way of showing various data to any remote locations with the help of connectivity to these technologies. Internet technologies are used as the vehicle in which the interaction between students and the teachers are a means of intellectual transportation that helps people span geographic distances (Moraes et al., 2003). The World Wide Web is a universal medium that everyone who has an Internet access can view. It is an international information delivery tool. The whole information required by the students such as course content, course pack, projects, etc. are readily available (Rao, 2003). Computer mediating conferencing uses text-based systems for interaction between learners and teachers. It has been singled out in the literature as a key development in distance learning because it is a means of support. Learners can support each other both directly and indirectly, by sharing their experiences, insights, concerns and reactions to the course and a sense of being part of a cohort of learners, thus reducing a sense of isolation (White, 2003). Choosing the appropriate delivery medium to enhance the interaction with the use of available resources is the key to successful interaction. Consortium for Educational Communication (CEC) an inter-university centre of University Grants Commission, creates e-learning material for higher education. In this process, CEC has also imparted capacity building programmes for teachers and technical personnel to use various multimedia software for development of e-content material on higher education. CEC is also responsible to maintain the quality of e-content material on higher education in terms of standard and quality material it puts for the benefit of students and teachers not only in India and for outside countries and especially Third World countries. All the CEC material will be available on website through Internet all over the world which can be accessed and used for educational purposes in most of the subjects taught in the country in two three years time.

## Discussion and Conclusion

The high degree of national commitment for increasing the reach of and access to education throughout the whole country has resulted in a surge in professional, technical and information technology education specially after globalization. Integration of ICT into basic education and in the uses of this technology for educational purposes has been a defining feature of education all over the world in recent years. In a rapidly changing world of global market competition, automation and increasing democratization, education must contribute to an individual's capacity to access and apply information in the proper context. This ability to access and effectively use information is no longer a luxury; it is a necessity for development. At the national level, IGNOU, NCERT, CEC, Department of Science and Technology are major users of EDUSAT network for distance education, school education, higher education and science education respectively. Spot beams are being used by several states to disseminate educational programmes in their respective languages. The Mana TV network in Andhra Pradesh with over 2000 receiving nodes across the state is the biggest network under the EDUSAT scheme as of now. The Mana TV network is slated for further expansion this year as 8000 more schools are getting connected to the network in the next three to four months. Other states which are active in the EDUSAT project are: Karnataka, Tamil Nadu, Kerala, Gujarat, Maharashtra, Madhya Pradesh and Orissa. The remaining states are at various stages of adopting the project.

The country has seen a very rapid and impressive expansion in ICTs which are wide spread in large parts of the countries after globalization and large-scale privatization of Indian education. The rapid pace of technological change offers hope that education in India can leapfrog into the new era of global knowledge at considerably less cost than the developed, industrialized countries have experienced. The scope of computer education was broadened to include computer applications in all walks of life, including administration, governance and management. Such ICT institutes have been set up by both government and privately-managed educational institutions across the country. The all-pervasive ICT has penetrated all sectors: education, research and development, business, industry, entertainment and service sectors such as travel. Today, getting railway reservations or paying electricity bills has become faster and much more efficient as a result of computerization. The educated youth as well as the elderly have begun to invest time, energy and money to become computer literate and to gain mastery over information technology.

In the age of techno-scientific revolution the country will need more and more educated and trained personnel to cope with the global demands. Teaching and learning methodology should be appropriate to the changing times. Access to higher education should be broad-based in view of changing socio-economic scenario of the nation. Globalization accelerated the ICT and ODL interaction resulting in networked learning which in turn enabled the education sector to reach global market creating online organizations. Consequently,

- Enrollment in educational institutions is going up as envisaged in the 11th Plan by the national policymakers, specially in distance mode.
- Number of online institutions are increasing in the world as well as in India.
- Need-based courses and programmes are written and rewritten to suit the modern mode of teaching and learning.
- Academic calendars are changed with changing pattern of education and global needs.

- Nearly 80 per cent of the universities started offering distance mode of education in addition to conventional for earning quick additional revenue to sustain conventional education.
- Online degrees awarded by American and European universities are very much available in India.
- Technical institutions have come up in thousands producing highly skilled technocrats for changing work places who are spreading across the length and breadth of the world.
- NRI remittances are fast increasing our foreign currency reserves.
- Teachers and institutions have readily accepted the challenge and change the organizations to suite the modern times that helped the nation in socio-economic development.
- Several foreign students started coming to India laying highways for international cooperation in real sense.

What started out as an alternative provision for higher education purposes ODL interacted with ICTs intensively after globalization transcending all sectors and potential playing crucial role in all aspects of human development in India. Opening the era of borderless nations with network learning lead the way for the formation of global village in consonance with our traditional concept of Vasudhaiva Kutumbakam that envisages prosperity not only for you but for the whole mankind. Further, the National Knowledge Commission's working group on Open and Distance Education has already sighted the light at the end of the tunnel "Open and Distance Education (ODE), enabled and delivered through information and communication technology (ICT), holds the promise to address questions of access and provide new, alternative forms of capacity building".

**Acknowledgements**

The author is grateful to Dr. P. Satyanarayana former Regional Director, IGNOU, Regional Centre, Hyderabad, Prof. C.K. Ramaiah, former Director, Virtual School of Higher Learning, Prof. D. Swaminathan, Vice Chairman, State Planning Board,

Govt., of A.P., Sri D. Suresh, Registrar, MGNIRSA, Hyderabad, Prof. J.S. Satish Kumar, Vice Chancellor, Prof V.R. Rajendran, Registrar, Prof. K. Rajendran, Dean (Research) Vinayaka Missions University, Salem, Prof. A.M. Pathan, Vice Chancellor, Maulana Azad National Urdu University, Hyderabad, Prof. K.R. Iqbal Ahmed, Pro-Vice Chancellor, Maulana Azad National Urdu University, Hyderabad for their help and encouragement during the preparation of this article.

## REFERENCES

Agarwal, Binod C., and Aghi, Mira B. (eds.) (1987), *Television and the Indian Child: A Handbook*, UNICEF, New Delhi.

Agarwal, Binod C., Karnik, Kiran S., Lai, C. and Viswanath, K. (1999), *Children's Television in India: A Situational Analysis*, Concept Publishing Company, New Delhi.

Anjanappa, K. (1989), *Manual for Coordinators,* 2nd Edition, Regional Services Division, IGNOU, New Delhi.

Barr, R.B. and Tagg, J. (1995), "From Teaching to Learning: A New Paradigm for Undergraduate Education," *Change,* November/December, 13-25.

Bates, A.W. (1990), "Interactive as a Criterion for Media Selection in Distance Education," *Interactive Communication in Distance education* (AAOU, 1990 Annual Conference Papers), Jakarta.

Blair, A. (1998), Forward to Connecting the Learning Society: *The National Grid for Learning,* The Government's Consultation Paper, HMSO, London.

Bush, V. (1945), "As We may Think," *Atlantic Monthly,* 176, 1, reprinted in I. Greif (1988) Computer-Supported Cooperative Work: A Book of Readings, Morgan Kaufmann Publishers, San Mateo, CA.

Daniel, J.S. (1999), "Mega Universities and Knowledge Media," *Technologies Strategies for Higher Education*, Kogan Page, London.

Dhanrajan, G. (2003), "Best Practices: Then and Now," in Prasad, V.S. et al. (eds.). *Best Practices in Open and Distance Education*, Booklinks, Hyderabad, India.

Garrison, D.R. (1987), "The Role of Technology in Continuing Education," *New Directions for Continuing Education.*

Gubernick, L. and Ebeling, A. (1997), "I got My Degree through E-mail", *Forbes Magazine*, http://www.forbes.com/forbes/97/0616/5912084a.htm

Hawkridge, D. (1995), "The Big Bang Theory in Distance Education," in F. Lockwood (ed.), *Open and Distance Learning Today,* Routledge, London.

Holmberg, Borje, (2003), Distance Education in Essence: An Overview of Theory and Practice in the Early Twenty-first Century, 2nd Edition, *Bibliotheks and information System* der Universitat Oldenburg.

Horgan, Barbara (1998), "Transforming Higher Education using Information Technology: First Step." http://horizon.unc.edu/TS/deafault.asp/show=article&id=490

Inglis et al., (1999), "Delivering Digitally", *Managing the Transition to the Knowledge Media,* London: Kogan Page.

Khan, A.W. (2000), "Collaboration and Cooperation in Specialised Education", Address at 27th World Marketing Congress, IIM, New Delhi.

Moraes De, M., Rodrigues Paz, C., Lumi Matuzawa, F. and Jantsch, P. (2003), Supporting Distance Students Using the Internet: *A Brazilian experience, the International Review of Research in Open and Distance Learning (online),* 4(1), http://www.irrodl.org/index.php/irrodl/article/ view/120/200

Moore, Michael, G. (1995), "American Distance Education: A Short Literature Review", *Open and Distance Learning Today,* Ed. by Fred Lockwood, Routledge Studies in Distance Education, London.

Murahari, B. (2007), "The Use of Multi Media in Open and Distance Learning", Conference proceedings of *Emerging Trends in the Use of Information & Communication Technologies,* National conference papers, Rajiv Gandhi International School of Information Technology, MGNIRSA, Hyderabad.

Nelson, T.H. (1990), *Literary Machines, Verson 901,* Mindful Press, New York.

Pask, G. and Curran, S. (1982), *Microman: Computers and the Evolution of Conscious*, Macmillan, New York.

Peters, Otto (2002), Distance Learning in Transition: New Trnds and Challenges, *Bibliotheks jund information System* der Universitat Oldenburg.

Rao, V.K. (2003), *Distance Education,* APH Publishing Corporation, New Delhi.

United National Development Programme (2006), About the MDGs: Retrieved from http//www.undp.org/mdg/ basics.html

White, Cynthia (2003), *Language Learning in Distance Education,* Cambridge University Press, Cambridge.

www.planningcommission.gov.in (National Knowledge Commission).

# 12

# In Search of Online Learning in India

*Sohanvir S. Chaudhary*

Indian education system is one of the largest in the world offering a variety of courses at all the levels: from early childhood care and education to post doctoral research. In the recent past, India has made moderate progress in terms of quality, equity and equality in education. The number of colleges from 700 at the time of independence in 1947 has increased manifold to around 25000. However, it continues to be grossly inadequate for a nation of this size and its requirements. India has set out an ambitious plan to establish another 700 odd universities and 35000 colleges over the next ten years. The plan has to be realized in collaboration with public-private partnership based on three pillars of education: access, inclusion and excellence (Lakshman, 2010).

To address the various needs and demands of the emerging society, the Government of India is trying its level best to impart quality education to its people for inclusive growth. With the liberalization policy, the expansion of education has become a serious concern for the policy planners as well as people at large. One of the most important issues is to improve the quality of higher education and increase access to institutions for higher learning. This is a difficult task for the government, as quality and access both are equally important instruments for development in all sectors (Alexander, 2009). The need of the hour is to provide quality education and make higher education more relevant to the emerging needs of the society.

India is equally concerned about the low Gross Enrolment Ratio (GER) in higher education. Educational planners feel that high GER is imperative to sustain economy as the educated youth contribute to the economic growth of the country. India is also concerned about the accessibility of quality education to a large number of youth in the country. Quality and access should get high priority as deserved but the moot question is: Whether it will be realistic to adopt a more moderate enrolment ratio and deploy more resources for improving the quality of education in the existing institutions? Thus, issues of access, quality and relevance of education having direct impact on the quantity and quality of the country's economic growth constitute important parameters for inclusive growth of society.

The government, according to Alexander (2009), will have to make a quick reassessment about the practicability of increasing the enrolment ratio from 12.4 per cent to 25 per cent and that too through the conventional system of education. India aspires to reach the gross enrolment ratio of 30 per cent between the ages of 18-25 years by 2020 up from the current level of 12.4 per cent (Lakshman, 2010). Taking into account the high, enrolment and retention of children in elementary schools, the government has resolved to universalize secondary education, which, in turn, would raise the enrolment in higher education and based on the positive trends of the recent past, these targets are likely to be achieved. Since this growth is not possible through the conventional system of education, multi-prong strategies are needed to achieve it.

### Learning Revolution in India

India is knowledge rich yet resource poor country with varied literacy levels across the vast nation (the illiteracy rate exceeds 35 per cent). It is also rich in traditional knowledge of its people which require to be transformed into electronic mode/version if it wants to benefit from both its own resources and those acquired from other sources (CSTD, 2003). The citizens, therefore, have to be technologically literate and acquire necessary skills to use these devices for storage, dissemination and retrieval of information as and when required.

The education system in India offers a variety of courses such as regular, part-time, week-end, flexi-time, etc. Classroom-based teaching continues to be the main form of education which requires high demands on physical infrastructure and human resource. Hence, the country is not able to impart education to every single child through classroom-based teaching. The ambitious aim of making education accessible to all can be accomplished if multiple modes of education such as formal, non-formal, conventional and unconventional are used. To fulfil the existing and emerging educational and training needs of the prospective learners, India has adopted several modes of education with mixed results including various generations of the Open and Distance Learning (ODL) system. All these modes are in practice in the Indian education system at all levels.

The ODL system has a history of about five decades in India and is the largest consumer of Information and Communication Technologies (ICTs) for delivery of content to a variety of learners. Starting with correspondence courses in 1962 by the University of Delhi to the recent web-supported learning all these modes exist and are likely to remain there for years to come. These modes aim to make out-of-classroom study more accessible to those learners who wish to pursue education/higher study for their professional growth as well as lifelong learning. In India, where major section of the population belongs to the middle level income group and cannot afford high fees of regular colleges, various institutions are engaged in offering a variety of courses through the ODL system to cater to their needs.

ICTs are recognized as a vehicle of success and growth of the nation and help the society at large to learn, communicate and share knowledge. India is recognized the world over for its information technology-enabled services (ITES) involving millions of low-cost English speaking professionals. Therefore,

India's biggest advantage is availability of skilled and qualified professionals for developing need-based courseware (Bhatti, 2008) for various purposes. In the light of these resources, the country needs a technology revolution if it has to move forward both educationally and economically.

The technological revolution of the country is being led by the young population and India can draw great economic leverage by developing this young human resource with right kind of education and skills. The increased investment in creating technological infrastructure reflects the commitment of the country in exploiting the potential of ICTs for development.

## Online Learning Resources

A UNESCO report states that the acquisition and sharing of knowledge, key to economic and social development, have been dramatically changed and accelerated by ICTs which enhance productivity of the teaching-learning process and offer unique and unconventional solutions to problems confronted by the education sector. Problems such as poor infrastructure facilities, dearth of qualified teachers, inaccessibility of a large chunk of people to quality education, lack of relevance of courses, etc. result in denial of education to thousands of aspirants. Hence, there is a reason to believe that online education—if used on a large scale—can emerge more economical as compared to the classroom-based teaching. It can also save the opportunity costs by making learning resource available to learners anytime, any place and at any pace.

Since the learners pursue study at their own pace and place (campus/home/workplace) they do not have to withdraw themselves from their work/job and they can pursue their course of study from different institutions/universities, even from different countries simultaneously—one learner can even seek guidance from more than one teacher/institution. As learners exchange information with the teachers through a variety of ICT tools, this can enable the learner to gain control of the learning process and achieve mastery in given subject/topic. Admissions and examinations can also be made flexible to suit the needs of the learners.

Among the various modes of education, online learning in India is becoming a need of the hour. The rapid growth of technology along with increased access to both the networked and stand-alone computers makes online learning possible in India. The number of Internet users worldwide is expected to touch 2.2 billion by 2013 and India is projected to have the third largest online population by then (*The Hindu*, 2009).

As in many developing countries, Internet access in India has largely been the preserve of the rich, urban and industrialised communities since www was born. Realising the importance of ICTs in improving the quality of life, the Government of India has initiated various schemes to connect remote areas so that digital isolation of rural communities in India can be addressed. As a result, substantial online growth rates would be higher in the coming years. The number of people online around the country will grow at a very fast pace; more than 45 per cent (*The Hindu*, 2009).

About one decade ago, access to the Internet was limited in a few major cities and that too under the government control with erratic and slow Internet service. In 2002, a large number of Internet Service Providers (ISPs) were allowed to be partner in this initiative thus ending the government monopoly. Now the ISPs have been permitted to establish their own gateways and they are using every opportunity to capitalize on the potential of online channels to engage a rising number of people in a variety of online activities. These include reading content, searching information, watching video, playing games, reviewing research literature, conducting financial transactions, etc.

India has progressed rapidly as technology connectivity and net usages have increased. It is estimated that at most seven per cent of the population have access to Internet, including kiosks and net cafes (*American Economic Review*, 2009). However, there is no accurate estimate of the current status of Internet users in the country. Apart from urban areas, nowadays, there is significant growth in Internet service and penetration in rural and semi-urban areas as well. Such a trend can be attributed to the growing literacy rates, easy availability and affordability of Internet access.

Considering the importance of ICTs, India has launched an ambitious initiative: National Mission for Education through Information and Communication Technology (NME-ICT), a centrally-sponsored scheme, which is aimed at connecting higher education institutions across the country through computer and the Internet. It aims to use ICTs to provide high quality personalized and interactive learning for higher education students. The mission has two major components: (a) content generation (the mission would generate high quality e-content for the target group of learners), and (b) connectivity along with provision for access devices for institutions and learners. Under this component, the mission would seek to extend computer infrastructure and connectivity to all the colleges in the country, including each of the departments of nearly 400 universities/deemed-to-be universities and institutions of national importance. This connectivity will help thousands of students exchange and share their views, doubts, problems, etc. related to their study.

The mission is a part of a bigger plan to establish a 'National Knowledge Network' in the country which will include connecting academic community to the world of knowledge in cyberspace, digital empowerment of academic community, content generation and management, development of new ICT tools, human resource database and certification of skills. This would help in preparing a knowledge-driven society for inclusive growth of the country. The mission aims to effectively use new methods and media for teaching and learning by focusing on appropriate pedagogy for online education, providing facilities of performing experiments through virtual laboratory, online testing and certification, online availability of teachers to guide and mentor learners, utilization of EduSat (educational satellite) and direct to home (DTH) platforms, training and empowerment of teachers.

Since the last one decade or so, with the increased use of the Internet as well as modern technologies, online learning is gradually becoming popular and some learners have started giving preference to it. It is hoped that it would have considerable impact on teaching, learning and training which is becoming increasingly international over the recent past. The learners are exploring new methods of acquiring knowledge and skills. According to Oblinger (2009), learning, discovery and creative expression are fundamental to higher education. Technology can help each of these areas. But learners want to know which emerging technologies are best and for what purposes.

With increased ICT connectivity, it has become mandatory for all the higher education institutions in the country to have a website to display their physical and instructional facilities. Even primary and secondary schools are being equipped with the Internet and satellite connectivity. The Government of India hopes that the ICT infrastructure would help in addressing the deficiency of quality teachers in institutions located in the rural area, for example, Kerala (a southern Indian State) has equipped nearly 20,000 classrooms in over 2,000 schools with computers and multimedia projectors to enable learning through ICTs (iGovernment, 2009). All the teachers have been oriented in the use of online system for teaching learning purposes. Similarly, the Govt. of Orissa has linked 40 schools in the state to the EduSat network which provides two-way video and audio communication between teachers at the studio and children in the remote schools, thus making class interactive (iGovernment, 2009). With its wide outreach, the EduSat network has the potential to cover all the schools in the state and impart online education.

ICT infrastructure has been set up for production of video-based teaching materials by the Indian Institutes of Technology (IITs), Indian Institute of Science (IISc) and Technical Teacher Training Institutes. Some institutions have also ventured into online distance education, for example, NIIT University offers online training to millions of students across 33 countries. Indian Institute of Management (IIM), Kolkata, has entered into strategic alliance with NIIT University to offer executive development programme through virtual classrooms.

Online learning is an opportunity as well as a challenge. There are two main components of online learning: generation of e-content and connectivity for institutions and learners. Once the connectivity is in place and the cost of e-devices come down, the penetration of broad band (Internet/Intranet) would reach rural, remote and marginalised areas. It would bridge the digital divide, i.e. gap in the skills to use computing devices for teaching and learning among rural and urban teachers/learners.

India has spent a lot of money and time on expanding the reach, access and overall quantity of students yet plenty needs to be done on the quality aspect. In spite of the potential of technology, the gap between its actual and realized potential in the country is large, primarily due to the lack of technically trained and educated teachers and students, inadequate infrastructure (particularly in the rural area), and a conservative mindset of both the teachers and learners towards teaching-learning through ICTs. In India, students gather information through traditional education system. But lately higher education students have started giving preference to the Internet. Hence, there is a growing demand of online courses as a source of information.

India is embracing online learning in a moderate way based on the experience of the developed countries. Some professionals have expressed their preference for online learning due to the inherent flexibility that online courses offer. Some business and industrial houses are also engaged in developing online learning materials. Educational institutions, however, are lagging behind in this initiative and they are been encouraged to make a shift in their teaching-learning strategies by adopting ICT-enabled solutions.

### Mobile Communication Technology

The mobile technology is expected to reduce the urban-rural digital divide in the country. Voice services, data access and video downloads are already being used in urban India while basic voice services in the rural area are far from satisfactory. It is, however, anticipated that 60 per cent of the India expected that 650 million subscribers will be rural (Mahapatra, 2009). The key areas of focus are affordability, accessibility and inclusion where everyone can have access to information and services. Affordability is the main concern in spreading mobile communication services across the remote, difficult terrain and unconnected areas. Mobile networks are growing and making it increasingly easy and inexpensive for those at the bottom of the socio-economic pyramid to afford mobile services.

Some educational institutions in the country such as the National Council of Educational Research and Training (NCERT) have planned to use mobile technology to help teachers across the country enhance their teaching skills by providing them access to a whole host of information on their respective subjects through their mobile phone (Kamat, 2009). The course details are being developed in various formats including graphics and animation. The project would include comprehensive course content in various subjects developed by a group of experts. Institutions are working for convergence of technology for enhancing the quality of education. Kamat (2009) elaborates that the NCERT plans to create a mobile phone portal where a database of teachers across India would be entered. This project will also help teachers to keep themselves abreast of the developments in the field of education (teaching, learning and evaluation). Such a facility would later be used for students for providing information on syllabus related subjects, career guidance and much more.

Indira Gandhi National Open University (IGNOU), the largest DL system in India, is creating a learning platform in collaboration with Ericsson that uses mobile devices to build educational excellence and exchange information for distance learners pursuing certificate course in Information Technology. IGNOU views this project as a classroom of future where learners will learn in 3G environment wherein they can download the content and get short message service (SMS) alerts. The 3G technology will create a wider scope for the learners—it is a small screen that has a browser to scan, stream and build capacities of the learners by getting learning material at the shortest possible application methods (e-government, 2009).

Some other institutions are also exploring the possible applications of mobile technology for educational purposes. MILLEE (Mobile and Immersive Learning for Literacy in Emerging Economies) project has been developing and testing mobile phone applications that enable children in the developing countries to acquire language literacy in immersive, game-like environments. The goal of the project is to make localized language learning resources more accessible to the underprivileged children at convenient time and place as compared to the regular schools. After more than ten rounds of field studies in the last six years, MILLEE is beginning a controlled experiment with 800 rural children in 40 villages in India, with early replication underway in Kenya and China (Kam, 2010) with a view to examining approaches to unsupervised mobile learning in rural India.

## Teachers and Students in Online Learning Environment

Good teachers are a rare resource all over the world—this holds true in the digitally divided communities. Some teachers have an apprehension that increased use of ICTs would replace them or affect their image in the mind of the students as online teaching is being designed and planned more systematically than the routine preparation by them. To overcome this barrier, the teachers need to be trained on different aspects of online learning to enhance their effectiveness—they can integrate audio, video, graphics and text to highlight what they are trying to teach. They should know that the students are more likely to learn and retain knowledge when they learn online (UNESCO, 2009). There are talented and motivated teachers but their potential needs to be unlocked and training would motivate them to use digital resources such as online and offline multimedia courseware, laboratory, library, etc. more frequently to make the teaching-learning process more effective. Research studies in India have shown a direct correlation between the access to broadband facility and economic growth of the people (Sivakumar, 2009). One of the important factors that contributes to the adoption of technology is education and training. More educated persons are seen to be adopting newer technologies for communication, business and education. Students mostly use Internet for educational information search and entertainment purposes.

It is a fact that under Right to Education Act (2009), there are not enough teachers to teach school children under the revised teacher-pupil ratio. But technology can help overcome both the problems of teacher shortage and standardized learning materials. For example, Microsoft India has trained 450,000 teachers of government schools. These teachers are also provided a common platform to share the lessons they create using ICTs for their students, making the lessons available to other teachers across the country. This is enhancing power of teachers to and in the process making learning more relevant for the children (Bajwa, 2010). Similarly, Intel Education has claimed that it has helped India transform through the Intel(R) Teach Program where over a million teachers have been trained to bring technology tools and resources into their classrooms for better learning. It has provided teachers with proven professional development and 21st century skills, promoting children-centred learning to engage them in appropriate use of ICTs for learning, creativity and communication. The agency claimed that this program has reached over 100,000 learners across 22 States and five Union Territories in India bringing about tangible change in technology knowledge, skills and attitudes giving young learners in developing countries opportunities to learn key skills needed for tomorrow's success (Otellini, 2010).

The premier public schools in India are being equipped with plasma television, connected to a computer with Internet access. Classroom teaching is imparted through the use of traditional textbooks along with multimedia capsules which include video clips and animations. Some schools are planning to introduce interactive board in their classrooms and these schools also have a repository of resource material that helps daily teaching. But these gadgets are not available in majority of the schools and colleges across the country. However, more schools are joining the ICTs highways with white boards that can screen the Internet, generate electronic notes, and assess students' performance and access information (Banerjee, 2008).

## Possible Future Challenges

As already mentioned, having a website for educational institutions is being made mandatory where the institution's infrastructure and instructional facilities have to be displayed. This facility has been scaled up and used for teaching, learning and tutorials/counselling purposes. Many institutions are gearing up their resources to exploit the potential of web-based teaching and learning in due course of time.

India has now realized that in information society, technological infrastructure/network is the capital for its development. Though the entire country is not yet wired, ICTs connectivity is gradually penetrating across the length and breadth of the country. India is poised to become the third largest country in terms of Internet users across the globe and it is estimated that an average growth of Internet users in India would be 10 to 20 per cent. The Government of India has elaborate plans to expand broadband and Internet access as part of many of its e-governance projects.

*Challenges*: The use of ICTs is, however, not without various challenges; let us examine some of these:

***Educational System Inertia***: The ICTs are being used in the Indian education system in the unchanged educational system. This implies that the education system in India is not dynamic enough to accommodate the emerging needs of the society.

***English Language Domination***: Most of the online courses are available in English and a large section of society including the general public and students find it difficult to communicate in English. However, gradually new courses are increasingly being made available in Indian languages. Greater efforts need to be made in designing and developing quality courses in Indian languages.

***Relevant Content***: The content of the online courses, already on offer by Indian or international organizations, is not relevant and affordable for most of the students hence the courseware developed by these agencies does not suit the needs of the Indian users. Some good quality online learning programmes are being developed in India by credible agencies and qualified individuals; this would increase the adoption of online learning in India. The use of online courses in isolation or stand-alone solutions is yet another challenge which needs to be addressed.

***Instructional Design***: Instructional design still lacks support from empirical research evidence. The courseware is not designed and developed based on the principles of instructional design in the Indian context. As a result, the courseware does not challenge the students to question, investigate, analyze, synthesize, solve problems, make decisions and reflect on their learning. Thus, in addition to infrastructure and networks, proper use of instructional design will increase the utilization of online courses. It has been observed that most of the online programmes are developed by technocrats and by the pedagogists. Such programmes may be glowing from commercial angle; they may not be pedagogically sound.

***Digital Divide***: There is a clear digital divide in the Indian community and it is a huge challenge to deliver the benefits of online learning to a heterogeneous group of users across the country. The digital divide has to be turned into 'digital opportunity' by bridging the gap between the sophistication of available technology and the knowledge of teachers and students. The relevant online learning materials should be easily accessible at affordable cost to majority of learners.

***Mindset***: The conservative mindset of some teachers and administrators also acts as a stumbling block in the use of ICT-enabled education. Many teachers still resist the use of technology in classroom for reasons such as ignorance about the scope and potential of ICTs in teaching, learning and training, etc. We have to change the conservative mindset of the teachers and students by introducing new strategies of teaching-learning through systematic training and motivation. The integration of ICTs creates challenges for teachers who need to invest extra time and energy in implementing new methods and media. All the stakeholders of online learning have to be oriented in the potential and utilization of ICTs for teaching, learning and management. Teachers' competency and empowerment can make a significant difference to develop a culture and environment in classroom that embrace ICTs as a natural partner in the teaching-learning process.

A review of the teacher education curriculum reveals that not enough importance is being placed to train teachers in designing, developing and utilizing ICTs appropriately. Hence, very few teachers and teacher educators have acquired the capability of developing and utilizing the potential of ICTs. The teacher education curriculum needs to be restructured to meet the requirements of online education.

There are deterrents at the level of students also who continue to look up to the teacher as a guide and facilitator of individualised and customised mode of teaching. Yet another factor is the administrative support which is crucial for the success of online education.

***Lack of Research Support*:** Research on the potential impact of ICTs on school environment is a must and the findings should bring out the impact of technology on school environment to encourage the teachers to adopt the use of ICTs.

***Low-cost Availability of Broadband and Internet Services:*** The Internet connectivity, availability and accessibility of computers to both teachers and students is essential. The high cost of technology and the need for substantial reorganisation of curriculum to make it compatible with online learning system are some of the factors which inhibit wide spread use of ICT-enabled education.

***Constant Power Supply*:** Power supply is yet another crucial factor for the adoption of technology as despite the outreach and availability, if regular power supply is not available, the use of ICT will be affected.

## Conclusion

In the present context, online learning can at best be complementary or supplementary to the conventional learning/training in India and may take some more time to emerge as an alternative mode of learning. Online learning system can make learning more responsive to individual needs as it can motivate both teachers and learners to take greater responsibility of their teaching and learning. The ignorance about its huge potential and unfavourable attitudes of the teaching community can hamper its growth. Online learning, like correspondence education introduced in 1960s, seems to be on a crossroad where the learners express diverse views about the credibility of the mode. On the one hand, many institutions and educationists see great hope in online learning and find it geared to meet the demand of new age learners while others put a question mark over the credibility and quality of this mode. The advantages of online learning need to be viewed with caution.

The challenge for the country at present is to reach out to the underprivileged and the marginalized sections of society and turn them into productive human resource. This challenge is gradually being taken up at various levels and the positive results are quite visible. Younger population is utilising new ICTs tools, collaborative sites and blogs, platforms like Facebook and Twitter, videoconferencing and mobile technologies in a big way. Teachers, however, need to master these techniques by learning to teach in virtual learning environment, play the role of a facilitator and provide greater control of learning to the students for lifelong learning.

Online education is likely to co-exist with other communication technologies and modes of imparting and acquiring knowledge, skills and value systems. Older methods and media of teaching, learning and training cannot be ignored at the cost of online education and will continue to be relevant for the heterogeneous group of learners. With easy availability and accessibility of computer hardware, the online mode would carve a niche for itself in both conventional and ODL systems. The need of the hour is to build sound infrastructure and provide basic amenities, particularly in rural and semi-rural areas, for the success of online learning.

## REFERENCES

Alexander, P.C. (2009), "Higher Education: A Matter of Quality", *Asian Age*, July 15, 2009.

*American Economic Review* (2009), Internet Usages in Asia: Internet Users and Population Statics for 35 Countries and Region in Asia (updated up to December 31, 2009), http://www.internetworldstat.com/status3.htm

Bajwa, Karan (2010), "The ICT Trends in India", *Digital Learning,* Vol. 6, Issue 6, June 2010.

Bhatti, Babar (2008), Comparison of ICT Infrastructure in China and India, http://telecomk.net, downloaded on July 16, 2009.

Banerjee, R. (2008), "Classroom Connected", *Times of India,* August 24, 2008.

CSTD (2003), Information and Communication Technologies: Current Status in India, 6th Session of Commission of Science and Technology for Development (CSTD), United Nations, Geneva.

iGovernment (2009), 20,000 classrooms in Kerala to be IT-enabled, http://www.igovernment.in/PrintStory.aspx?Id=9330, October 15, 2009.

iGovernment (2009), IGNOU to offer distance education using 3G, http://www.igovernment.in/PrintStory.aspx?Id=9390, October 26, 2009.

iGovernment (2009), Orissa school education system goes hi-tech, http://www.igovernment.in/PrintStory.aspx?Id=8885, September 1, 2009.

Kam, Matthew (2010), Mobile Phone and Language Literacy in Rural Communities, http://web.worldbank.org/WEBSITE/EXTERNAL/NEWS/0,contentMDK:22525186-menuP, down loaded April 6, 2010.

Kamat, Vasudha (2009), New Cellphone to Help Teachers Enhance Skills, *The Hindu News* Update service.

Lakshman, Narayan (2010), "Sibal Pitches US-Indian University Partnerships", *The Hindu,* June 3, 2010.

Mahapatra, M. (2009), *Valued Added Services in Rural India,* Paper presented at Ccnnect-World India, downloaded on July 16, 2009.

Oblinger, Diana (2009), 2009 Horizon Report Profile Six Key Emerging Technologies for Higher Education, UNESCO, Bangkok.

Otellini, Paul (2010), "Working with India for Progress", *Digital Learning,* Vol. 6, Issue 6, June 2010.

Sivakumar, R. (2009), Fuelling the Modern Economy, Paper presented at Connect-World India, downloaded on July 16, 2009.

*The Hindu* (2009), "India to have Third Largest Online Population by 2013", July 27, 2009.

UNESCO (2009), Satellite Education: Providing Quality Education under Extreme Conditions.

13

# New Technologies for Teaching and Learning in the Information Age

*Bucherla Murahari* and *V. Vijaya Kumar*

New technologies like web-based PCs, mobile phones, satellites and wireless technologies, and Internet, etc. are helping the teachers and the students to gather and disseminate information which is normally not possible through any other means. Unlike the previous society, the present information society has accepted the new technologies for faster development and growth due to the global competition. Today, higher education is considered as an important form of investment in human resources development. Youth with high end scientific and technological specializations is considered the first rate human capital for economic growth of the nation and proved as the new engine of the world economy. The goal of media is to communicate. Media communication is both an art and a science. Multimedia technology supports communication and interaction that transcends traditional language-based and cultural-based communication forms because of multimedia communicates to multi-senses. So, several universities, colleges, schools, educational institutions and even corporate training centers are increasingly utilising the distributed networks and multimedia to supplement or enhance classroom instruction and to provide open/distance learning.

## Demand for Higher Education and ICT

After independence, India has made great strides in the growth and development of education. The successive

Education Commissions piloted by Radhakrishnan, Kothari and other eminent educationists had thrown open education to all sections of our society, i.e. rich and poor, men and women, rural and urban, backward and weakest of the weaker sections. There has been an impressive growth of colleges from about 700 to 20,700, universities from 25 to 435 and student enrollment from one lakh to 1.16 crore. However, literacy rate today is 52 per cent only; out of which 77 per cent people are in urban areas and 23 per cent are in rural areas. Further, only about 10 per cent of the population in the relevant age-group are enrolled in higher education and a mere five per cent graduates with degrees. This is far below the world average of 23 per cent and is less than one-fifth of the ratio in developed countries (55%). It is grossly inadequate to meet the huge magnitude of demand in any meaningful way for a developing nation like ours. India's growth prospects will depend on our ability to make available the latest and most useful knowledge and skills to our youth, making use of latest educational technologies. With the rapid growth of the service, knowledge and associated sectors in the economy due to globalization, it is imperative that the populace is equipped to contribute to and benefit from these developments. The urgency to step up the educated youth ratio to at least 15 per cent by the end of the Eleventh Plan is now projected by our planners. Five per cent net increase will require an additional increase of about 85 lakh students in the universities and 60 lakh in the colleges during the Plan period. It is unlikely that traditional universities and colleges would respond to the needs of this sector. To meet the growing demand for higher education we need to go in for a rapid expansion setting up new institutions and augmenting additional capacity in the existing institutions. The traditional universities and colleges with their limited seats have to change their strategies and envisage new approaches to instruction based on communications and technology in order to meet the challenges of 'learning on demand' and 'learner-centered' instruction in the face of sinking resources Manjulika and Venugopal Reddy (2006). Though it is difficult to quantify the size of this constituency, it is only reasonable to assume that their hopes and aspirations rest primarily with the open and distance learning system. Recent proposals to establish 30 more central universities and 6,000 new colleges would still not be able to absorb the projected growth in the conventional system fully. Substantial part of it would still have to look for non-formal channels like open universities and DEIs, though it would be unrealistic to assume that a specific proportion among them could be targeted by the ODL system. Indian Government is insisting the education monitoring organizations and universities to find ways to reduce the cost and increase the availability of education as envisaged in the 11th Plan enrollment projections. IGNOU is the largest Open University in the world with over 17 lakh students on rolls. There are about 60 regional centres, 1900 study centres and 50 overseas centres (Rajasekharan Pillai, 2008). UGC, IGNOU, AICTE, MCI, etc. which navigate higher education and Distance Education Council (DEC), which monitors distance education in the whole country, are taking adequate steps to achieve the enrollment targets of 11th Plan projections.

To achieve the targets of Planning Commission (2007) and Knowledge Commission (2007), our educational sector must use a variety of new technologies to replace or supplement the classroom teaching. The technologies include use of computers, IT, audio and video conferencing, computer conferencing, networks, Internet and multimedia in teaching for all levels of education. While these technologies can be used to reach geographically dispersed students, minimum attention is being paid to the effectiveness of each and a combination of technologies, for education. Its potential for flexible education delivery, scope for self and lifelong learning and cost effectiveness make IT instrumental in meeting the needs of individual and communities at this juncture—in the rapid transition being made from the industrial to the information age. As Bates (1995) puts it, "the value of technology is its ability to reach learners not well served by conventional education institutions, to meet better the newly emerging educational needs of an information society, and to improve the quality of learning". As the number of technologies increases and the range of delivery techniques grows, it is important to examine the issues in developing multimedia-based instructional material and evaluate the effectiveness of the technologies for distributed instruction. Distance learning allows classes to be spread over longer periods with shorter face to face meetings so those students could more easily fit into their schedules. Research in advanced countries shows that these technologies motivate the students and improves collaborative learning, provide greater understanding, improve designing skills and develop critical thinking and better social interaction through networks. This paper attempts to analyze the following areas of distance learning and gives an overview of the technological developments in field. Web-based teaching, its advantages and disadvantages in teaching and learning, and impact of Web-based teaching.

## Instructional Methods

A flexible instructional system is the most important innovation introduced in the Open University System. Since most of the open university students are likely to be employees and housewives, and are scattered over a wide area including the interior and remote villages, they may find it inconvenient to be physically present in a classroom for lectures at stipulated time and place. These inherent limitations make it imperative to explore alternatives and exploit the modern communication technologies for the advantage of the distant learner. IGNOU adopted an integrated media approach, in the form of print materials, broadcasting and audio-visual aids, supported by tutorial system, contact classes, summer schools and other methods. While print materials will be provided for all courses, use of other communication media—radio, television, audio and video—will depend on circumstances and the nature of the courses. Today, radio is within the reach of most of the people, but other means such as video and audio players and television sets are scarce. Such equipment is installed at the study centres. While television broadcast has the advantage of the coverage, its time may be inconvenient to the viewer. As against this, a student could use a video player at the study centre whenever he wants and as often as he wants it. It is also a practice to use computers for certain types of programmes like MCA. As it has been pointed out earlier, the choice of the technology would depend on the nature of courses and circumstances.

The credibility enjoyed by distance education today is mainly because of its multimedia approach. Media eliminates the problem of distance and carries education to the door-step of the learners. In this approach, services of a few experts are made available for the whole nation. Media not only compliment to face-to-face method, but also off-set the disadvantages of the face-to-face teaching. Blend of media gives maximum benefit to the students so that the multimedia approach not only multiplies classrooms and teachers but also creates enthusiastic environment to the learners in distance teaching. The multimedia used in open universities and Directorates of Distance Education where techniques of distance education are followed in imparting knowledge are through print, radio, television, audio-video cassettes, satellite, computer, etc. (Anjanappa, 1988). Print is the backbone of all open universities and Directorates of Distance Education (Diana Laurillard, 1996). Audio-Video technology has emerged as an important tool in imparting knowledge for a distance learner. Radio the sound medium is another affective tool in non-formal education specially for hilly, rural and remote area learners where there is no power supply. By replacing the traditional teachers of conventional education the Education TV has transformed innumerable viewing rooms into classrooms. Computer revolutionised information storing and retrieving processes. It is one of the most important aids to distance education instruction and management today. Mobile Telephone is widely used in distance student counseling by tutors and coordinators of several open universities in India and abroad.

### Use of Multimedia for Distance Education

In traditional teaching, the teacher selects a body of knowledge, organises it into a single course package and transmits that to students in one way (mostly) flow of communication in the form of lecture to students. The students in this model are considered as passive recipient of this information. Simply providing information either directly or access to electronic information resources is not enough. Learners should be given opportunities to discuss their understanding with others, search from other information of their interest or unknown concept/topic and build conceptual connections to their existing knowledge base. While print still tends to be the core medium of distance education, there are examples of highly sophisticated multimedia systems in use throughout many parts of the world as detailed by Binod C. Aggarwal (2005) A.W. Bates (1990, 1995), M.M. Chaudhari (1997), Croft (1991), Duning (1990), John Dekkers (1990), Paul Kawachi (2005), Sanjay Mishra (2005), Sohanvir Chaudhary and Santosh Panda (2005), Murahari (2007, 2008), Mishra (2008), Murahari and Vijaya Kumar (2008) and several others. World Wide Web provides such kind of environment for producing, linking and organising multimedia-based instructional materials for all levels of people. The most important advantage of web is that it allows the publication of rich array of learning resources. The course is built in Hypertext environment highlighting cross-links to other related topics/disciplines. For example, the course on Information Science is linked to course on IT, Communications, Publishing, Management, etc.

In the classroom, multimedia can bridge the chasm between theory and practice by giving students the opportunity to practice what they have learned in safe and controlled environment. By making the theory real, multimedia engages students, turning them into active rather than passive learners. However, this is somewhat limited by the relatively low number of computers per student within most classrooms. Usually, a given classroom will have only one or two, often aging machines, without the capability to run the latest multimedia applications. Another new aspect of education is the distance learning. College courses, training courses and seminars have become available using multimedia networks or CD-ROMs. These types of courses usually provide the convenience of self-paced training as well as savings in both travel costs and time.

### Designing Multimedia Courseware for DE

Designing a good MMCW require total commitment in terms of time and resources. Most crucial decision in the design is selecting appropriate multimedia authoring tool for the development of a OHP and screen colour slides, slide projector and screen, computer, LCD projector and screen, computer and Internet connection. An authoring system is software that helps the developers in designing an interactive courseware or application or presentation more easily than with conventional languages. Once authoring tool is purchased and time is spent in learning that, it will become very difficult to change to another, if all does not perform quite well or flexible as expected. So, one should be careful in selecting the authoring tool. For instructional courseware design, multimedia is the latest and best tool that allows the designers in integrating text, graphics, animation, sound and video information (real time). If the designers provide control over the information presented on screen, the resulting courseware becomes interactive multimedia. Normally multimedia does not become interactive, however, adding hypertext links to that makes the presentation interactive, interesting and meaningful.

**Web-based Teaching/Learning**

According to Aggarwal (2000), during the past two decades, telecommunication technologies combined with web-enabled technologies have created a new technology-based focus called web-based teaching and learning. This new area has changed the concept of education around the world, creating new challenges and opportunities offered by this new technology-based concept. Web-based teaching technology can be utilised to enhance the teaching and learning environment (Fulantelli et al., 1999). There is little doubt that the World Wide Web is the most successful educational tool to have appeared in a long time. It combines and integrates text, audio, and video, with interaction amongst participants. It can be used on a global scale and is platform independent. While largely an asynchronous medium, it can also be used for synchronous events. It is not surprising, therefore, that trainers, distance education providers and teaching institutions at all levels are increasingly using the web as a medium for delivery (Keegan, 2002).

One way of using the web for supporting teaching and learning is to simply transfer aspects of one's normal practice as a teacher onto the medium of the web. For example, at the most basic level course content such as course notes, lecture notes and administrative detail can simply be posted on the web, and at a more complex level, relevant web-based resources can be linked to course notes and lecture notes to form interactive learning materials. Discussion groups can also be set up using web-based conferencing software; students can be required to produce assignments on the web; and multimedia simulations can be made available via the web (Maddux, 1999). By using the web as a delivery or communication method as mentioned in the instances above, teachers actually make learning easier and more flexible for students to gain access to learning opportunities and resources. However, the standard processes of teaching and learning in higher education remain the same as teachers continue to direct what is to be taught, in what sequence, and how. That is the content of learning remains under the teacher's control (Martin, 1998).

In web-based teaching courses, the role of teacher changes from that of instructor to that of a facilitator. They need to be competent in using computers and in accessing the Internet. They got to learn how to operate and design web-based teaching courses, as well as generate and disseminate knowledge and information through web-based teaching (Newton et al., 1998). They should be encouraged to plan curricula, discuss innovative instruction methods, and exchange ideas with other teachers, either within or outside their institutions. Furthermore, they need to provide instructional resources and materials which they help students to access. Finally, they may need to guide and facilitate students' critical and creative thinking in a collaborative learning environment (Aggarwal, 2000).

## Advantages and Disadvantages of Web-based Teaching/Learning

### *Advantages*

Web-based Teaching (WBT) courses provide students with access to resources and expertise outside their own institution. No space or time restrictions are present in a virtual course. Web-based materials are easily distributed across multiple platforms, that is, they can be accessed by Apple Macs or IBM

PCs. The technology is relatively easy to use. Sources are available across the entire web. Web-based materials are easy to update, providing student access to current information. The web provides a student-centered learning environment. And a variety of learning opportunities can be provided to accommodate learning style differences (Martin, 1998).

WBT is a powerful solution to many of the issues that confront teachers in secondary and higher education such as the need to innovate in course delivery and to accommodate increasing number of students, sometimes at physically distant sites, without an associated increase in resources (Cann, 2000). On-line, interactive WBT delivered through the World Wide Web (WWW), is a dynamic open learning resource that has many advantages over pre-authored, fixed platform CAL packages. Besides being of advantage to students, such systems also provide powerful and flexible tools for course administration (Cann, 2000). Web-based type of courseware has many advantages, those including:

- They are available outside normal class hours with limitations only by necessary security arrangements. They are also available to students anywhere on any computer platform.
- They allow self-administered learning/revision/ assessment and students can learn at their own pace, with no direct teacher involvement.
- They provide visual images which are important elements in many subject areas. The visual images are a mix of diagrams, full colour images and text, with interaction by means of hypertext indicators.
- They allow selectivity. Hypertext enables individual students to either concentrate on a particular topic or browse more widely through the subject.
- Last but not least, they allow adaptability. Unlike expensive CD-ROM materials, which are platform-restricted and liable to become rapidly outdated, in web-based courseware new CAL material can be easily incorporated and present materials can be updated.

*Disadvantages*

Courses may focus on the technology rather than the content. Web-based course materials may be time consuming for teachers to develop. Teachers must change their mindsets and accept a new teaching paradigm, that is, from teaching to facilitating and managing learning rather than disseminating information. Some students are technophobic just like some teachers. The active learning required by web-based course activities may be difficult for students conditioned by prior courses to be passive. Copyright violations may be easier to commit on the web and are certainly more public. Students without web access are excluded. The financial cost incurred to access the Internet and to use the computer could be very high and it varies from institution to institution and from individual to individual (Martin, 1998).

## Impact of Web-based Teaching

With Web-based teaching (WBT), course materials for traditional classroom courses can be delivered on the web. These materials can be updated frequently and can even be interactive. Since the course material is always available, there is no longer a need for students to incessantly take notes in class. Students who are shy to speak up in class can use the web technology to foster better dialogue with their teachers by asking questions related to the subject taught through the e-mail, discussion group, list serves, etc. The privacy and individual attention afforded by a computer can relieve some students of the embarrassment of giving an incorrect answer publicly or of going more slowly through lessons than other classmates. The simple act of making the learners aware of the learning objectives, including the criteria for evaluation and the conditions under which they will be evaluated, helps them develop confidence. WBT courseware can free teacher time from some classroom tasks so that a teacher can devote more time to individual students (Johnson, 1991).

WBT provides perhaps the best opportunity for student self-guided learning. It is self-paced and self-planned, with the students themselves choosing their own paths through the mass of information encompassed by the package. Successful use of such packages will increase students' knowledge as well as require them to develop other important skills such as self-assessment and planning of studies, information technology skills, creativity and self-motivation (Rosen, 2000). Interactive web-based courseware represents a move towards active learning, that is, student self-guided teaching and can be used as a constantly available learning resource for students.

Conducting a class with WBT can free-up some of the teachers' curriculum time for developing more web-based courseware. The web can also provide information resources that are very current and that might otherwise be difficult to find. Teachers and students can communicate through the web with other students, teachers and experts in a particular field online conferencing, list serves, e-mail, newsgroups and chat rooms (Newby, 2000).

Students and teachers can access valuable resources and a wealth of up-to-date information located far beyond the walls of the college building. This information is available on the web in the form of databases, documents, government information, online bibliographies, publications and computer software. Students and teachers alike will need to develop skills that will enable them to effectively wade through all of the possibilities to find which is most relevant and determine its quality. Here are a few examples of how the unlimited information can be accessed to enhance students' learning experiences (Newby, 2000):

- Monitor current events through online newspapers and magazines. The web allows students and teachers to get up-to-the-minute information on critical news stories from a variety of sources. Besides, students can also access and read what their local newspapers have to say about some current event and immediately compare that with what is being written by the national news organisations and those from countries around the world.
- Finding information on what to teach and how to teach is now easy. Databases of teaching methods, instructional strategies, and lesson plans are now readily

available and accessible on the web to give ideas to both new and experienced teachers.

The web is a quick and inexpensive method for sharing ideas. Students' work and teachers' teaching ideas can be posted on the web for people around the world to read. Many schools, teachers, and students have their own home pages nowadays. An increasing number of schools and colleges are using the web to post their students work for public viewing. This idea can be very motivating to the students and posting students' hypermedia projects to the web gives parents, grandparents and members of the community an opportunity to keep tabs on what is happening in the school and college. Students and teachers develop web pages and offer many opportunities for classroom activities (Newby, 2000).

## Web Authoring Tools for Developing Instructional Materials and Their Strengths and Weaknesses

Today's web authoring tools can give anyone, from an experienced coder to a relative novice, the power to build an interactive, animated, state-of-art website suitable for anything from a personal web page to a mid-size business site. An authoring tool is a software that lets us create CAL courseware without the need for high-level programming. There are many authoring tools available and it may be difficult to know which one to choose. Some are expensive, so it is important to choose carefully to avoid a costly mistake. Important tools are classified into three categories as low-end, medium-end and high-end authoring tools are listed below under each category.

### *Low-end Authoring Tools*

A low-end authoring tool contains only the basic features that are necessary for creating web pages.

- Adobe Page Mill
- Altrax the Web Publisher
- Drumbeat
- Net Objects Fusion
- Homesi Hot Dog Professional
- HoT Metal PRO

- HTML Assistant Pro
- Hyper Studio
- Microsoft Front Page Editor 2000

*Medium-end Authoring Tools*

A medium-end authoring tool contains some advanced features (not available in the low-end authoring tool) for creating multimedia content in web pages, e.g. Macromedia Authorware Professional.

*High-end Authoring Tools*

High-end authoring tool is more efficient than the low- and medium-end authoring tools. It has more sophisticated features for creating web-based courseware and e-learning environment. Some of these high-end tools have been developed using the low-end tool (e.g. FrontPage) to be integrated into their web authoring tools (e.g. Blackboard).

- Dreamweaver 4
- ToolBook II Instructor
- Director
- Blackboard 5
- CourseBuildeConclusion

We are on the road to a big leap in higher education. Many universities and colleges are heavily investing in multimedia technologies, computers, CD-ROMs, Internet, and high speed networks (ISDN). With the emergence of relatively cheap multimedia delivery systems, many universities in developed and developing countries started their distance education programs. Although multimedia courseware is originated on standalone platforms with custom configurations, the Internet has solved several problems and delivering multimedia content across networks. Multimedia technology provides major benefits over conventional teaching for the distributed learning:

- Less instructional cost and reaching more students in less time.
- Provides effective institution learning.

- Multimedia courseware prepared by a single source can be utilised by many users.
- Large number and geographically diverse population can participate in the distributed learning.
- Lower cost of instruction.
- Improved learning.
- Anybody can access these instructional material from any place and time.
- Universities, business houses, hospitals, transport, government offices, etc., can use it to train or educate.
- Encryption provides the security to authorised learners and protects data.
- Multimedia courseware allows students to interact with the instructor almost real time with the help of new technologies. The web is emerging as the global distributing multimedia courseware for distance learning. With the emergence of computer TVs, online educational institutions, virtual schools, colleges and universities will be able to provide instruction at home to all the people (including rural areas) in a much more cost effective way.

Finally, the observation of Manoj Kumar (2008) "the education is one of the most important inputs that influences the all-round development of any nation—economic, physical, social, cultural, ethical and spiritual. With General Agreement on Trade in Services (GATS) becoming fully operational under the WTO regime, it will be difficult for India to survive as a nation without developing our intellectual knowledge through diligent monitoring, expansion, strengthening with new technologies and reorientation of our educational system as per the ever-increasing demands of the market" is really a timely reminder that cannot go unnoticed. As web-based education has become so exiting and enjoyable in the present-day digital world, Xingfu Ding (2002), China's eminent distance education expert puts a question to the world of educationists "Will the web-based teaching and learning become the only form of education and training in the future instead of the face-to-face provision in the past several centuries?" However, our answer to Dings optimistic question is—partly Yes.

## Acknowledgements

The authors are grateful to Dr. P. Satyanarayana, former Regional Director IGNOU and Prof. C.K. Ramaiah, former Director, Virtual School of Higher Learning, MGNIRSA, Hyderabad, for their valuable suggestions. The writers are thankful to Prof. D. Swaminathan, Vice Chairman, A.P. State planning Board, Sri D. Suresh, Registrar, MGNIRSA, Hyderabad, Prof. VR. Rajendran, Vice Chancellor and Prof K. Rajendran, Dean (Research) Vinayaka Missions University, Salem, Prof. A.M. Pathan, Vice Chancellor and Prof. K.R. Iqbal Ahmed, Pro-Vice Chancellor of Maulana Azad National Urdu University, Hyderabad for their help and encouragement.

## REFERENCES

Aggarwal, A. (2000), *Web-Based Learning and Teaching Technologies: Opportunities and Challenges*. Hershey PA: Idea Group Publishing.

Aggarwal, Binod C. (2005), "Educational Media in India", *Perspectives on Distance Education: Educational Media in Asia*, Commonwealth of Learning, Vancouver, BC, Canada.

Anjanappa, K. (1988), *Manual for Coordinators of Study Centres,* IGNOU publication, New Delhi.

Bates, A.W. (1990), "Interaction as a Criterion for Media Selection in Distance Education", *Interactive Communication in Distance Education* (AAOU, 1990 Annual Conference Papers), Jakarta.

Bates, A.W. (1995), *Technology, Open Learning and Distance Education*, Routledge London.

Cann, A.J. (2000), On-Line Interactive Computer-Assisted Learning. Retrieved on from http://horizon.unc.edu/ projects/monograph/ CD/Professional_Schools/Cann.asp

Chaudhari, M.M. (1997), "The Limits and Challenges of Educational Technology in the Paradigm of Sustainable Development of India". In *Educational Technology 2000: A Global Vision for Open and Distance Learning* (conference papers). Singapore (August 15-17, 1996). The Commonwealth of Learning, Vancouver, BC, Canada.

Chaudhary, Sohanvir and Panda, Santosh (2005), "Educational Television and Teleconference", *Perspectives on Distance Education: Educational Media in Asia,* Commonwealth of Learning, Vancouver, BC, Canada.

Dekkers, John (1990), "Implementation of a Community-based Open Learning Center Network Using Interactive Communications Technologies for Access to Education and Information", *Interactive Communication in Distance Education* (AAOU, Annual Conference Papers), Jakarta.

Ding, Xingfu (2002), Ten Challenges Facing ODL Worldwide at The Dawn of The 21st Century, Towards Virtualization, Open and Distance Learning, Kogan Page India Private Limited, New Delhi.

Duning, D. (1990), "The Coming of the New Distance Educators in the United States: The Telecommunications Generation Takes Off", *Distance Education,* 11, 1.

Fulantelli, G., Corrao, R. and Munna, G. (1999), "Enhancing User Interaction on the Web". *WebNet 99 World Conference on the WWW and Internet Proceedings*, Honolulu, Hawaii.

Johnson, D.M. (1991), "Second Language and Content Learning with Computers: Research in the Role of Social Factors", in P. Dunkel (ed.), *Computer-Assisted Language Learning and Testing: Research Issues and Practice.* New York: Newbury House.

Kawachi, Paul (2005), Computers, Multimedia and E-Learning, Perspectives on Distance Education: Educational Media in Asia, Commonwealth of Learning, Vancouver, BC, Canada.

Keegan, Desmond (2002), *Globalisation of Distance Learning: Challenges in the New Millennium, Towards Visualization, Open and Distance Learning*, Kogan Page India Private Limited, New Delhi.

Kumar, Manoj (2008), "Economic Education in India: Need for a Market Friendly Curriculum in the Globalised Regime", *University News,* 46 (27).

Laurillard, Diana (1996), *Rethinking University Teaching: A Framework for the Effective Use of Educational Technology,* London and New York.

Maddux, C.D. (1999), *A University Class in Web Design for Teachers: Content and Rationale.* SITE 99: Society for Information Technology & Teacher Educational Conference, San Antonio, Texas.

Manjulika, S. and Venugopal Reddy, V. (2006), *The Changing Concept of Higher Education in the 21st Century Towards Virtualization, Open and Distance Learning*, Kogan Page India Private Limited, New Delhi.

Marian, Croft (ed.) (1991), Report on Round Table on Student Support Services. The Commonwealth of Learning, Vancouver, BC, Canada.

Martin, K. (1998), Some Advantages and Disadvantages of Web-based Teaching and Learning. Issues of Teaching and Learning, 4(7). Retrieved from http.7/www.csd.uwa.edu.au/newsletter/issue0798/plusminuswbi.html

Mishra, R. (2008), "Evolutionary and Revolutionary: Information and Communication Technology", *University News*, 46(01).

Mishra, Sanjaya (2005), Audio, Radio and Interactive Radio, Perspectives on Distance Education: Educational Media in Asia, Commonwealth of Learning, Vancouver, BC, Canada.

Murahari, B. (2007), The Use of Multi Media in Open and Distance Learning, National Conference Volume, Emerging Trends in the Use of Information and Communication Technologies, Rajiv Gandhi International School of Information Technology, MGNIRSA, Hyderabad.

Murahari, B. (2008), "Teaching Today for Tomorrow", *University News*, 46(15).

Murahari, B. and Vijaya Kumar V. (2008), "Acceleration of ICT and ODL Interaction due to Globalisation", *University News*, 46(31).

Newby, T.J. et al. (2000), *Instructional Technology for Teaching and Learning*. Upper Saddle River, NJ: Prentice Hall, pp. 190-205.

Newton, R., Marcella, R., MacLennan, A. and Middleton, I. (1998), *Using the Internet to Support Lifelong Learning: The Role of the Librarian*. The Challenge to be Relevant in the 21st Century, International Association of Technological University Libraries) IATUL Conference, Pretoria, South Africa.

Rajasekharan Pillai, V.N. (2008), Vice Chancellor's Report 19th Convocation, IGNOU, New Delhi.

Rosen, L. (2000), The World Wide Web: Taking on the Pedagogical Challenge. Retrieved from http.//horizon.unc.edu/projects/monograph/CD/Instructional_Technology/Rosen.asp

www.planningcommission.gov.in (National Knowledge Commission-2008).

14

# M-Learning: A Novel Avenue to Erudition

*S. Parthiban* and *B. William Dharma Raja*

Learning occupies a very important place in our life. Most of our behaviour is mainly influenced by what we learn and how we learn it. It is a lifelong process that involves constant change, adjustment and development. Our instincts, attitudes, appreciations, skills and abilities are primarily the product of learning (Bhatnagar et al., 2004). Learning implies acquisition of knowledge and skills on one hand, modification of behaviour on the other hand. It is measured in terms of improvement of behaviour. In the words of Skinner, learning is not acquiring knowledge or skills by mere mechanical repetitions. It is a process in which the learner organises different elements and experiences to reach a particular goal (Dash and Dash, 2003). Advancement in science and technology makes the learning process so easy and possible without geographical barriers (Singh, 2005). The usage of non-print media such as educational radio, educational television, and computers enhance the process of learning. With the help of Internet, learning became learner-centred process (Venkataiah, 2004).

## Mobile Phones

Now very recently mobile phones are used for the purpose of learning without geographical barrier. The mobile phone has become an aestheticized object that resembles clothing, increasingly incorporated into their appearance. Through the mobile phone appearance youths seek to manage the expression of who they are and to whom they are connected. This is the process of defining the self, perceiving others and redefining the self (Sugiama, 2006).

Mobile phones were invented just for communication and now they play an important role in the process of media transformation. Mobile phones are General Packet Radio Service (GPRS) tracking devices, video and cameras, wireless Internet connections and pocket calculators. They are also used to deliver texts, audio clips and digital pictures. Now, mobile phones have the ability to talk and walk at the same time in a global village that makes learning a process very easy.

Mobile phones allow interacting with other people at anywhere and anytime through voice and through the exchange of written messages. These devices are also used to accessing content, reached through interconnection. Wherever one looks, the evidence of mobile penetration and adoption is irrefutable, no demographic is immune from this phenomenon. From toddlers to seniors, people are increasingly connected and are digitally communicating with each other in ways that would have been impossible to imagine only a few years ago (Wagner, 2005). Instant messaging enables real time and often simultaneous connections among co-workers, friends and family wherever there is a access to a wireless communication network.

### Mobile Learning

Mobile learning (M-learning) aims at making the learning process more flexible, accessories and personalised. M-learning is the acquisition of any knowledge and skill using mobile technology, anywhere, anytime that results in an alternation of behaviour. It can be defined as "learning that happens across locations or that takes advantages of learning opportunities offered by portable technologies" (Wikipedia, 2007). The term covers mobility of the learner, interacting with portable or fixed technology, learning in a mobile society, etc.

M-learning facilitates performance support at the point of operation, and enables workers to learn what they want, where they want, and when they want. M-learning improves access to information, that people can update their knowledge continuously to satisfy the demands, which want to improve cultural experiences of life.

### M-Learning—Current Practices

People in Asia and Europe are finding that their connectivity and computing needs can be met through mobile phone (Wagner, 2005). The learners used to share photos and news with classmates and teachers through the mobile phones. M-learning provides an opportunity to get touch with the group to reach learners.

Every student participates in mobile learning has equal opportunity to make quality presentations, communicate with faculty and access course materials without waiting for the campus computers (Quinn, 2006). Students have access to test and assignments and results. Students use mobile phones to collaborate with peers, faculty and experts in their area of study.

Mobile devices have been mainly used for:

- gathering responses from students
- participatory simulations
- collaborative data gathering
- supporting communication among group members
- helping the co-ordination between the learning activities
- enhancing the student engagement
- having effective interaction between students and teachers
- autonomy, anonymity and motivation to the learners
- easy adoption to students and teachers
- accessing word, phrase translations, and practicing new words in language learning
- ensuring all students have equal data
- creating learning community

- accessing to a variety of learning resources
- enhancing self-directed learning, etc.

Mobile phones use the wireless Internet to exchange voice messages, e-mail and web pages at anywhere and anytime. Since most students already carry mobile phones, most classes are already equipped. Portability, connectivity, simplicity and low cost make them valuable educational tools and running cost and text input speed restricts its usage.

Mobile phone e-mail produced learning as superior to desktop e-mail mobile web and paper (Houser, 2002). In Singapore, courses already offered through mobile phones, due to the people's convenience, they were planning to offer an entire distance education course through mobile phones even with limitations of tiny size of phones, less memory and screen (Ring, 2001).

**Researches on M-learning**

***Distance Education.*** The main advantage of mobiles in the higher education is collaboration between students, with the sharing of information and questions resulting in both are asking and answering questions they may not otherwise have thought of. Certainly, the interactive nature of learning is increased compared to a textbook. The use of mobile technology in distance education could provide more flexibility for learning (Ally, 2005). The mobile learners in distance education need to be able to perform tasks such as studying the course materials, making notes, writing assignments, accessing a forum, sending and receiving e-mails and communicating with a tutor (Rekkedal, 2002). The use of mobile technology in distance education could provide more flexibility for learners (Ally, 2005). Existing course materials must be converted into new ones developing for delivery on mobile technology to improve the learning efficiency of the learners (Rekkedal, 2002).

***SMS and MMS Facility.*** SMS (Short Message Service) system makes the students to feel positive, convenient and personal than web and e-mail system. SMS system was considered as significant to spread information about lectures and classes, corrections in the schedule, etc. (Divitini et al., 2002, Stane et al., 2002). Students of Oslo University are using the technological devices to read information and discuss problems with colleagues, to organize social events mainly by sending SMS (Smordal et al., 2002). Introduction of MMS (Multimedia Message System) among teachers will lead to more and more possibilities for M-learning (Seppala, 2002).

***GPRS.*** Blue tooth and GPRS (General Packet Radio Service) are used in University of Taiwan so-called paperless education, when the traditional classrooms were replaced by electronic tools, the students were strongly encouraged to communicate and learn together (Chang et al., 2002).

***Language Learning.*** The abundant features and availability of mobile technologies enhance the feasibility of mobile language learning. The mobile learning with smart phones has the measurable impact on second language learning than online learning with personal computers (Shih, 2007).

***PDA.*** Trinder, Magill, Roy's (2005) case study highlighted the immediate readiness of PDAs (Personal Digital Assistants) that they can be switched on and used straight away with no 'boot up' time, making it so useful for learning at where even a laptop would not be possible.

## Challenges to M-learning

The main technical challenges to the mobile learning are connectivity, battery life, interacting with small devices, displaying useful content in small screen devices, continuing expansion of broadband wireless networks, low resolution of displays, diversity of operating system. The other challenges are to develop an appropriate theory of learning for the mobile age, design of technology to support a lifetime learning, tracking of results and proper use of this information, how to assess learning outside the classroom, how to support learning across many contexts (Wikipedia, 2007).

The training of M-learning has challenges like widely dispersed staff/student base, constant mobile workforce, rapid deployment of training, etc. Wireless access in the classroom will encourage or enable cheating is a question mark (Wagner,

2005). Mobile devices are often disconnected because of the lack of access in certain places but also because of the high prices in most of the cases, challenges to the security of the device and its data.

**Future of M-learning**

Mobile devices with their small screens and poor input devices lead to the assumption that they cannot replace desktops. But users can use their small fragments of waiting time for learning by reading small pieces of data. Screens have to be made bigger and better, systems have more memory, more refined methods for inputting data, more multimedia capabilities will make them more effective (Megreal, 2005).

Informing learners that training is available, minimises the barriers that prevent people from training, enable organisations to be more responsive to changes in the environment, making the learners aware of the appropriate content available on M-learning, redesign of learning content for mobile delivery, utilize the infrastructure to deliver content will make the M-learning more effective and meaningful.

Despite the drawbacks, it will be more useful in collaborative projects and fieldwork, in a classroom alternative to books or computers, where learners are widely dispersed. Engage with learners who in the past have felt excluded. More access to specific information, easy access at any time, anywhere, non-work hour training, learning at outdoors, etc. will make the M-learning a significant role to be played in education at all levels. It will allow the collaboration to happen regardless of physical location, in real time and to include text and rich media as well as voice. When the existing course material is converted into new ones for delivering on mobile technology, the learning efficiency will be high (Rekkedal, 2002).

The characteristics of mobile devices like ubiquity, access, richness, efficiency, flexibility, security, reliability, interactivity have to be improved to reach the high efficiency of mobile learning for the future generations (Wagner, 2005). Thus, the M-learning facilities became an unavoidable source into the process of learning without which the future learning may not be possible. Let us move towards mobile learning for mobilising more learners and more learning.

## REFERENCES

Ally, M. (2005), "Use of Mobile Devices in Distance Education". Paper presented at M-learn 2005, October 25-28. Cape Town, South Africa.

Bhatnagar, A.B., Bhatnagar, M. and Bhatnagar, A. (2004), *Psychology of Teaching Learning Process.* Meerut: R. Lall Book Depot.

Chang, C. and Sheu, J. (2002), "Design and Implementation of Ad Hoc Classroom and Schoolbag Systems for Ubiquitous Learning". *IEEE International Workshop on Wireless and Mobile Technologies in Education.* Vaxjon, Sweedon.

Dash, B.N. and Dash, N. (2003), *A Text Book of Educational Psychology.* New Delhi: Dominant Publishers and Distributors.

Diviniti, M. et al. (2002), "Improving Communication through Mobile Technologies: Which Possibilities?" *International Workshop on Wireless and Mobile Technology in Education.* Vaxjo, Sweden.

Houser, C. et al. (2002), *Mobile Learning: Cell Phones and PDAs for Education.*

Kulkulska, A. (2007), "Mobile Usability in Educational Context: What have We Learnt" <www.irrodyl.org> retrieved on 15.11.2007.

Mcgreal, et al. (2005), "The Athabasca University Digital Reading Room: Library Resources for Mobile Students". Paper published in the proceedings of the 2005 *IADI International Conference on Mobile Learning* <www.irrrodl.org/index.php/irrdyl/article/view/356> retrieved on 18.11.2007.

Quinn, V. (2006), "M-learning: Mobile, Wireless in Your Pocket Learning" <www.linezine.com> (retrieved on 15.11.2007).

Rekkedal, T. (2002), "M-learning for PDAs: Enhancing the Flexibility of Distance Education". PowerPoint presentation delivered to Ericsson Education, November 22, Dublin, Ireland.

Ring, G. (2001), "Case Study: Combining Web and WAP to Deliver e-learning", *Learning circuits,* www.learning circuits.org/2001/jun2001/ring.html.

Seppala, P. (2002), "Mobile Learning and Mobility in Teacher Training", *IEEE International Workshop on Wireless and Mobile Technologies in Education.* Vaxjo, Sweden.

Shih, Yuhsun, E. (2007), "Dynamic Language Learning: Comparing Mobile Language Learning with Online Language Learning". *Dissertation Abstracts International,* 68, 04, p. 1426-A.

Singh, V. (2005), *Practical Approach to Educational Technology.* New Delhi: Akandha Publishing House.

Smordal, O. et al. (2002), "PDAs in Medical Education and Practice". *IEEE International Workshop on Wireless and Mobile Technologies in Education.* Vaxjo, Sweden.

Stane, A. et al. (2002), "SMS and Interactivity—Some Results from the Field, and its Implications on Effective Uses of Mobile Technologies in Education". *IEEE International Workshop on Wireless and Mobile Technologies in Education.* Vaxjo, Sweden.

Sugiama, Satomi (2006), "Fashioning the Self: Symbolic Meaning of the Mobile Phone for Youths in Japan". *Dissertation Abstracts International.* 67, 11, p. 4039-A.

Trifonava, A., "Where is Mobile Learning Going?" <www.hpl.hp.com> (retrieved on 15.11.2007).

Trinder, J., Magill, J. and Roy, S. (2005), *Expect the Unexpected: Practicalities and Problems of a PDA Project. Mobile Learning: A Handbook for Educators and Trainers.* London.

Venkataiah, S. (2004), *Education via Internet.* New Delhi: Anmol Publications.

Wagner, E.D. (2005), "Enabling Mobile Learning" <www.educause.edu/er/erm05.asp> retrieved on 15.11.2007. http://knowledge free.flexiblelearning.net.au/edition06/download/geddes.pdf (retrieved on 21.07.2008).

http://its.dc.voit.ca/mobile/advantages.php (retrieved on 15.11.2007).

www.m-learning.org/how/how-can-I-use learning.html (retrieved on 15.11.2007).

www.m-learning.org/how/how-can-I-use-m-learning-html (retrieved on 15.11.2007).

www.tatainteractive.com/mlearning/html (retrieved on 15.11.2007).

www.wikipedia.org/wiki/mlearning (retrieved on 21.12.2007).

15

# Blended Learning as a Strategy of Innovation in Education

*Sreekala E.*

We now live in an increasingly complex world of rapid expansion of knowledge, scientific development, space exploration and globalisation. All these made education a process where quality is the major deciding factor. The quality in education becomes increasingly important today because we live in an integrated world where every nation is able to contribute to improve the lives of not its own but throughout the globe. There is a demand for innovative ways of educating the young for long-term quality involvement in learning to help them contribute to the growth of the nation and in turn helping them to maintain quality in life. This kind of innovative methods in education will help them to face the challenges of a society which allows the self-conscious, intellectual and artistic efforts of individuals to express enrich and distinguish themselves. These methods should also emphasise higher order thinking and independent learning. This requires certain supportive values, particularly liberty. This is because the thought process cannot develop without freedom. An individual must be left to govern himself, he must have large amounts of freedom, which is necessary for innovation and creativity. In a democracy like ours, an individual must have the freedom and opportunity to channelize the free flow of ideas in a globalised society. He/she must have access to free flow of information. The creativity of an individual and the originality of the work produced are the factors important in independent learning. A person who is capable of producing his own outlook possesses the spark of independence in him. Then it becomes possible for him to adopt independent learning. It is not to forget that the originality of the information used for independent learning is important.

### Role of E-learning in Independent Learning

E-learning fosters independent learning. The use of e-learning in educational activities in various fields has introduced new methods to enhance and transform teaching and learning. E-learning helps in better communication and collaboration being an integral part of educational programmes. Though our country has still not equipped itself to adopt these approaches for every student, a lead is already taken in this direction. Access and equity are assured in independent learning provided high quality materials and highly qualified teachers are made available for all, irrespective of their caste, religion or region. Internet and a vast array of digital resources and content are used for the purpose. E-learning provides vast information required for independent learning to students which otherwise is not available in the traditional facilities of a classroom. E-learning also provides individualised attention to the students. Moving out of the restrictions of the schools, e-learning increased the quality of teaching-learning in the form of vast resources available to them. Independent learners can now learn differently according to the difference they possess. It has also challenged them to engage in learning in a way they prefer while also challenging them to learn in other ways of preference.

### The Learner, Teacher, Content and the Community—The Disconnect

Apart from the edge e-learning possesses, this paper also discusses the problems associated with a complete dependence on e-learning. It is true that e-learning has many advantages over traditional methods of teaching and learning. But it lacks a connect between the teacher, learner, the content and the community. This method is largely loosing face because of the absence of face-to-face pupil-teacher interaction and peer interaction since they play a vital role in the social development of students. Leaving the real classroom interaction totally for e-learning will be premature. Traditional methods of gaining knowledge have not lost its importance. High technology might produce highly skilled people but total dependence on e-learning might separate the individual from the rest, they might gate themselves to be loners in the virtual company of technology. This might lead them to serious psychological problems. Affective exchange of ideas through eye contact, in real face-to-face interaction in the classroom situation is vital in the life of a learner in any age group.

Mere imparting of knowledge will not help in attaining quality in education. Producing emotionally and socially intelligent individuals is one of the main aims of quality education. Most research studies show that people with high emotional and social intelligence are happier, healthier and successful. They possess the qualities which are valued and accepted in any society in the whole world. Now, how do our children attain these qualities being loners in a virtual world, in social isolation, away from the peer group, the community around and away from the interaction of teachers? Human interaction is essential in attaining emotional maturity and emotional sensitivity. Leading the children with empathy and compassion is essential especially, since we are going through the worst of times. Proper education cannot take place in isolation from the rest of the community. Character development is to be the foundation of the society where selfishness, violence and out of control emotions tear apart the goodness of day-to-day life of people.

The Education Commission (1964-66) remarked, "Of all the different factors that influence the quality of education and its contribution to national development, the quality, competence and the character of teachers are undoubtedly the most significant". Teacher is the backbone of educational system. The role of teachers and the students have been redefined due to the tremendous changes that happened worldwide due to the scientific development, turn out of learning theories, expansion of knowledge and globalisation. It is foolish to throw away the traditional methods of teaching and learning blindly to embrace new technologies. Blending these different methods in such a way that it prepares the young to be independent, creative and at the same time help them to face the world with confidence, will be an intelligent solution.

Children become the teachers of themselves and each other through 'cooperative learning', group learning, peer tutoring and student directed learning (Venkateswarlu, 2006). Even if study for its own sake is a dying pursuit with so much emphasis now being put on the acquisition of marketable skills, there should be more emphasis on independent learning. The broader our knowledge, the better we can understand the many different aspects of our environment. Such study encourages greater intellectual curiosity, sharpens the critical faculties and enables people to develop their own independent judgements on the world around them. But it did not decrease the role of teachers, rather made them more responsible and creative.

Traditional methods also have certain advantages over the web-based media. The development of memory skills is an excellent tool for countering the overpowering stream of instant information put out by the media. It would be dangerous to conclude that there is no point in people's improving their memory skills because of the vast amount of information storage and distribution capacity available in web. Methods of memory training conventionally used in our classrooms with the active interaction between the teacher, student and the community still have not lost its importance. It is dangerous to discontinue various traditional exercises in schools simply because they are considered to be boring.

We have different national as well as international values such as equality, fraternity, democracy, freedom, etc. in our educational system. There are also topics related to history, culture, religion, etc. But these days, students do not prefer to read much, especially regarding art subjects from where they get awareness about our culture, tradition, value system, brotherhood, social living, adjustment, adaptations, etc. The active involvement of a teacher is significant here to inculcate these values in the children.

Therefore, the need of the day is a blend or a hybridisation of different learning methods to prepare the young to take part actively in democratic life. This could be accomplished using blended learning.

## Blended Learning

Blended learning is learning that is facilitated by the effective combination of different modes of delivery, models of teaching and styles of learning, and founded on transparent communication amongst all parties involved with a course (Heinze, and Procter, 2004). This is the process of incorporating many different learning styles that can be accomplished through the use of 'blended' virtual and physical resources. A combination of technology-based materials and face-to-face sessions are used together to present content. This method is a balanced blend of use of web-based technology and traditional methods in education.

It is to be noted here that blended learning mentioned in this paper is not really just a combination of traditional methods and e-learning. It is a unique method of teaching and learning which requires suitable methods of instruction, content development, and teacher skills. Methods of instruction are to be planned well in advance. Content is to be developed and users are to be given training. Methods of evaluation also are to be planned. It needs to be designed according to the content prepared to be imparted. These steps are necessary because it is not simple use of face-to-face teaching methods in an online class, and vice versa. At the same time, blended learning is not a readily available module which can be used for both the type of teaching and learning. This is to say that a truly blended course is not exactly a face-to-face course that incorporates a few digital elements. In a nutshell, the communication should be significantly web-based as required, the content and interaction must be managed by a properly and well-planned systematic management system so that the communication is facilitated to the maximum extent possible. Well-suited software can also be used to organise content and facilitate communication.

When a content to impart is blended with the best of both the environments of online and face-to-face, the learning objectives are to be clarified in specific manner. There are certain things that can be conveyed best through face-to-face than online and vice versa. Blending has to be done keeping the purpose in mind. It must relate to the objectives of teaching and learning. It has to assist the teachers and the students. It should give more access to information.

At the end it is to be mentioned that even without an exact definition of blended learning many institutions and individuals are somehow blending e-teaching and traditional teaching in various mixes. The extent of mix or blend is not very important, what is important is a serious interest towards using this kind of innovation so that the students and teachers involve themselves in the teaching learning process and enjoy teaching and learning. As mentioned earlier it is difficult to bring in these kinds of innovations in our classrooms because of the heavy inertia our education system and the society itself has, still it is imperative.

## Conclusion

No doubt, India is fast becoming what we call as Electronic India, with aspirants in every field. The technology helps us to produce skilled manpower. But it is to be done in the context of the culture which had been nurtured and created through centuries. Maximising productivity and establishing a nation which is internationally competitive is important, but this should not overshadow the personal and cultural experiences of individuals. Learning should lead one to excellence, at the same time it is also a social experience. If the knowledge provided fails to encourage the learner it is of no use. Here is the gap for blended learning which can take care of the technological as well as social aspects of education, blending the online and face-to-face environment in a planned and pedagogically opportunistic way.

## REFERENCES

Heinze, A. and Procter, C. (2004), "Reflections on the Use of Blended Learning" in *Education in a Changing Environment.*

Picciano, A.G. and Dzuiban, C. (2007), *Blended Learning: Research Perspectives.* Needham, MA, The Sloan Consortium.

Graham, C.R. (2005), "Blended Learning Systems: Definition, Current Trends, and Future Directions", in Bonk, C.J. and Graham, C.R. *Handbook of Blended Learning: Global Perspectives, Local designs.* San Francisco, CA, Pfeiffer, pp. 3-21.

Garrison, D.R. and Kanuka, H. (2004), "Blended learning: Uncovering its transformative potential in higher education", *The Internet and Higher Education*, 7(2), 95-105.

Kirschner, P.A., Sweller, J. and Clark, R.E. (2006), "Why Minimal Guidance during Instruction does not Work: An Analysis of the Failure of Constructivist, Discovery, Problem-based, Experiential, and Inquiry-based Teaching". *Educational Psychologist*, 41(2), 75-86.

Venkateshwarlu, D. (2006), "Changing Role of Teachers", *Journal of Indian Education*, Vol. XXXI, pp. 35-39.

Goleman, D. (1995), "Emotional Intelligence: Why it Matters more than IQ?", *Bantam Books,* New York.

# 16

# 'Technophobia' Among the Teaching Community

*Z. Zayapragassarazan* and *E. Ramganesh*

Social, economic and technological changes of the past decades are making teaching more crucial than ever. The information and knowledge society needs a continuous change in the role and the working of teachers. Being a teacher in the knowledge society, one has to deal with new knowledge and new ways for accessing knowledge, networked world with new types of co-operation and collaboration, and a society in which knowledge plays a crucial role and lifelong learning.

Information and Communication Technologies (ICT) have brought new possibilities into the classroom, at the same time they have placed more demands on teachers. ICT exemplified by the Internet and interactive multimedia are obviously of great significance for teachers. It needs to be effectively integrated into the formal classroom teaching and learning conditions. The integration of ICT in teaching in general and higher Science education in particular is the need of the day. Its adequate recognition and fulfillment of relevant needs is crucial for integration and effective utilization for quality education programmes. The use of ICT can make substantial changes both for teaching and training mainly in two ways. Firstly, the rich representation of information changes learner's perception and understanding of the context. Secondly, the vast distribution and easy access to information can change relationships between teacher and learner. ICT can also provide powerful support for educational innovations. Every day new technologies emerge but the latest technologies also have capacity to integrate with older analog technologies and retrieve information stored in older technologies and to develop link between the old and the new. So the choice of technology is important for a specific purpose of classroom teaching.

Now the question is that how many teachers use technology in the classroom? How many teachers have a positive attitude towards using technology in the classroom? How many teachers are skilled in using ICT? How many teachers are aware of educational technology for use in teaching and training at higher education level? In the present context of globalization, the goal of quality education for all is not possible without the use of technology in classroom. As there are a lot of chances and it is evident that teachers may be left without the knowledge of educational technology if proper policy changes are not made in education. Moreover, it is essential to assess the level of knowledge, awareness, attitude and skills with respect to ICT in order to understand technological divide among the teachers to frame necessary strategies and policies to make teachers of higher education as e-literates and technology users.

Many factors contribute to the attitude and skill of using technology in the classroom by teachers in higher education. One important factor is 'technophobia' where teachers show fear of or revulsion to modern technology. Sometimes the term is used in the sense of an irrational fear while others defend that the fears are justified. The main cause of technophobia is ignorance. The people who shun technology are generally the people who do not understand it. Most people who hate technology hate it for the simple fact that it is not what they are used to. Usually, technophobia inflicts the older generation, the generation who has not grown up with computers, computer games, complicated acronyms, or even calculators. Another thing that they do not like is the fact that they are being taught by those younger than them, either a young adult or maybe even a child, which is the exact opposite of how the usual passing of knowledge system works.

### What is 'Technophobia'?

- Technophobia means any negative psychological reaction to technology, either mild or severe. "Technophobia" and "computerphobia" are terms which can be used interchangeably. Although "technophobia" can be called "computerphobia", technophobia is not restricted to computers. In fact, technophobes can be uncomfortable with many forms of technology, including VCRs, ATMs, fax machines, computers, voice mail systems and even digital watches. However, since computers represent the most frequently used aspect of new technology, technophobia is discussed with respect to computers in this article.
- There are two kinds of anxiety: *trait* anxiety "a relatively stable personality characteristic pertaining to feelings of anxiety induced by a broad and diverse set of conditions" and *state* anxiety "a transient condition, centralized upon and specifically related to certain situations", and typically, computer anxiety is considered to be a specific example of state anxiety.
- Technophobia is not a fear of the actual dangers of technology such as job loss or the effects of screen radiation, but an irrational one, and the technophobes acknowledge this.

### Various Factors for Technophobia

*Age*: The younger ones are more computer-anxious. The key in explaining this is the expectancy of computer literacy. Because younger people are expected to be more computer literate, it results in greater computer anxiety. On the other hand, since older people are expected to be less computer proficient, this results in less anxiety.

*Race*: The results from various studies about the relationship between computer anxiety and race are more or less consistent over time. For example, as the study by Marcoulides in 2004 reported, American students studying in America and Chinese students studying in China showed a similar degree of computer anxiety. This is also true when comparing students from the UK and Hong Kong in the study by Brosnan in 1998. All of these studies strongly suggest that computer anxiety is a universal phenomenon.

*Biological Sex vs. Psychological Gender*: Research shows that females reported more computer anxiety than their male counterparts. Furthermore, recent research suggests that this is due to the differences of psychological gender, rather than the differences of biological sex.

*Early Experience*: Studies demonstrate that many technophobes were introduced to technology by parents and teachers who themselves were uncomfortable with technology. Through these early experiences, discomfort with technology gets passed on to the learner; eventually, the technophobia begins.

*Social Status (Education and Occupation)*: Research reveals that, on the one hand, educational level did not seem to have an impact on the respondents in a particular study; on the other hand, occupation shows a moderate relationship with technophobia, with those in both low and high occupational statuses being less computer anxious.

*Residence*: Research shows that rural residents and residents of large urban areas were less computer anxious.

*Religion and Religiosity*: Research demonstrates that religiosity was not related to technophobia.

## Types of Technophobes

*Anxious Technophobes*: Individuals who show classic signs of being anxious when using a computer (e.g. excessive sweating and shaking).

*Cognitive Technophobes*: Individuals who may appear cool, calm and collected externally but are experiencing negative cognitions internally (e.g. 'I am going to lose all my work in my computer').

*Uncomfortable Users*: Individuals who show negative attitudes or slighter anxiety as they lack sufficient information about computers to use them efficiently.

## Some Statistics of Technophobes

*In the U.S. in general*: According to a recent study by Dell Computers, 55 per cent of all Americans are technophobic.

*In the industrial world in general*: It has been reported that, on average, between 1/4 and 1/3 of the population of the industrial world are technophobic to some degree.

*In business setting*: Thirty per cent of the business communities who use computers experience some level of computer anxiety.

*In education community*: Research demonstrates that about 46 to 52 per cent of teachers experience some level of computer anxiety, especially among female teachers.

## Symptoms of Technophobia

The following are the behaviors that were identified as being indicative of computer anxiety:

- Avoidance of computers and the general areas where computers are located
- Excessive caution with computers
- Negative remarks about computers
- Attempts to cut short the necessary use of computers.

Also, the following are symptoms of technophobia:

- Breathlessness
- Dizziness
- Excessive sweating
- Nausea
- Dry mouth
- Shaking
- Heart palpitations
- Inability to speak or think clearly
- A fear of dying
- Becoming mad or losing control
- A sensation of detachment from reality or a full blown anxiety attack.

## Overcoming Technophobia

Careful and early introduction of technology is the key to avoid technophobia. For example, technology should be introduced as a subject in individuals' early school years. Also, studies show that, with careful and informed introduction, technology can become not only comfortable but enjoyable.

## Guidelines to Overcome Technophobia and Use Technology Comfortably and Successfully

1. The person who is teaching computers (or any form of technology for that matter) must be comfortable with that technology.
2. The person who is teaching technology must be calm, clear and very open to questions.
3. The teacher should walk the learner through the process of using a technological device first with the learner pushing the buttons.
4. The introduction of technology should be in a evaluative atmosphere.
5. It is important to learn about technology by 'playing' with it.
6. It is crucial not to try to pack learning experiences into too short a time.
7. People who have negative reactions to technology should be told very clearly that they are not unusual.
8. Consulting someone who is knowledgeable in both psychology and technology to introduce technophobes to modern offices is recommended.'
9. Technophobia can be overcome by introducing technophobia reduction programme.

## REFERENCES

Brosnan, M.J. (1998), *Technophobia: The Psychological Impact of Information Technology*. Routledge: New York.

Frideres, J.S., Goldenberg, S., Disanto, J. and Fleising, U. (2006), "Technophobia: Incidence and Potential Causal Factors", Nov. 2007, www.springerlink.com/index/_GG813 11214028407.pdf

Marcoulides, G.A., Marcoulides, L.D. and Stocker, Y.O. (2004), "Examining the Psychological Impact of Computer Technology: An Updated Cross-Cultural Study", *Educational and Psychological Measurement,* 64(2): 311-18.

Rosen, L.D. and Weil, M.M. (1996), "Psychologists and Technology: A Look at the Future", *Professional Psychology, Research and Practice,* 27(6): 635-38.

# Total Quality Education

# 17

# Five Suggestions to Improve Quality in Education

*Mahabir Singh Dhankhar*

A lot of discussion is going on regarding reforms in the education system in general and higher education in particular. In the present scenario when we talk about any system, the prevalent market forces have a strong effect on it. As far as system of education up to matriculation level is concerned then we should forget the market demand. Presently, I think there are two types of systems, one for rural India and another for the population living in cities. To do away with the examination at Xth level is not a good idea, this will increase the sense of non-seriousness among students and teachers. Without a serious evaluation procedure you cannot judge whether a student is fit for professional studies or research or any other profession. The State Education Boards are doing good job by conducting central examination of state, we should improve the quality of evaluation process in such a manner that the examination fear is reduced to a large extent. We have seen the results of doing away the examination at primary level in government schools. Today most of the students up to primary level come from labour class to earn food and some money. When these students enter VIth class they do not know ABC of any subject. The teachers at primary level also remain busy with the implementation of social schemes of State Governments like distribution of food to students, pension to old-age persons and many other works of similar nature. This is causing a very serious threat to primary education. Keeping in mind this experiment of doing away the 5th standard examination, one can think of what will happen if we scrap the 10th board examination and what quality of students we can expect at senior secondary level. In place of doing away with the examinations and diluting the course contents we should have very serious and strict evaluation process at XIIth level so that the talent can be judged in a transparent and fair manner.

I have observed in my 21 years teaching career that many students, particularly girls in rural areas, who have performed exceptionally at XIIth level join the courses like JBT or Nurses training because there is job security by doing such courses. If this talent is brought into higher education then certainly we can have very good researchers. The government must ensure that the talented students are not diverted to petty job training courses. Truly meritorious students after passing their XII class be diverted to higher education and research, because if the system of higher education is unable to fetch good students then we cannot think of quality faculty in the institutions. Today, there is very serious problem of quality teachers in the institutions of higher education and our universities are not performing well in the area of research. To achieve the objective of quality in higher education, there are few suggestions listed below:

### Joint Syllabus Designing Committee (JSDC)

In most of the subjects which are being taught in colleges there is a big gap between the syllabus at senior secondary level and at UG degree level and in some cases there is repetition of course contents. In addition to this, the courses to be taught at UG level are decided by teachers those who are teaching PG classes. The State Governments should form JSDC to design the course contents of a subject in such a manner that the subject is covered in a uniform way in five years. The syllabus of all the subjects of all universities in a state up to UG level be same and if possible there should be uniform syllabus at national level for UG classes. The JSDC must consist of teachers of high reputation from universities, colleges and schools.

## Quality Books

Today, most of the books which are being taught in our schools and colleges are not authored by competent teachers and in same cases very cheap help books are recommended to students. The private publishing houses print these books by simply cutting and pasting from some old books and then put the name of a teacher who is teaching in a big school or college. Without reading quality books one cannot understand the true concept of a subject, it is better who do not know a concept than who knows wrong concepts. As far as my subject of mathematics is concerned, I have noticed that in many books which are being taught in colleges even definitions are not given correct. To do away this evil the universities can choose competent teachers who can write quality books of their subjects and each university or if possible State Government can print these books. This will reduce the cost and increase the quality of course contents. If good literature of any subject is not served to the students then the very purpose of education is defeated.

## Teachers Training Institutes (TTI)

Today, there are training institutes for the teachers at school level only. For college and university teachers there are orientation and refresher courses run by academic staff colleges. These courses are not serving any purpose except a mandatory requirement for higher grades. There should be an institute in each university which provide very serious training to a teacher before he/she joins teaching profession in a college or university. The training must include the social concept, concerned subject matter and knowledge about ordinance and scheme of examination as well as the purpose of evaluation of students. These training institutes can train the teachers about latest techniques of teaching like power point presentation and education through EDUSAT, etc. For every teacher in a college or university it must be a necessary condition to serve TTI at least for 2-3 years, therefore there is no need to recruit permanent staff for these institutes. By doing so we can overcome the problem of not having quality teachers for the institutions which are coming in large numbers every year.

## Choice Based Credit System (CBCS)

The system of examination and process of evaluation are most important components of any education system. Keeping in view the present scenario evaluation after every six months by external examiners and a continuous evaluation by internal examiners after every 1½ months is suggested. The curriculum should be designed in such a manner that each subject has a certain number of credits equal to number of teaching hours in a week. It must be compulsory for every student to earn a certain number of credits to pass a course and in addition to this there should be some optional credits based on the interest/choice of a student which a student can earn from other disciplines. The CBCS has more flexibility and a meritorious student can earn more credits than others in a subject of his/her choice. For example, if a student admitted in B.Sc. course has interest in journalism then he can earn credits in journalism course if available in the same university/college otherwise he can attend the classes of that course in the neighbouring university/college. If the system is uniform at the national level then it becomes very easy to transfer credits in case of migration of a student. Deenbandhu Chhotu Ram University of Science and Technology, Murthal (Sonepat) has taken a lead in this matter by implementing credit based system for each course at UG and PG level w.e.f. session 2008-09, the evaluation consisting of internal and external components is done after every one month and six months respectively. The Vice Chancellor has already constituted a committee to implement CBCS in the next two years.

## Human Resource Evaluation Centres (HREC)

Today, most of the organizations/recruitment agencies conduct entrance examination to select quality manpower and it has become a challenge to conduct fair examination for this purpose as well as board/university examinations. Therefore, it is suggested that each university should have its own HREC so that examinations/interviews can be conducted in a transparent manner or such type of centres can be constructed at district level by State Government. These centres should be equipped with facilities like computers and OMR scanners so that results can be declared in time. The approximate cost of construction of one such centre having capacity to examine 3000 students in approximately ₹ 10 crores. Most of the universities nowadays have Distance Education Programmes which are run by private study centres. The product of these study centres is very poor because the examinations are not conducted in a transparent manner by them, these HREC can be utilized to examine the students of private study centres so that quality of education can be maintained in Distance Education Mode. In addition to this, the universities can earn from HREC by conducting the examination for organizations like banks, insurance companies, etc.

It is my belief that every system has merits and demerits and there are not so many demerits in the present system of education but it requires some flexibility and quality improvement which can be achieved by implementing above five suggestions. Certainly, we can have quality education system if its parameters are decided by a team of honest and unbiased persons and implemented by a team of committed educationists.

# 18

# Quality Education and Human Development

*S.K. Singh*

I would like to start my paper with a Sanskrit slok:

Vidyadadati vinayam, vinayad yat patratam Patratvad
Dhanamappnoti, Dhanad Dharmah Tato Sukham

Education makes man courteous, and polite, from courtesy one gets competence and ability, from competence, money comes, from money, a person can perform his duties and can do righteous things, from right actions a person can live happily.

P. Ramanatha Aiyar Law Lexicon (1997) has defined quality as the degree of excellence, a mental or moral attribute trait or characteristic. Quality is that which is inherent in the thing and co-exist; the property is that which belongs to it for the time being; the attribute is the quality which is assigned to any object. The word quality is also related to client satisfaction. Quality reflects the worth of a product or a service as professed by the producer/provider and as perceived by the consumer/client.

The term is generally used in term of quality of life, which means improvement of lifestyle of people, their enlightened life-styles and their access to civil rights and freedoms. In the management studies, the term quality is used to connote a move in a positive direction, i.e. from good towards better. When we talk about the term in reference to education, it means how far education is in a position to provide an individual a quality life. Needless to say that quality education is that which enhances quality of life. The quality education may be defined as that which transforms the consciousness of a person and leads him from darkness to light in the knowledge area.

Sa vidya ya vimuktaye

That is the education which gives freedom to a person. Quality education gives a human being perfection in life. It does so by imbibing the following four capabilities:

(i) To think logically, analytically and critically.

(ii) To enable an honourable living, i.e. employability by learning occupational skills and work experience.

(iii) To realize one's potential for self development in terms of physical, emotional, intellectual, aesthetic and moral attainment.

(iv) To acquire concern for equality, justice, civility, harmony and cultural pluralism.

In order to be able to import quality education, our education system has to acquire the following qualities: (i) quality syllabus, quality faculty, quality teaching and evaluation, quality research and quality character. Some of the indicators of quality syllabus are: it is regular updating and upgradation, it is advanced theoretical and experimental thrust, credibility of content, interdisciplinary orientation, sensitivity to emerging intellectual developments and social sensibility and above all, relevance for self and social development. Similarly, some of the essentials of quality faculty include their academic and research eminence, intellectual competence as measured by command over subject, ability to build and argument in a cogent and coherent manner, communicative competence as reflected in clarity of thought and expression and above all their creative competence as signified by reflective character of teaching. Likewise, indictors of quality teaching and evaluation are: teacher student ratio, modes of teaching, its interactive and participatory character, innovative teaching methods, regularity of classes, sanctity accorded to completion of syllabus, student keenness to attend classes without compulsion of attendance, positive feedback by students, affectivity in teacher student relationship, regular and continuous assessment, thorough mode of evaluation objectivity, impartiality and transparency in evaluation. In the area of research, the quality research is: discovery of new fact, research publication, acknowledgement by way of frequency of citation. Last but not least, the quality of character and outlook of faculty is as important as is the quality of its intellect. In fact, it is this which constitutes the bedrock of quality education.[1]

## Historical Aspect of Education System

### *(a) Ancient Education System*

Since ancient times, education is viewed as the transmission of values and accumulated knowledge of society. Success of any country depends on the qualities of the students. India has glorious tradition of teaching and learning, where education was pursued for the sake of knowledge and *mukti* and not for materialistic benefits. Knowledge is regarded as highest virtue of man. According to Radhakrishnan Commission,[2] our ancient teachers tried to teach subjects and impart wisdom. Their idea was wisdom along with knowledge. Plato emphasized that no amount of factual information would make ordinary man into educated man unless something is awakened in him. Education is treated as both training of mind and soul. Education was for *mukti* and self realization. Social service was the greatest ideal of scholar. A scholar drew satisfaction in social service which gave him the joy of achievement and excellence. There was no special arrangement for salaries of teachers. They normally maintained on their personal earnings or on *gurudakshina*. King provided land for Gurukul Ashrams, but there was no interference from the king. The teachers had full freedom and enjoy highest respect in the society, which was the greatest motivation and incentive for them. Education was never subordinate to political power.[3] Thus, education in ancient times emphasized to impart values to students. Teaching was personalized and the students used to be in close association with teacher. They used to imbibe the values of teacher and treat him as a role model. Teaching was regarded in high esteem.[4]

### *(b) British Education System*

The Indian Education System under British rule became subordinate to political system and the main thrust was for supplying clerks to run the administration and not to create any intellectual tradition in any field. Job in administration has become a dominant social value than studentship. East India Company did not provide any education to Indians for more than two centuries. In 1813, they felt the responsibility of education for Indians. There were different groups supporting either elite education or mass education. There were two strongly opposing groups one for Western education and other for Oriental education.[5] Some of the Britishers encouraged Sanskrit and Arabic Colleges whereas some Indians favoured Western education and stated that it would be best suitable for keeping the country in darkness. He wanted the future generation of India to march ahead on the path of progress along with Western countries.

Macaulay (1835)[6] strongly supported English education and stated that we are forced to pay for our Arabic and Sanskrit students, while those who learn English are willing to pay us. Britishers wanted to form a class of persons, who were Indian in blood and colour, but English in taste and opinion, who could work as interpreters between Britishers and Indians. Thus, the Britishers introduced English education for preparing better civil servants. But in practice, this minor group of English learnt people developed a superiority complex and isolated themselves from masses.

### *(c) Education in Free India*

In independent India, rapid growth of universities and colleges started across the country. Emphasis was also given to technical and professional colleges. There was quantitative growth of higher education system rather than qualitative.[7] India's higher education system rose to the second largest system in the world and is having third largest pool of science and technology manpower.[8] Despite these, there was concern about the quality. During last decade of 20th century, there was mad rush for market-driven courses. Just to cash demand colleges without any proper infrastructure either human or material came up. The thrust for completing the degree was the priority than anything else. With such anomalies, the education system entered 21st century.

*(d) Education in 21st Century*

In 21st century, the education has been globalized with the advancement of information technology. Any person on the globe can offer its education to any person of any country. A prospective student is aware of availability of quality education and is ready to go and study anywhere. Under this liberalization, privatization and globalization, the demand will be for quality only. A prospective student may not give preference to quality provider institution in comparison to a institution having a glorious history. Twenty-first century needs a flexible generalist rather than a specialist. The flexible generalists are persons equipped with necessary level of knowledge, skills and values to adjust readily to different job settings and life situations. They should be adaptable to multiple career changes.

## Concept of Quality Education

Quality may be defined as skill, excellence, perfection, standard, competence for work and value for money.[9] Quality may also be defined as combination of competence with virtue, excellence in performance and capability of delivering goods. To understand quality education, it must be mentioned that what are the skills, which describe quality education: These are (1) time management; (2) ability to work under pressure; (3) accuracy and attention to detail; (4) oral communication skills; and (5) managing different tasks at the same time.[10] The UNESCO document on "Thematic Debate: The Requirements of World of Work" has added a few more to this list, as flexibility innovativeness, creativity, entrepreneurship, versatility and teamwork.[11]

These skills are the parameters by which the quality of higher education is assessed. Such education enables persons, societies and even nations acquire competencies required for living meaningful life in a competitive globalized world.

## Need for Quality Education

In a developing country like ours, there is quest for quality education due to incredible growing importance for knowledge in society. Taking stock of the higher education scene in the developing world, very few are enrolled in educational programs of high quality, the rest are taught by poorly qualified, poorly motivated, poorly compensated faculty, with inadequate facilities and out model curricula. This large majority which is deprived from quality education are given the task of nation building. They are called upon to provide good governance, develop future businesses, build health and educational infrastructure needed for raising the standard of living and improving the quality of life. Therefore, it becomes essential for developing nation to focus on the quality of education they impart.

Under the General Agreement on Trade in Services (GATS), India has to allow the opening of foreign university campuses on Indian soil and admit Indian students to their courses as a reciprocal measure. Indian universities can also open their campuses on foreign soil and admit their students too. This will have an impact on the higher education scene in India. It will improve quality of education through competition and improve access by increasing the number of institutions, which the government is unable to do due to resource crunch.

## Ensuring Quality of Teaching, Research and Extension

The three dimensions of higher education, namely teaching, research and extension, should be strengthened. Institutions of higher educations work on the assumption that research is prestigious while teaching is not so. It is good to have few institutions that are strong in research but we should have all the institutions strong in teaching. Good research should be encouraged but it should not be at the expense of teaching. Therefore, when the institutional performance is assessed, performance in teaching should be prime agenda and research and extension should come next. The National Assessment and Accreditation Council (NAAC) gives a prime place to the quality of teaching. In the overall institutional score of 100 points, the teaching—learning and evaluation—carries substantial weight. While the universities carry 25 per cent weight, the autonomous colleges have 30 per cent and the affiliated colleges carry the weight of 40 per cent. In most of higher education institutions, the prime function is teaching and evaluation of the students. If we consider the students as beneficiaries, the 88 per cent of the total students enrolled in higher education are at undergraduate level, 9.5 per cent are in post-graduate level, remaining 2.5 per cent are at diploma and doctoral level students do not constitute one per cent of total student enrolment in higher education institution.[12]

Selection of teaching staff is based on research credentials even in general education universities, selection committee look for publications and research potential of the candidate. It is like assuming that anyone good in research can be good in teaching staff are hired as teacher but evaluated as researchers. Probably, this is the only profession in which one can become a success without satisfying the primary stake holder, namely students in the primary responsibility of teaching. However, it does not imply total research and extension has less importance.

For quality education, one of the most essential ingredient is "scholarship". Scholarship means not only engaging in original research but also includes looking for connections, building bridges between theory and practice and communicating one's knowledge effectively to students. The work of professoriate should be (1) scholarship of discovery; (2) scholarship of integration; (3) scholarship of application; and (4) scholarship of teaching. Scholarship of discovery means what is to be known, what is yet to be found, while scholarship of integration means making connection across disciplines. Today researchers feed the need to move beyond traditional disciplinary boundaries, communicate with colleagues in other field; the scholarship of application means applying research findings to consequential problems. The scholarship of teaching is about communicating one's knowledge effectively to students. A scholar acquires knowledge through research, through synthesis (integration), through practice (application) and through teaching—teaching becomes well recognized. If seen as a scholarly enterprise, teaching beings with what the teacher knows and therefore those who teach must be well informed and has knowledge of one's fields, he should be a scholar who are intellectually engaged.

For quality education, the teachers of higher education are required not only to engage in teaching, the already existing body of knowledge, but are also expected to facilitate the creation of new knowledge by future researches. The aim of education is not only to produce knowledgeable students, but also to develop students as critical thinkers which is essential to succeed either at their work or at home. Good researches in Indian universities should be encouraged but it should not be at the expense of teaching.

## Human Development

Development of nation is directly related to the development of human being of that nation. Following capacities should be built up among the students by providing them quality education:

### 1. Capacity for Research and Inquiry

We must give our students the skill with which they can search knowledge which has been created by the intellectuals and scholars. This is possible through advancement of science and technology. Research is necessary to satisfy some natural human curiosity. The cause and urge to inquire into a phenomenon are basic to human advancement. Exploring into the unknown or unfamiliar comes naturally to all living beings.

### 2. Creativity and Innovation

Quality education makes a person creative. He becomes capable to produce some new thing by his intelligence. He becomes competent to make a change by introducing a novelty and can and do a material change in established method.

### 3. Capacity to Use High Technology

Every student in our institution should learn to know, how to use latest technologies for aiding their learning process. Universities should equip themselves with adequate computing equipments, laboratory equipment, and Internet facilities and provide an environment for students to enhance their learning ability.

### 4. Entrepreneurship

The aptitude for entrepreneurship should be cultivated right from the beginning in the university environment. We must teach our students to take calculated risks for the sake of larger gain, but within the ethos of good business. They should also cultivate a disposition to do things rightly. This capacity will enable them to take up challenging task later.

### 5. Leadership Quality

The quality education is also responsible for the development of leadership quality in the human being and he become capable of guiding others. A person having leadership quality encourages the persons working in the establishment hence become responsible for its development. Such types of persons should be given key positions in the organisations.

The inquiry, creativity, capacity to use technology, entrepreneurship and leadership quality are the five capacities required to be built through the education process. If we develop in all our students these five capacities, we will produce, "Autonomous Learners", self-directed, self-controlled, lifelong learners who will have the capacity to both, respect authority and at the same time be capable of questioning the authority in an appropriate manner. There are the leaders who would work together as a self-organizing network and transform any nation into a developed nation in a time-bound manner.[13] Quality education opens up new vistas of development of humanism. It transform human being into a noble soul and an asset to the universe. The quality education enhances dignity and self respect of human being. If quality education is given to each individual and carried forward in every field of human activity the world will be better place to live.

## NOTES

1. S.L. Sharma, "Rethinking Quality Parameters in Higher Education", 42, *University News* (2004), p. 3.
2. R. Sivaswaroop, "Resilience of Ethics and Values in Higher Education: Pre-requisite for Providing Value Orientation", 43, *University News*, p. 13.
3. C.P.S. Chauhan, *Higher Education in India* (1990).
4. *Supra* note 2, at 14.
5. Hetukar Jha, *Colonial Context of Higher Education in India*, 25 (1985).
6. Macaulay's dispatch dated 02.02.1955.
7. Kothari Commission Report, 1964-66.

8. Prem Kirpal, "Role of Universities as Agent of Change", in J. Veer Raghvan (ed.), *Higher Education in the Eighties: Opportunities and Objectives* (1985).

9. Pratibha Khanna, "Changing Scenario of Higher Education: Challenges to Quality Assurance and Sustenance", 43, *University News* (2005), p. 4.

10. *Ibid.*

11. UNESCO (1998), *Higher Education in the Twenty-First Century: Vision and Mission*, www.unesco.org

12. Antony Stella and A. Gnanam, "Primacy of Teaching in Assessing Institutional Quality", 43, *University News*, p. 3.

13. A.P.J. Abdul Kalam, "Education System for Developing Capacities of Learners", Speech delivered on 5 November 2004 at J.N. Tata Auditorium NT Bangalore. 43, *University News*, p. 16.

# 19

# What Ails Quality in College Education?

*M.S. Kurhade*

K'uan Tzu a great thinker (551-479 BC) once said:

> If you plan for a year, plant a seed. If for ten years, plant a tree. If for a hundred years, teach the people. When you sow one seed, You will reap a single harvest. When you teach the people, You will reap a hundred harvests.

The philosophy of K'uan Tzu is the 'soul' of education. It is the combination of Virtue, Value and Validity of human life. It has multidimensional implications. It means there is a need to understand the criteria that can help in the development of human beings.

Proper education process is a passport to a good, comfortable and secure life. This process is transmitted through commitments and sharing of the teacher-pupil relationship. Education is not merely imparting knowledge in a particular faculty or subject. Education should be training in pragmatic and logical thinking and should help the coming generations adjust to the available environment. Education should make the student community think and become worldly wise.

A great number of colleges have come up in India during the last six decades. Education in the British period was guided by a policy which can be summed up in Macaulay's words, "To create a class who would be interpreters between us and the millions whom we govern, a class of persons Indian in blood and colour, but English in tastes, in opinions, in moral and intellect"; a class who would be loyal to the British Raj. Since 1947 (after independence), the expansion of higher education has led to ways and means of achieving quality in education. Down the corridors of the time, many colleges have been founded on the commitment to search for and disseminate knowledge. The role of colleges has always been important but perhaps never so in man's history than today. In the modern world, quality education and research are crucial to the development of students. In the rapidly changing modern world, one thing is certain: Yesterday's educational system will not meet the needs of today, and even less so, the needs of tomorrow. Betterment of quality in education alone can provide the foundation to the nation's progress, security and welfare.

Today, there is a strong feeling that the education imparted at the college level does not match the needs and expectations of the employment sector. Therefore, there is need for a comprehensive programme for college improvement. The college improvement programme is based solely on the efforts of management, principal, teaching, non-teaching staff and students. But the present scenario indicates that the rigidity in the process of planning and its implementation has reflected very badly on the Indian Education System. The effort of college authorities and staff are directionless and therefore ineffective. As a result, development in college education has been receiving low priority in the Indian government. If our education system does not encompass the necessity for students to become optimistic and an integrated part of society, the credibility of our colleges will be doubted. Skeptics, pragmatics and even scientists would voice their apprehension about the present teaching-learning practices. Some basic questions may well be asked of the colleges: How far have the colleges succeeded in helping the students? How far has the college culture changed the life of the students? What are the main educational programmes, offerings, and services? Why have the colleges failed to bring in the expected standard? These are critical questions that need to be asked continuously even though the answers to them are difficult.

A major task before the colleges now is to create new strategies, policies and programmes of a revolutionary nature which can bring about quality in education. A disheartening fact of the colleges in India is that there is no fundamental or social understanding in the college campuses. There is no education which can enrich human life. Who is to ensure that the quality is maintained? Is it only the principal or the teachers too? Yes, as per the statutory provisions, the entire college staff is responsible for maintaining the standard of education. But our higher education system is such that it does not attempt or even inspire to match the international standards. If the objective is to build a world class system then "Degrees" or "Certificates" would not be enough for faculty recruitment.

In view of the ever-increasing number of colleges, and the ever-increasing student populace, the problem of providing students with quality education has assumed a serious dimension. Until and unless we have sufficient infrastructures and the best teaching-learning facilities in every corner of the country, the aims and objectives of higher education are sure to suffer a setback. So, the need of the hour is to build quality institutions in India. The aim and purpose of imparting education must change in response to economic and social changes. The traditional rigid approach to planning and implementing will not work any more. To achieve these objectives, experts within and without the system are to be mobilized for working out higher education programmes.

Our colleges are unable to transform our huge human resources into an asset. Unfortunately, the colleges have not yet come out of conventional courses of studies. It is equally true that our education fails to teach team work and communication skills. There is no fine tuning of teachers and students. The indiscipline, protest and disruptive activities on the part of students are at times instigated by the teachers themselves as well as political parties. The teachers, students and non-teaching staff unions instead of taking up educational causes, frequently take-up populist causes and easily succeed in disrupting the daily functioning of a college. Politics and groupism in colleges have damaged the standard of higher education. Therefore, our graduates have no demand in job markets. The colleges in India seem to be far behind their counterparts in USA, UK and Australia in terms of quality education and research. What is disconcerting and worrisome is that the non-academic environment of the colleges has the worst impact on educational and moral values of the society. Although India has more than 415 universities and 20,000 colleges with more than 5.5 lakh teachers catering to 11.5 million students, it caters to only nine per cent of the relevant age group. But in the larger context it is found that there is no alternative device to ensure international standards in higher education. The major problem lies in sticking to a teacher-centric environment, which largely focuses on the convenience of the teachers and ignores expectations of the students. The mechanical way of useless teaching, lack of understanding about the aim of higher education often results in going away from the philosophy of higher education. The universities are awarding degree certificates to students without ensuring anything related to quality. This has surely and steadily affected the present education system in an adverse manner. It is a fact that people pursue a degree for the status it carries.

The teachers deliver lectures without employment of a proper teaching methodology. Many a times, the teacher does not have the time or the inclination to ensure whether the students could follow the lecture. Sometimes, we come across teachers who merely dictate notes. There are instances of teachers just reading out the textbook or the guide on the subject. It is also observed that learning at college level does not include acquisition of habits or skills. Evaluation and testing stress upon rote memory. The curriculum design is mere 'collection' of topics and subjects. There is no genuine comprehension or critical evaluation. The accumulation and presentation of data alone cannot become the criteria for quality education. Promoting students from one class to another for maintaining the workload of the teachers is a common phenomenon. It means the colleges are plain enrolment centres and examination bodies. They are not bothered about the quality of teaching. Neither is there any procedure to check the kind of teaching that is imparted at the college.

In the light of the above-vitiated scenario, there is a need for fresh thinking on the issue of college education. Francis Marion Crawford rightly said "It makes little difference what the trade, business, or branch of learning is, in mechanical labour, or intellectual effort, the educated man is always superior to the common laborer. One who is in the habit of applying his powers in the right way will carry a system into any occupation, and it will help him as much to handle a rope as to write a poem." It means the philosophy of right kind of education resulting in provision of suitable culture where students can develop their creative, intellectual and mental personality is of utmost significance. The present-day needs of colleges are:

- to realise that education is a dynamic and a continuously changing process and
- to realise that a college is not merely a building but a part of the global village.

To meet the above-cited needs, the colleges require a very innovative approach and thinking. It is a fact that growth of colleges has taken place without commitment and proper infrastructural facilities, as a result of which a large number of unproductive students are produced. If this is so, what should the colleges do? It would be a big help if efforts are made to:

- Establish the links between colleges and industry with the social and economic goals of the society in mind.
- Improve the governance of colleges.
- Mobilize the resources.
- Introduce multi-disciplinary approach to education.
- Create working environment in colleges.
- Make provisions of well-equipped laboratories, employment of modern technology and good libraries.
- Improve quality, relevance and standards of higher education through renewal of curriculum.

The colleges neither care for the community nor respect the welfare of others. No importance is given to human relations which is a much pertinent matter required for effective education. There is no encouragement or appreciation of virtues of responsibility and self-discipline. There is no projection of the college as the servant of the society. The words of William James, a great Psychologist are much relevant in this regard:

Sow an action and
You reap a habit
Sow a habit and
You reap a Character
Sow a character and
You reap a destiny

It means colleges should provide hope and open new avenues for the student community. Colleges should enable students to become contributory members of the society by providing knowledge, skills and character development opportunities. Every student should be enabled to acquire the tools and qualifications necessary for earning his living. The purpose of higher education is to prepare the students for good citizenship in a democratic society where tolerance, goodwill, responsibility and accountability is deeply integrated in life.

At present, the college administrative system is following a redundant and a non-effective procedure. Imparting quality education not only means providing the necessary facilities, but also creating an intellectually stimulating environment. In this context, the novel and creative skills of the students should be encouraged. For exposure and training in modern technology, there is a need for teachers who are innovative and enterprising besides being learned and qualified. But at the college level, the teachers' apathy towards student development is deplorable. Students are not motivated to improve their self-study skills. Therefore, it is high time that the colleges made an integrated effort to meet the various challenges of the modern day by broadening the vision and progressing in the right direction.

While deliberating upon the problems in the field of higher education one has to perceive the entire picture in totality. Colleges are unable to lead the students towards the fulfillment of social needs or a complete adoption of advanced technological skills. Colleges should become knowledge-based learning centres. There has to be a definite change in the attitude of students, teachers, principal as well as the management. Without adopting a humanistic approach, colleges would fail to achieve the goal of quality in education. Therefore, it is time to rethink and revise the environment in the college campus and devise a strategy that would work towards a quality culture. When there is no compromise in the quality of education, change is certain and progress would be inevitable.

20

# Accreditation, Assessment and Recognition in the System of Higher Education

*Dinesh Kumar Paliwal*

The credibility of the academic awards has always been an issue of concern. With the rapid expansion of the education system and growing trend of international education, this issue has assumed more significance. In developing nations, governments take prime responsibility for coordination and maintenance of the standards of education, whereas in developed countries non-governmental organizations play an important role, through peer review system, especially for higher and professional education.

## Need for Accreditation and Assessment

India, in the recent past, has witnessed sizeable expansion of its higher education system especially in the private sector. Some of the private institutes, in operation, are offering programmes leading to award of degrees without obtaining requisite approvals from the concerned regulatory authorities. This state of affairs has created a situation of confusion among the students, academic institutions and employers in respect of recognition of degrees/diplomas awarded by various institutions for the purpose of academic pursuit as well as employment, thereby generating a need for evolving a process for recognition of the degrees. A systematic system of assessment, accreditation and recognition for the institutions of higher education may provide a viable solution to deal with this situation as well as to provide seamless mobility of the graduates of Indian universities to international educational institutions.

**Explanation of the Terms**

In general, accreditation, assessment and recognition may be defined as under:

(a) The word accreditation is derived from the latin word '*Credito*' which means trust. Accreditation of the institute or the education programmes offered by that institute means granting credit or to the institute that maintains standards and/or its programmes as the case may be. This may also make it eligible to receive financial aid or loan from government agencies. Accreditation of courses or programmes, more precisely, means evaluation of the academic programmes in terms of its academic enrichment, relevance and suitability in respect of its outcome. The assessment of the quality of the faculty engaged in the teaching/research in the discipline of the programme as also the resources available with the institute to teach and undertake research in the discipline of the programme.

(b) Assessment is, usually, done to rate the institutions in terms of their physical and academic infrastructure as also financial soundness and grade them accordingly.

(c) Recognition of an institution by the concerned statutory authority or government may be understood as granting the permission or license to an institution that fulfills minimum eligibility criteria prescribed to offer/run the concerned education programme. This may be appropriately incorporated in a suitable Act to facilitate expansion of higher education system (in consonance with the recommendations of National Knowledge Commission and Prof. Yash Pal Committee Report) by granting permission/license to award degrees. This provision may also require suitable amendment to UGC Act, 1955.

### Current Status

Presently, India has a system of assessment and accreditation through National Assessment and Accreditation Council (NAAC) established by the University Grants Commission (UGC) in accordance to the provision under Section 12(ccc) of UGC Act, with the objective to assess and accredit the institutions of higher learning, i.e. colleges and universities, etc. NAAC, through the prescribed mechanism, assesses the physical and academic infrastructure of the universities and colleges imparting higher education and on the basis of the evaluation, assigns them appropriate grading. This often is referred to as accreditation by NAAC.

National Board of Accreditation (NBA) is another autonomous body created under AICTE Act, 1987 in accordance with provision under Section 10(u) of the Act and undertake the job of evaluation of the technical/professional programmes offered by technical and professional educational institutes. However, at present, NBA does academic evaluation of only those technical/professional programmes, which are in operation, atleast for four years, conducted by the institutions/universities and if it is found that the programme conforms to the standards prescribed by NBA, it is certified as accreditated by NBA. Presently, NBA is confined to evaluate the technical programmes only and not the institutions, obviously the technical education institutions. Whereas, NAAC is confined to the assessment of institutions (colleges and universities) imparting General Higher Education and not to the programmes offered by them.

### Accreditation and Licensing of Profession

To understand the whole issue with more clarity, especially in the light of internationalization of education and entry of private education providers in the Higher Education System, in a big way, the issue of coordination and maintenance of standards of higher, technical and professional education has assumed new dimensions and the term recognition, assessment and accreditation may need to be appreciated accordingly.

In the era of education, especially in developed countries, all the professionals like teachers, lawyers, engineers and doctors are required to take their licenses from designated agency after successful completion of the programme and learning, required degree before entering into the practice, e.g. if a teacher wants to teach in a school after completion of his/her degree in education, he/she is required to obtain the license for teaching. In the US licensing varies from state to state in certain professions. Licensing of teachers is highly decentralized, Medicine, Nursing, and Engineering are more centralized and national. If the Licensing Law is governed by State Boards, it may or may not have reciprocity with other states. The license, generally, is issued, if the concerned person has earned the degree from an accreditated institution or after completion of the accreditated programme and qualifying the examination conducted by the licensing authority. This license is renewable after a prescribed term for which the concerned person is to qualify an examination, which is conducted in order to assess the updation of the knowledge of the person in his/her field of profession. Similar is the process for professionals in other fields like lawyers, etc.

### Accreditation in United States

The accreditation in US is usually granted by the non-government professional bodies on the basis of evaluation of the programme for its academic strength, relevance and outcome by a team of professionals from academic institutions as well as field.

In US, usually, academic institution of higher learning is supposed to have membership from association/body which grants the membership only to such institutions which conform to their standards. There may be two, three or four such bodies with varying standards. Recognition or membership in other body in some way indicates the level of academic institution.

The accreditation of the academic programme is done by the professional body in its own field. It means, if an institution is offering ten different programmes in ten different disciplines like Management, Engineering, Medicine, etc., it may require to seek accreditation from the relevant body of each discipline. In a nutshell, if an institution is offering a programme without accreditation, the graduate of that institute in that particular unaccredited programme faces difficulty in pursuing further education in reputed institutions as also in getting employment or practicing the profession. All the reputed institutions usually give admission to the students, who have completed accredited programmes only.

**System of Accreditation for India**

Since India needs a lot of expansion in the Higher Education System, it may require to have two separate systems, one for maintenance of standards of higher and technical education and the other for promotion and coordination in the system. The role of the statutory authority like UGC and AICTE in present or any other form may be limited to facilitation, promotion and ensuring planned growth of the higher education in their respective domain, especially in order to remove regional imbalances as well as for manpower planning. These bodies may continue to provide grants to the universities and colleges under their jurisdiction. In a nutshell, these bodies may act as mentor for the institutions in their respective field. This may require appropriate amendments in their respective Act.

For maintenance of the standards, the existing system of assessment and accreditation by NAAC and accreditation of programmes by NBA may be integrated and modified to address the situations in the current environment of participation of the private sector in higher education and internationalization of higher education. A body with representatives from the government, University Grants Commission, All India Council for Technical Education and other statutory bodies like National Council of Teacher Education, Medical Council of India, Dental Council of India, etc. and persons representing various professions and professional bodies may be established by providing one-time grant, i.e. for one plan period. Thereafter, the said body should be expected to generate sufficient funds from its resources to maintain and carry out its activities. This statutory body may introduce and coordinate a two-tier system for maintenance of standards in higher and technical education.

The first tier of the mechanism may involve assessment and grading of the institutions of higher learning by the above referred body. The assessment could be of physical and academic infrastructure; administrative set up and procedures; and financial position. The body should evolve and adopt a detailed and transparent system of assessment of the institutions and their grading. For the purpose details in respect of all possible parameters of the assessment of physical and academic ratio of full time as well as part time qualified faculty, administrative set up and procedure and financial position, etc. should be identified with different levels of grading. These parameters along with the procedure of assessment and evaluation should be placed on the website of the body before undertaking any assessment. The format of the report should also be devised and posted on the website. The assessing team should substantiate their assessment given in the report with appropriate evidence. The assessment reports should be made public after their consideration by the statutory authority on a designated section of the website of the statutory authority. This system of assessment may also have a mechanism of filing the dispute before an authority to be constituted along with the proposed body.

The team for assessing the institution may be constituted out of different panels of experts, e.g. one panel could have the experts from the area of educational administration, the other panel could have the expert in finance and accounting, another panel could have experts from academia, etc. The panel should be approved by the top executive body of the suggested authority/body. The secretariat of the body should ensure that the representation of the experts on various teams should be fairly even, i.e. all experts on the panel must be given equal opportunities as far as possible. A discrete mechanism of having feedback about the performance of the assessors from the above referred panels should be put in place and this feedback should be considered by the apex body of the statutory authority for appropriate action.

The assessment report of an institution/college or university may be considered as the base for examining the proposal of that university for release of the grant by bodies like UGC, etc. For instance, if assessment report indicates the weakness of an institute in terms of its library facility, the commission or the funding body should emphasize the institute to seek the grant for strengthening the library system so that the same can come up to the mark. A follow-up visit by an accreditation team may also be provided to ascertain whether the grant was properly used to strengthen the weaknesses pointed out earlier by the accreditation team. All the institutions of higher learning may be strongly encouraged to go for assessment by the assessing body under reference every five years. Needless to mention that this body should be mandated to assess all institutions of higher learning irrespective of the discipline of education and training they are imparting.

The assessment report/reports should essentially be considered along with other parameters like accreditation of the courses (dealt in later section) for considering the request of the institution to grant deemed university status or giving license for starting autonomous programme leading to award of degree. In case an institution declared as deemed to be university is rated below the minimum prescribed grade by the assessing agency, the institution should be advised to take remedial steps in a time bound manner and subjected to re-assessment. If the institute fails to achieve the desired level, the report of the assessing team should be considered seriously by the commission to recommend to the government for withdrawal of the deemed to be university status. Similarly, in case of the university established by or under a State or Central Act, if the university fails to maintain minimum level of grading, the suggested body may recommend to the commission and State Government in case of State Universities and Central Government in case of Central Universities, to take necessary measure for upliftment of the grading of the university to the desired level or to consider to take appropriate corrective measures including to repeal the Act by which establishment of the university concerned was established, if need be. There should be no discrimination between publically funded and privately funded institutions.

The second tier of the mechanism may involve accreditation of programmes offered by institutions of higher and professional education. For this purpose the suggested body should be empowered for facilitation (including by giving one time grant) of establishment of various professional bodies in different disciplines of education and training, monitoring and coordinating their activities for the purpose of accreditation of the various programmes leading to award of diplomas and undergraduate, postgraduate and research degrees as well as some special courses offered by institutions of higher learning, including colleges and universities. These bodies should be essentially represented by the professionals, employers/industries and technical community in their respective fields. The functioning of these bodies should also be on the same lines as suggested for the proposed body.

The above said professional bodies should consider to undertake the accrediation of the programmes of only such institutions which are assessed and graded by the assessment body. Like the assessment body, these professional bodies too should meet out their expenses out of the fee charged by them from the institutions for their assessment/accreditation of their programmes and become self-reliant financially in due course. The existing councils and bodies like Indian Council of Social Science Research (ICSSR), Indian Council of Historical Research (ICHR), Indian National Science Academy, etc. may be approached by the suggested body to assist the said professional bodies of their area, in accreditation of the programmes under their respective fields.

The suggested body may also be entrusted with the responsibility of evaluation of the Indian as well as International degrees in consultation with concerned professional bodies and recommend for their recognition for academic pursuit and employment and accordingly issue advisory to the institutions/colleges/universities assessed by it and also to the employers.

The suggested body should be responsible for maintaining and publishing the list of the institutions and the programmes assessed and/or accreditated by it and/or concerned professional bodies along with their degrees, recognized by it.

This body may be established by the government under Societies Registration Act, as an independent autonomous body and thereafter be converted into a Statutory body by an Act, if need be.

# 21

# Quality Assurance in Examination System: Challenges and Strategies

*Sambit K. Padhi*

Examination is a sub-system in a wider system of evaluation, which measures both qualitative and quantitative aspects of a young human mind. It reflects the changes that take place in different domains (cognitive, affective, psychomotor) of one's personality as a result of a structured instruction. The basic purpose of such instruction is to train one's head, heart and hand, i.e. (3H), so that they become useful for self as well as the society. The examination process must be capable of revealing the potentialities, which are latent in young ones in addition to assessing their achievements. In the system of examination, public examinations are usually conducted annually and half yearly in an academic year which is a public debate in present time.

## Quality Assurance in Examination

Examination reform is an age-old responsibility for the educationists since independence. Several commissions and committees have presented their reports to reform the system of education in general and examination system in particular. But as such eye catching movement has not done yet.

Quality is an industrial concept adopted and integrated now in the educational surrounding. It is defined as the totality of features and characteristics of a product or service that bear its ability to satisfy implicit needs. It is a dynamic idea used in day-to-day conservation as an absolute. Most of us admire it, many of us want it, and few of us can have it. Quality is not the end in itself but a means by which the end product is judged to be up to standard. In an era of globalization, industrialization, and liberalization, 'quality' is chanted as catchword of every product or service. One may come across the level of ISO, ISI, AGMARK, TQM as a quality symbol on products and services. The dimensions of quality symbols pertain to areas of input or output or process or to the totality of the system. In the context of education, quality refers to the features of education, which have to satisfy the needs of students, parents and society at large by developing appropriate knowledge and skills. Quality assurance in examination system implies ensuring the maintenance in setting of standards from the beginning (planning) stage to the end of the programme. Since quality assurance implies a real concern for standards even before any programme commences, its coverage is from the initial to final stage on a continual basis.

In other words, quality is a continuous improvement in performance to satisfy the customers' needs and expectations. Thus, quality is conformity to requirement like excellence, standards and values, quality has become a highly talked about concern in our society.

Assuring quality in examination system is imperative from the stage of paper setting (developing need-based question papers), conducting smooth examination and adopting appropriate evaluation technique.

## Evolution of Examination System

Since time immemorial, examinations are the inseparable components of educational system because these are the well-accepted parameters to ascertain the level of excellence of the students. Examinations are no doubt good servants as they help to evaluate the achievements of the students. They are great touchstones for measuring the amount of knowledge acquired or the degree of skill achieved. In Western countries, its first traces were found in the history of China where individuals were selected for high office of public responsibility as far back as 909 AD, through a well-designed examination system. The Indian mythology is also replete with instances of examination of intellectual and physical powers. The oft-cited name of Arjuna and Ekalavya in Mahabharat are prominent examples under the examination system. The concept of examination came into play clearly into India when Panini, great grammarian of ancient India graded his students on the basis of errors made in reciting the tests. In course of time various institutions have started their own system of examinations like Taksyashila University (150 BC to 180 BC) had no such tight system for obtaining admission. Then Nalanda University (450 AD to 850 AD) introduced admission test but that was oral, Mithila University (14th century) introduced "Salorkha Pariksha" Method (Needle examination method). After that Nadia University (12th century), now located in West Bengal followed the dialectical method of evaluation. From time-to-time, examination system took number of turns; with all these process of developmental stages the examination system has reached such a condition, where it is a great debatable feature.

Nowadays, it is a great challenge before the nation. By alternative day, the magnitude of problems related to these matters are multiplying. Here are some ongoing problems noted below those that have frequently occurred from nursery to university level

- Leakage of question papers
- Cancellation and shifting the dates of examination
- Unfair means of conducting examinations
- Unfair involvement of the staff
- Lack of standard question papers
- Unscientific techniques of evaluation and tabulation
- Unfair way of declaring results/certifying the students/ awarding degrees.

## Challenges in Examination System

Most of the issues related to the existing examination system do not have any state or national boundaries. These are the concern of educationists across the globe. We are convinced that our system of education is very much examination ridden.

Examinations have been dubbed as a 'gamble' and a 'necessary evil'. Award of marks and declaration of results have become the focus in the whole examination system, any improvement in other areas of the system stands completely neglected. An analysis indicates three broad areas under any examination system, viz.

**Questioning**

The importance of questioning in examination system can never be neglected. Questioning is the important area of discussion on the said topic. Standard/quality of examination depends on the pace with which we questioned and the speed with which we received the responses. The success of this part is purely in the hand of the question setter/framer. It is therefore very important to give a careful attention to the structuring of questions and their assemblage into a question paper. Before selecting a question setter, administration should have idea about his/her expertiseness/competency in framing the question papers. Besides this, a clear-cut guideline on kinds of questions, number of questions, time duration, maximum marks, weightage of marks along with syllabus need to reach sufficiently before the commencement of examination to the question setter. While constructing the question paper, one should have an insight to the guidelines and the characteristics of good/ quality questions. Question setter should ensure the following vital points during and after the preparation of a question paper:

- Questions are clear, purposeful, brief, natural as well as adaptable to the level of class and thought provoking.
- Questions really measure what they intend to measure.
- Questions are free from superfluous words and terms, precise, unambiguous.
- Questions are fit in accordance with time duration.
- Questions cover the objectives (knowledge, understanding, application and skills) in right proportion.
- Questions state the subject matter in a correct and accurate way.

- Questions are not challenges or threats but as a tool for assessment.
- Questions are off factual, analytical, explanatory, critical and judgmental.

**Conduct of Examinations**

The way now examinations are being conducted in various institutions is really precarious. The University Education Commission, presided over by Dr. Radhakrishnan wrote, "For nearly half a century, the examination has been recognized as one of the worst features of Indian Education." The Secondary Education Commission summarizing the glaring shortcomings of our examination very aptly and emphatically stated, "External examinations are exercising a restricting influence over the entire field of education to such an extent as almost to nullify its real purpose." W.H. Rybrn strongly criticizes and writes, "It goes without saying that examinations are the enemies of creative works at least as they are usually conducted." Again to quote the Secondary Education Commission, "The present system of examination does not test any thing except memory and certain kind of verbal felicity." Views of all the above committees and commissions agree in one point, i.e. huge decay of standard/ quality in examination system. Analysis indicates that there are four prime components that affect the total system, i.e. students, teachers (supervisors), the support and the system. The most deplorable aspect of the matter is that students, parents and teachers are only concerned with examination marks and not with the means by which the marks are obtained. This accounts use of unethical and unfair means like mass copying, individual copying, impersonation, fake degrees, etc. It is surprising to note that in many places unauthorized examinees are substituted in place of authorized examinees for writing the examinations. To attract the number of student, few institutions have the provision of mass copying, special arrangement of sickrooms to specific students, dictation of answers through electronic devices, writing the answers in blackboard of the exam halls, etc. There are number of other ways like paying handsome price to the invigilators, centre superintendent and flying squad members. When all the strategies fail they use their muscle power to capture and threaten the invigilators.

## Evaluation

Evaluation is a part and parcel of all examination system. It is widely used to determine the strength and weakness of the students in specific areas of study, and awarding degrees/certify the students is the particular educational practice. There is a common saying; existing system of evaluation is suffering with serious maladies. By presenting the clear-cut picture on drawback in the present evaluation system, the committee of examination, appointed by CABE, Ministry of Education and Social Welfare outlined that "Learners evaluation is a process of collecting, analyzing and interpreting evidences to judge the level of achievement acquired by an individual learner or a group of learners in all areas of domain. The method by which learners' evaluation is practiced in a majority of cases leaves much to be desired. Apparently, learners' achievement is established through the prevailing examination system which takes into cognizance only specific aspects, the other aspects are totally ignored". Truly, the present system does not provide any scope for the application of multiple techniques of assessment of the learners' potential in more valid and reliable ways. Besides this, the current practices of terminal examinations, semester system, home evaluation of M.Phil., Ph.D. work, suffer a lot of discrepancies caused due to a variety of errors. Another significant challenge before us is the selection of right evaluators. It is obviously observed that inter and intra-examiner variability are with respect to time, situation, mental set up, environment, etc. Besides this, imperfection of tools, sampling of contents, sampling of objectives within the content, arbitrary or very less time limits for answering individual questions, testing situations affect the evaluation system.

## Strategies for Quality Assurance in Examination System

The present time demands the multifaceted functions and responsibilities of examination system. To achieve the success in this field, right type of planning and strategies to be implemented are essential. The following are some suggested statements which may be taken care for maintaining the quality in examination system.

- Improving questions by making them specific in terms of objectives content and language along with appropriate weightage to objectives, content areas.
- Improving scoring procedures by developing scoring keys, marking scheme with suitable instructions to examiners.
- Expanding the techniques of evaluation to continuous-comprehensive evaluation (internal as well as external).
- Framing suitable rules for admission to an examination.
- Appointing appropriate paper setters with right qualification and experience.
- Developing scientific mechanism for conducting smooth examination.

For this, some steps should be taken before, during and after the commencement of examination.

- Secrecy should be maintained regarding setting, printing, stocking, mailing of question papers.
- To minimize impersonation, stress should be on admit card along with photograph and request for centre change should be discouraged.
- To overcome the chances of malpractices, strict instruction should be given to reach at least 15 minutes before the commencement of examination, so that mass checking could be possible.
- The seating arrangement and invigilators schedule at the exam halls should be frequently changed.
- Strict instructions should be given to both examinees and invigilators regarding their work during the examination hours.
- External observers and flying squads should be appointed for each exam centre.

- Toilets (permanent and temporary), bathrooms should be checked time to time before and during the examination hours.
- No stranger should be allowed into the boundary of exam centre.
- Two same class students should not sit at one place, right gaps/distance should be maintained among them.
- Exchange of question papers and answer papers should be prohibited.
- Opening of question papers packing and dispatching of answer papers must be carefully supervised by superintendent along with observer on duty.
- Coding and decoding of answer papers should be done confidentially.

After completion of all the evaluation works, suitable methods should be adopted for declaring results and issues of certificates. There should be provision for re-evaluation and rechecking and also provision for supplying Xerox of evaluated answer papers to the candidates.

The existing examination system will never be a qualitative one unless and until it gets active cooperation from every packet of educational sphere. As students are the real beneficiaries, they need to understand the importance of an examination in their life system, which will empower the students in several ways. No doubt, there are many shortcomings in the existing examination system; its complete solution is next to impossible. There is an urgent need to develop awareness among students, teachers, administrators, as well as among the parents for minimizing into certain extent. Let us join our hands and hope for the better quality of examination in upcoming days in comparison to the existing system.

## REFERENCES

Brophy, J. and Good, T. (1986), "Teacher Behaviour and Student Achievement" in M. Wittrock (ed.), *Handbook of Research on Teaching* (3rd ed.), Macmillan, New York.

Good, T.L. and Brophy J.E. (1987), *Looking into Classrooms* (4th ed.), Harper and Row Publisher, New York.

Grossier, P. (1964), *How to Use the Fine Art Questing*, Teachers' Practical Press, New York.

Kothary, D.S. (1964-66), Kothary Commission Report, GoI, New Delhi.

Vernal, L. (2004), "Questioning as a Communication Tool for Pedagogy", *University News*, New Delhi, Vol. 42, No. 21, May 24-30.

Radhakrishnan, S. (1952-54), University Education Commission, GoI, New Delhi.

# 22

# Designing Tests and Evaluation Approaches

*A.K. Singh* and *Surya Rathore*

Classroom tests play an important role in the evaluation of students' learning. They provide relevant measures of many important learning outcomes and direct evidence concerning others. The validity of the information they provide however depends on the care that goes into planning and preparation of the test. The terms test, measurement and evaluation are easily confused because all may be involved in a single process. We generally ask our students to answer a series of questions concerning our subject, obtain their scores by counting the number of correct answers and conclude that all the students are making good learning progress. Here, we are concerned with all the three concepts, i.e. test, measurement and evaluation. A test is a set of questions, measurement is the assigning of numbers to the test results according to specific rule and the evaluation adds the value judgment. The specific meaning of each term, as applied to classroom evaluation, is summarized as:

**Test:** An instrument or systematic procedure for measuring a sample of behaviour. (Answers the question, how well does the individual perform—either in comparison with others or in comparison with a domain of performance tasks?).

**Measurement:** The process of obtaining a numerical description of the degree to which an individual possesses particular characteristics (Answer the question "How much?")

**Evaluation:** The systematic process of collecting, analyzing and interpreting information to determine the extent to which students are achieving the instructional objectives. (Answers the question, "How good?")

Evaluation is much more comprehensive and inclusive term than measurement and testing is just one type of measurement. The term measurement is limited to quantitative descriptions of students, that is, results of measurement are always expressed in numbers. It does not include qualitative descriptions nor does it imply judgments concerning the worth or value of the obtained results. Evaluation, on the other hand, may include both quantitative and qualitative descriptions of students. In addition, evaluation always includes value judgments concerning the desirability of the results.

The process of evaluation will be more effective when following principles are taken into consideration:

*Clearly specifying what is to be evaluated has priority in the evaluation process*

The effectiveness of evaluation depends as much as on a careful description of what to evaluate as it does in the technical qualities of the evaluation instruments used. Thus, specification of characteristics to be measured should precede the selection or development of evaluation devices. When evaluating students' learning, this means clearly specifying the intended learning outcomes before selecting the achievement measures to use.

*An evaluation technique should be selected in terms of its relevance to the characteristics or performance to be measured*

Evaluation techniques are frequently selected on the basis of their objectivity, accuracy or convenience. Although these criteria are important, they are secondary to main criteria—Is this technique the most effective for measuring the learning or development to be evaluated? Each technique is appropriate for others. In testing students' achievements, for example, we need a close match between the intended learning outcomes and the types of test items used.

*Comprehensive evaluation requires a variety of evaluation techniques*

No single type of instrument or procedure can assess the vast array of learning and development outcomes emphasized in an educational programme. Objective tests of achievement are useful for measuring knowledge, understanding and application outcomes but essay type tests and other written projects are needed to measure the ability to organize and express ideas. Observational techniques are needed to assess performance skills; various aspects of students' behaviour and self-report techniques are useful for evaluating interests and attitudes. A complete picture of students' achievements and development requires continuing the results of many different techniques.

*Proper use of evaluation techniques require an awareness of their limitations*

Evaluation techniques range from highly developed measuring instruments (e.g. standardized aptitude test and achievement tests) to rather crude assessment devices (e.g. observational and self-reporting techniques). Even our best educational and psychological measuring instruments, however, yield results that are subject to various types of measurement errors.

*Evaluation is a means to an end, not an end in itself*

The use of evaluation techniques implies that some useful purpose will be served and the user is clearly aware of this purpose. To blindly gather data about students and then file the information away in the hope that it will some day prove useful is a waste of time and effort. Evaluation is best viewed as a process of obtaining information on which to have decision.

**Types of Testing and Evaluation Procedures**

The role of the distinctive features of the evaluation process is the use of wide variety of procedures. These may be classified and described in many different ways depending on the frame of reference used. This classification is based on the basis of most useful application in the area of teaching.

### Maximum Performance versus Typical Performance

In the first category are those procedures used to determine a person's abilities. Procedure for this type is concerned with how well an individual performs when he/she is motivated to obtain as high a score as possible. In short, the evaluation results indicate what an individual can do when he puts forth his best effort. Aptitude and achievement tests are included in this category. A distinction between these two types of tests is commonly made in terms of the use of the results rather than the qualities of test themselves. An aptitude test is primarily designed to predict success in some future learning activity, while an achievement test is designed to indicate degree of success in some past learning activity.

The second category includes those designs to reflect a person's typical behaviour. Procedures of this type are concerned with what individuals will do rather than what they can do. Methods designated to evaluate interests; attitudes, adjustment and various personality traits are included in this category. Here, the emphasis is on obtaining representative responses rather than high scores. This type of evaluation involves various methods such as interviews, questionnaires, ratings and various other self reports and observational techniques. None of these techniques when used alone provide an adequate appraisal of typical behaviour but combined results of number of them enable the instructor to make fairly accurate judgments concerning students' progress.

### Placement, Formative, Diagnostic and Summative Evaluation

Tests and other evaluation procedures can also be classified in terms of their functional role in classroom instruction.

*Placement evaluation*: To determine student performance at the beginning of instruction, i.e. measures entry behaviour.

*Formative evaluation*: To monitor learning progress during instruction, i.e. mid-term exam.

*Diagnostic evaluation*: To diagnose learning difficulties during instruction, i.e. identifies causes of learning problems.

*Summative evaluation*: To evaluate achievement at the end of instruction, i.e. measure end of course achievement.

## Types of Tests

Needless to say, conventional evaluation fosters competition rather than collaboration. Formal assessment tends to be governed by 'what is easy to assess' rather than 'what is to be assessed'. Therefore, traditional written examination, which has more transparency, is used. Some of the types of tests, which are frequently used, are as follows:

*Informal versus Standardized Tests*: Informal tests are those constructed by classroom teacher, whereas those designed by specialists and administered, scored and interpreted under standard conditions are called standard tests.

*Individual versus Group Tests*: Some tests are administered on one-to-one basis, whereas others can be administered to a group of individuals.

*Mastery versus Survey Test*: Some tests measure the degree of mastery of a limited set of specific outcomes, whereas others measure a student's general level of achievement over a broad range of outcomes.

*Supply versus Selection Tests*: Some tests require examinee to supply the answer (e.g. essay test), whereas others require them to select the correct response from a given set of alternatives (e.g. multiple-choice test).

*Speed versus Power Tests*: A speed test is designed to measure the number of items an individual can complete in a given time, whereas a power test is designed to measure level of performance under ample power conditions. Power tests usually have the items arranged in order of increasing difficulty.

*Objective versus Subjective Tests*: An objective test is one in which equally competent scores will obtain the same score (e.g. multiple-choice test), whereas a subjective test is one where the scores are influenced by the opinion or judgment of the person doing the scoring (e.g. essay test).

An adequate evaluation programme must include evaluation, development of desirable physical and mental health, social relationships, critical thinking appreciations, creative expression, interests and attitudes. Successful teaching calls for the competent use of evaluation of all three types of learning—cognitive, affective and psychomotor.

**Steps in the process of Evaluation**

The major objectives of a curriculum should be developed cooperatively by the administrators and the teachers according to the needs of the students and the society they live in; some examples of major objectives are:

(a) To develop an understanding of the diversification of agriculture.

(b) To develop abilities basic to successful agriculture development.

(c) To develop an understanding of various vocations those are possible in agriculture.

(d) To develop a positive attitude towards farm family as a basic unit of agricultural development.

Definition and classification of these objectives in terms of specific knowledge, abilities, skills and attitudes.

*Major Objective*

- To develop abilities basic to successful agriculture development.

*Knowledge*

- To develop an understanding regarding the role of agriculture for increasing production.
- To know the sources of various nutrients.

*Abilities*

- To develop an ability to plan sustainable agriculture projects.
- To be able to plan low input agriculture cultivation.
- To be able to produce low input sustainable varieties.

*Skills*

- To develop skill regarding mushroom cultivation practices.
- To develop skill regarding production of value added products of bamboo.

*Attitude*

- To develop a positive attitude towards low cost sustainable agriculture.

*Selection of available tests or measures for each major objective*

Example:

*Knowledge* – objective test

- Planning a lay-out for a kitchen garden.

*Ability* – Practical of budding, grafting, flower arrangement

*Construction of needed tests, scales and other techniques*

Example:

Preparation of –

"True and false items"

"Multiple-choice items"

"Short answer test items".

It is true that the main objectives of tests and examinations are mastery, diagnosis and reporting progress. In fact, the purpose of test should affect the kind of test given. Thus, a formal selection examination will normally cover a large number of skills and topics lightly and questions should be of middle difficulty level whereas mastery tests on a particular unit will be more intensive with several questions on each of a few topics to see whether they are mastered or not. Some tests might be relatively hard for all pupils (e.g. diagnostic tests). Some on the other hand would be lengthy and formal with elaborate marking schemes (e.g. end of year examination).

## Conclusion

Tests and evaluation play an important role in the instructional programme of an institution. Basically, they provide information that can be used in a variety of educational decisions. The main emphasis in classroom evaluation, however, is in decisions concerning students' learning and development.

# 23

# Teacher Stress: An Emerging Area of Research in Teacher Education Institutions

*Deepa Sikand Kauts* and *Minakshi Vig Aggarwal*

> The teacher is the most important element in any educational program. It is the teacher who is mainly responsible for implementation of the educational process at any stage. No amount of investment in improving the physical and educational facilities can improve education unless there are adequate number of well qualified teachers who can and willingly implement the educational process in such a way that it brings about the desired educational development of the students. It is, therefore, important that the teacher is well prepared to do his/her work efficiently and effectively. The quality of teacher depends, to a large extent, on the quality of teacher education received by him/her.
>
> —Quality Concerns in Secondary Teacher Education, NCTE, 1998

Ironically, today's technically super advanced life with lots of stress and strain hardly provides any congenial atmosphere for any thinker to think, any policymaker to do constructive framing of policy and above all any teacher to teach with sincerity and dedication. The daily interaction with pupils, co-workers and the incessant and fragmented demands of the teaching in general, often lead to overwhelming pressures and challenges, which further lead to stress and strain. Particularly, the teacher educators (who are preparing teachers for the schools) come across many pressures from different directions vis-à-vis:

- Norms and standards set by NCTE.
- Rules and regulations set by the concerned university.
- Various conditions set by DPI/State Level Agency.
- Expectations of NCERT from the institutions to go hand in hand with the changing times.
- Competitive attitude of the institutions for the attainment of higher grade from NAAC.
- Management's expectations for optimum utilization of minimum resources.
- One's own pressure to develop professionally.
- Voluntary organizations like CTE, AIAER and others who seek voluntary membership from teachers.
- Frequent changes in the time-table across the academic session to meet the needs of the curriculum detailed in the calendar of activities suggested by NCTE.
- Unending co-curricular activities to meet the needs of the quality school functioning required in future.
- Lesser span as also lesser number of full-time faculties available for the pupil teachers to be trained for tomorrow.
- Wide range of expectations of the special investors in the form of fees either from pupil teachers or their parents.
- Extra cordial relations with staff and heads of the practicing schools.

Above all, society entrusts responsibility of producing quality teachers on teacher educators. But in adverse circumstances of unlimited circumference as discussed earlier, it is hard task for a teacher educator to accomplish all the specified task objectives with a required level of commitment and competence. All the time, teacher educator is on the toes, which unconsciously take him/her to stress and then to distress.

## The Concept of Stress

In common parlance, the terms 'stress' and 'strain' are used synonymously in a non-scientific manner. But what really stress refers to and what does it mean in the real sense? Derived from the Latin word 'stringere', stress was popularly used in the seventeenth century to mean hardship, strain, adversity or affliction. In eighteenth and nineteenth centuries, it was used to denote force, pressure, strain or strong effort with reference to an object or person.

But the research literature finds difficulty in pin-pointing a single definition of the term stress. A frequently cited definition of stress has been provided by Hans Selye (1956) "the non-specific response of the body to any demand made upon it."

Mason (1975) reviewed literature on stress and concluded that there was confusion and a lack of consensus regarding its definition. The term stress has been approached in at least four different ways. First, as the stimulus or external force acting on the organism; second, as the response or changes in the physiological functions; third, as the interaction between an external force and the resistance opposed to it, as in Biology; and finally, as a comprehensive phenomenon encompassing all the three.

For want of more definitive terminology, the term stress has survived surveying definitions; Cox (1978) has described three classes of definitions. Stress can be variously thought of as a response, i.e. the stress response to an extreme stimulus, as a stimulus, i.e. as the stressor itself; and as an intervening variable. In contrast to the response and stimulus definitions, definitions in which stress is referred to as an intervening variable come closest to the everyday meaning of the term. Such definitions lay emphasis on the individual's perceptions of the demands made by the environment and his ability to meet those demands. It is the mismatch between these personal resources and environmental demands that leads to the condition called stress. Examples of such conceptualizations are found in the P-E Fit theory and Lazarus' (1984) theory of stress. These definitions lay great importance on the emotional component of stress commonly referred to by clinical practitioners and behavioral scientists alike. A diagrammatic representation of the term stress is presented in the figure below:

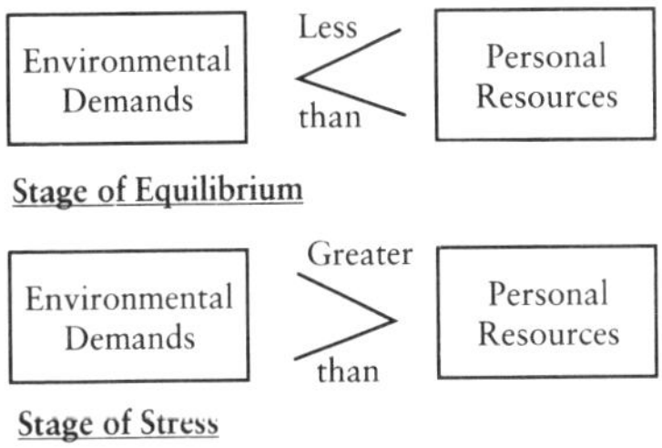


**Fig. 1:** A Diagrammatic Representation of Stress.

But the question is, who decides whether personal resources (capabilities, time, money, material) exceed environmental demands or not? It is an entirely subjective matter, since it is the individual who takes this decision. What is the basis for a decision? It can be another subjective process-perception of the individual. A person may feel or perceive that he does not have enough time to perform his duties both at home and at office and may experience stress. At the same time, others (including the boss and the spouse) may feel that the person has all the time in the world but what is lacking is efficient time management. Regardless of the ways in which others perceive the situation, so long as the person's perceptions regarding time on hand remain unchanged, the person will continue to be under stress.

The seminal work and conceptualization of Selye (1983) has undergone a change. There are three different viewpoints or approaches—medical, psychological and sociological. While the first construes stress typically as a defensive bodily response to environmental demands and involves physiological component; the second places greater emphasis on cognitive appraisal (mental picture) of threatening environmental conditions (the I cannot cope the type of situation) and the ensuing coping process. The third analyses stress as the resultant of stressful societal conditions. These three foci have produced a large body of research and practice, extremely active and variegated in terms of methodology, samples and conceptual analyses.

A fairly comprehensive definition arrived at on the basis of the findings in both research and practice can be—"Stress consists of any event in which environmental demands, internal demands, or both, tax or exceed the adaptive resources of the individual, social system or tissue system" (Farmer, Monahan and Hekeler, 1984).

## Teacher Stress

Although educational institutions tend to be viewed as microcosms that exist within, yet operate separately from, their local communities, they are essentially workplaces for people who choose the profession of teaching. Yet the experience of stress for teachers is qualitatively different from the work stress experienced by many others in the work context. Teaching is characterized by great responsibility, with no freedom to leave the classroom for more than a few moments and pressure to control one's emotions. The unproductive levels of stress might be harmful to teachers and can affect their teaching, personal lives and most importantly their students.

So far as the formal concept of stress is viewed in the context of formal teaching, a particular time cannot be pin-pointed regarding its inception but an idea for the same can be assessed.

> Teacher stress has continued to be studied since 1930s, when article on the health and happiness of teachers began to appear in various educational journals.
>
> (Smith and Milstein, 1984)

## Studies Related to Teacher Stress

Teacher stress has been a subject for some of the studies in the past in the relevant literature identifying the main job stressors facing teachers. There are also a number of studies (though fewer in number) focusing on specialist samples of teachers such as teachers in special schools, teachers of primary or secondary schools, newly qualified teachers, university teachers, teachers working in an open climate, teachers of professional and non-professional courses, college teachers, etc.

Mishra (1991) found relationship between organizational climate in school, teacher stress and burn-out in relation to teacher's personality.

McCormick and Solman (1992) examined the nature of occupational stress for teachers, with an emphasis on blame as the behavioral externalization of low job satisfaction amongst teaching professionals. Analysis revealed four factors likely to engender teacher stress: (i) supervision, (ii) extrinsic factors such as low salary levels and poor working conditions, (iii) school culture, and (iv) low satisfaction with advancement opportunities. The human relations element of supervision along with school culture, were suggested as logical target areas for improvement to reduce teacher stress.

In an investigation of teacher stress by Boyle, Borg, Falzon and Baglioni (1995), dimensions of stress were workload, student misbehavior, professional recognition needs, time/resource difficulties, and poor colleague's relations. Student misbehaviors and workload emerged as the strongest predictors of stress and were entirely consistent with studies reported elsewhere. However, results for time/resource difficulties and professional recognition needs contradicted the findings of other researchers. Poor relations with colleagues failed to emerge as a direct predictor of stress in its own right, in contrast to results generally reported by other researchers. Regardless of the apparent contradiction in some of these results, the study still offers support for the notion of multiple sources of teacher stress, in line with similar research.

A study by Punch and Tuetteman (1996) revealed the relationship between support found in the work environment and amelioration of teacher stress in Western Australian secondary schools. The four stressors identified in the study were (i) inadequate access to facilities, (ii) intrusion of school related work into recreational time, (iii) student misbehavior, and (iv) excessive societal expectations. Potential avenues for remedy were cited as (i) support received from colleagues, including principals and (ii) praise and recognition.

Czubaj (1996) cited several studies that explored how the effectiveness of one's stress coping may be related to motivational differences in the face of objective stressors. Some of the variables identified as intrinsic motivators were internal locus of control, self-efficacy, outcome expectations, psychological attachment to the teaching profession, and failure tolerance. In contrast, people who were higher on external locus of control and lower on the remaining dimensions were more likely to experience stress or burnout when external stressors accumulated. The results highlighted the idea of stress as transaction between person and environment, and points to a need for robust supportive cultures to counterbalance individual variation in stress coping.

> Teaching can be a stressful occupation. The daily interaction with students and co-workers and the incessant and fragmented demands of teaching often lead to overwhelming pressures and challenges, which may lead to stress. Where work stress is unrelenting, some negative physiological, psychological and behavioral consequences may result. (DeRobio and Iwanicki, 1996)
>
> Many teachers would agree teaching is not only hard work, it can be full of stress. Pressure due to reform efforts, inadequate administrative support, poor working conditions, lack of participation in decision-making, the burden of paperwork and lack of resources has all been identified as factors that can cause stress among staff. (Hammond and Onikama, 1997)

Indira (1997) reported stress and work orientation in relation to teacher effectiveness. Bhatt (1997) reported a correlation study of job stress, job involvement and job satisfaction of teachers.

Able and Sewell (1999) investigated differences in the sources of stress between rural and urban schools. Significantly, greater stress was found for urban versus rural schools from (i) poor working conditions, including inadequate resources, (ii) lack of recognition and advancement prospects, and (iii) poor staff relations, including unfriendly atmosphere, and lack of support from both colleagues and school administrators. For both urban and rural schools, student misbehavior and time pressures were the leading sources of stress, with no significant differences between groups.

Davis and Wilson (2000) examined the results of efforts to empower teachers to reduce stress and improve job satisfaction and motivation. They conceptualized personal power as part of intrinsic motivation, and included cognitive and behavioral aspects such as competence, meaningfulness, impact, and choice. Competence was defined as a belief in one's capacity for performance, meaningfulness as the value one places on task goals according to personal ideals, impact as the degree to which one perceives their behavior is producing intended effects, and choice as the intentional selection of actions of desired outcomes. Findings revealed that the more principals participated in empowering behavior, the more teachers were encouraged to make effective choices in fulfillment of job tasks. While no direct relationship was found between principals empowering behaviors and stress or job satisfaction, a moderately strong positive association was found between both variables and improvements in teacher's sense of personal power:

> Many teachers find the demands of being a professional educator in today's schools difficult and at times stressful. When work stress results in teacher burnout, it can have serious consequences for the health and happiness of teachers, and also the students, professionals, and families they interact with on a daily basis. (Wood, 2002)

In the studies reviewed above, it is evident that teacher stress has been investigated in a number of ways. For example, some authors utilize purpose designed measures to examine the sources and nature of teacher stressors while others use instruments designed to tap specific components of stress, including psychological distress, behavioral disengagement, strain reactions, health consequences, etc.; and many others in more varied ways. Still we need further investigation and elaboration in the right perspective.

"Teacher stress is a much talked of phenomenon, however there is little consensus between different professional groups regarding its etiology, or how to tackle it. Based on a review of international research, it is concluded that teacher stress is a real phenomenon and that high levels are reliably associated with a range of casual factors, including those intrinsic to teaching, individual vulnerability and systemic influences. Limitations with the current research base of teacher stress are identified. We have a reasonable understanding of the etiology of teacher stress, but little is known about the effects of reducing or mediating the impact of stressors. There are very few studies of effective interventions and none involving large samples or long term follow up. There are serious problems in generalizing findings from stress-management in other occupational sectors. As well as addressing these gaps in our understanding, future research based on a social representations approach is needed to allow teachers and stress management practitioners a shared understanding of stress" (Jervis, 2002).

**Probable and Divergent Directions for Future Research in Teacher Stress**

In this age of Science and Technology, life has become more complicated and arduous. This is exactly a time of chances and challenges. The value of time has to be taken as a moment lost is lost forever. Tempo of achievement once attained is to be maintained at all costs. Every moment brings for the humanity a vista of new and peculiar challenges, which have to be accepted and faced in all fairness. All this has to be managed with single method and the method is education. Hence, the modern 21st century education system must inculcate and assist in developing personality, improving communicational skills and help to choose a career. It must teach about time management and stress management. It must nurture qualities of creativity, innovativeness and enterprise. Value-based education, technical and psychological ideas are very essential to make a person perfect and highly competitive. So, it is necessary to adopt new dimensions in education due to globalization and InfoTech revolution.

Mushroom growth of education colleges over the last decade propelled by the highly speculative requirements at the national and global levels have resulted in severe degradation of quality education. We have started believing in quantity rather than quality. Like higher education, teacher education system in India is no longer the same as it was a decade ago. In the light of teacher stress so described, if the penultimate and the ultimate states of stress, which are detrimental in longevity, be described as loss of idealism and enthusiasm to work, the associate causes for the same. Stressors, which come across the way of smooth process of teaching to the quality educators, cannot be ignored in any sense. Most teachers seem to work under stress. Recognizing that stress is a hurdle to effectiveness, it may be a priority area to identify how teachers can avoid and cope with stress which is their lot. The effect of growing stress and tensions on teacher's life and work requires carefully designed rcsearch.

After reviewing the studies, it is evident that although the related literature covers a broader compass in general, there are few studies in the area of teacher stress in teacher education institutions and specifically in Indian context. These need further investigation and elaboration in the right context and perspective. Let us further try to enlist major areas of concern in relation to teacher stress and introspect the phenomenon in terms of the factors/variables that affect the stress among teacher educators and suggest ways to minimize problems towards the enhancement of quality teacher education as also school education in present scenario.

## Teacher Stress and Emotional Intelligence of Teacher Educators

In the last decade or so, science has discovered a tremendous influence about the role emotions play in our lives. Researchers have found that our emotional awareness and ability to handle feelings rather than our IQ will determine our success and happiness in all walks of life. Many intellectual problems contain emotional information that must be processed (Mayor and Salvoey, 1990) and utilized to solve such problems.

Although the construct of Emotional Intelligence (EI) is relatively new, it has enjoyed unprecedented attention from scholars and corporate gurus.

Salovey and Mayer (1990) conceptualized the term emotional intelligence as the subset of social intelligence that involves the ability to monitor one's own and others feelings and emotions, discriminate among them and to use information to guide one's thinking and action.

Goleman (1995) formulated the best known theory of emotional intelligence. Goleman's explanation of the construct was based on Salovey and Mayer's (1990) theory. Among other claims, Goleman theorized that emotional intelligence is equal to, if not more important than IQ as an important indicator of success in one's professional and personal life. Elaborating further on the construct, Goleman (1998) explained that an individual's emotional intelligence can affect one's work situation. He also applied his conceptual understanding to organization as a whole.

Baron (2005) proposed a new model of emotional intelligence. Based on Baron's model, to be emotionally and socially intelligent is to effectively understand and express oneself, to understand and relate well with others, and to successfully cope with daily demands, challenges and pressures.

Numerous studies have been conducted in the field of emotional intelligence highlighting its application and use in daily life.

Cherniss and Goleman (1998) estimated that by not following training guidelines established to increase emotional intelligence in the workplace, industry in the United States is losing between $5.6 and $16.8 billion a year. They found that the impact of training employees in emotional and social competencies with programs, which followed their guidelines, was higher than for other programs, and by not implementing these programs companies were receiving less of an impact and consequently losing money.

Cherniss (2000) outlined four main reasons why the workplace would be a logical setting for evaluating and improving emotional intelligence competencies.

- Emotional intelligence competencies are critical for success in most jobs.
- Many adults enter the workforce without the competencies necessary to succeed or excel at their job.
- Employers already have the established means and motivation for providing emotional intelligence training.

- Most adults spend the majority of their waking hours at work.

A strong interest in the professional applications of emotional intelligence is apparent in the way organizations have embraced EI ideas. The American Society for Training and Development, for example, has published a volume describing guidelines for helping people in organizations cultivate emotional intelligence competencies, which distinguish outstanding performers from average ones (Cherniss and Adler, 2000).

Ciarrochi, Chan and Caputi (2000), for example, posit that emotional intelligence may protect people from stress and lead to better adaptation. They opine that an objective measure of emotion management skill is associated with a tendency to maintain an experimentally induced positive mood, which has obvious implication for preventing stress.

It has been revealed that various investigators have suggested different techniques to raise emotional intelligence at workplaces with various strata of learners such as for leaders, employers, organizers, superintendents, etc. However, no study has been conducted for analyzing the effect of emotional intelligence among teachers and students. Realizing the importance of emotional intelligence, study efforts need to be made to seek relationship of different levels of emotional intelligence and teacher stress in the present scenario for the benefit of the learning society at large.

### Teacher Stress due to Introduction of Modern Science and Technology

The whole notion of teacher as disseminator of knowledge is now turned on its head. While in the old scenario, the teacher was the boss: in the new scenario, the teacher becomes the facilitator. Teachers, who employ knowledge in the classroom, do not funnel information into their students' heads. They guide them to information, to be accessed, and interacted with. He is becoming less central to the learning process. Learning with technology has to start by educating the teachers. There is considerable hope, and some positive evidence that technology can expand and improve education at all levels, with special reference to the design and content of instructional materials, delivery, assessment and feedback.

Considering the teacher, one can realize the great service provided by technology, for the betterment of the teaching-learning process.

- It renders its services in explaining the purpose and functions of different forms of applications, equipment, audio-visual material and mass media.
- In providing training in acquiring and handling the technological apparatus and appliances.
- It also helps the teacher in showing the relevance and the utility of the subject.

Keeping all this in view, the importance of knowledge and the skills that the teacher provides is easy to summarize its utility to the teacher as follows:

- Teacher has to know the impact of technological advancements in the field of education in vivid terms.
- They have to actively participate in the preparation of software that is within the reach and learn to utilize the hardware that is kept in their custody to the advantage of their students.
- The teachers need to be acquainted with their equipment and material to achieve the goal of education.

Thus, in educational technology and technology-enhanced learning, the role of the teacher is expected to be quite different from what it is in traditional classroom teaching. In the latter, the teacher is the author, playwrite, actor and director, with the actor's role assuming the major significance; while in the former, he will be more of a director, and a coach/facilitator. Teacher stress experienced, if any, needs to be explored in relation to the multidimensional impact due to the introduction of educational technology.

## Teacher Stress and Privatization of Teacher Education Institutions

The present education policy is complimentary to the economic policy of our government. As we all know today that the focus of economic policy has shifted towards liberalization, privatization and globalization. The mantra of privatization and globalization is being tried in education as well. Private institutions are being encouraged to provide education on commercial basis. Cutting down expenditure on education by the government, amplifying materialistic attitude in general and many more reasons have left with no alternative than privatization of higher as well as professional education.

In the Indian context, privatization is not suitable as the majority of population lies below the poverty line and do not have the means and access to education. The policy of the government to motivate privatization, on the one hand, will widen the socio-economic gulf and would go against the constitutional obligation of providing equal opportunities of education to all at different levels, whereas, on the other hand, this policy will lead to financial and academic exploitation of the trainers as well as of the trainees in the teacher education institutes in particular. The privatization of education has given birth to social tensions in the society. The teacher's health is being affected and in turn will affect student's learning environment and their professional careers in future. Lack of professional autonomy, improper human relations among teachers, political interference, autocratic attitude of bureaucrats and denial of teacher's professional rights will lead to dissatisfaction.

Hence, special attention is sought in this context. Teacher stress should be studied in depth, researched in the entirely changed scenario of globalized and privatized system of education and suggestions for future be made accordingly.

## Conclusion

The growth of any nation depends on the holistic development of its various sectors. "Education" is the key instrument in this process. Technical advancement of education is becoming a reality and India being a prominent figure cannot afford to ignore the challenges posed. Like other centers of higher learning, teacher education institutions are being confronted with new issues, challenges, threats and so on.

Now, it is the high time that these institutions do the introspection and identify major areas of stresses.

Members of the teaching profession are vulnerable to stress because of the demanding nature of the work and the stressors involved. Relatively speaking, teachers need help and hurt. They are not as satisfied as they want to be with the role of teaching. Unless they are able to reduce or eliminate their problems or attain their goals, they will feel considerable stress and burnout (Cruickshank, 1981).

In the present context, there is a need to lay stress on the quality of teachers and basically teacher educators who are to act as luminaries in the field of pre-service and in-service training to the teachers who will in turn be in the same process of luminaries for the nation builders of tomorrow. In today's rapidly growing and dynamic environment, the role of teacher educator is becoming more complex. The teacher educator is being challenged with the task of increased teaching load, research responsibility and continuous improvement in skill set. The performance demands have increased tremendously. It is upon them that the entire burden lays; the responsibility of producing quality teachers; is one of the greatest liabilities. Any minor ignorance or slacken in them will prove detrimental to the cause of advancement in the country as well as an important loss to the entire humanity.

## REFERENCES

Baron, R. (2005), "The Baron Model of Emotional-Social Intelligence", *Psichotema*, 17.

NCTE (2002), Calendar of activities for B.Ed. Programme (A Model), Document 2002/68, National Council for Teacher Education.

Cherniss, C. and Abler, M. (2000), *Promoting Emotional Intelligence in Organisations*. Virginia: ASTD.

Cherniss, C. and Goleman, D. (1998), *Bringing Emotional Intelligence to the Workplace*. Retrieved in September, 2003 from www.eiconsortium.org

Cherniss, C. (2000), "Social and Emotional Competence in the Workplace" in R. Baron and J. Parker (Eds.), *The*

*Handbook of Emotional Intelligence*. San Francisco: Jossey-Bass.

Ciarrochi, J. Chan, A. and Caputi, P. (2000), "A Critical Evaluation of the Emotional Intelligence Construct", *Personality and Individual Differences*, Vol. 28, pp. 539-61.

Cox, T. (1978), Stress. London: Macmillan.

Cruickshank, D.R. (1981), "What We Know about Teachers' Problems", *Educational Leadership*, 38, 402-06.

Derobbio, R.A. and Iwanicki, E. (1996), "Factors Accounting for Burnout Among Secondary School Teachers". Paper presented at the *Annual Conference of the American Educational Research Association*, New York, NY.

Farmer, R.E., Monahan, L.H. and Hekeler, R.W. (1984), *Stress Management for Human Services*. Beverly Hills, CA: Sage.

Goleman, D. (1995), *Emotional Intelligence: Why it can Matter more than IQ*, New York: Bantam Books.

Hammond, O.W. and Onikama, D.L. (1997), *At Risk Teachers*, Honolulu, H.I.: Pacific Resources for Education and Learning.

Jarvis, M. (2002), "Teacher Stress", *Stress News*. January Vol. 14, No. 1.

Lazarus, R.S. and Folkman, S. (1984), *Stress Appraisal and Coping*, New York: Springer-Verlag.

Mason, J.W. (1975), "A Historical View of Stress Field", *Journal of Human Stress*, March 6-12.

Mehrotra, R.N. (1998), *Teacher and Teaching: Sixth Survey of Educational Research*, Quality Concerns in Secondary Teacher Education, NCTE.

Salovey, P. and Mayor, J.D. (1990), "Emotional Intelligence", Imagination, *Cognition and Personality*, 9, 185-211.

Seley, H. (1956), *The Stress of Life*. New York: McGraw Hill.

Seley, H. (1983), "The Stress Concept: Past, Present and Future" in C.L. Cooper (Ed.), *Stress Research: Issues for Eighties*, Chichester. Wiley, pp. 1-20.

Smith, D. and Milstein, M.N. (1984), "Stress and Teachers: Old Wine in New Bottles", *Urban Education*, 19, 39-51.

Wood, Teri-Mccgrathy, Chris (2002), *Understanding and Preventing Teacher Burnout*. ERIC Clearinghouse on Teaching and Teacher Education, Washington DC.

# Perspectives Across Disciplines

24

# Science Education in Independent India: An Overview

*Subimal Kumar Chatterjee*

Before independence, entire education system of India was traditional and conservative. Negligence of British rulers was reflected in all spheres of education including science education. In 1943, Norwood Report was published where a chapter on science teaching was included. Sir Cyril Norwood, Chairman of the Secondary School Examination Council, perhaps visualized the approaching sun rays from independent India and suddenly realized that they should not delay any more to make Indians believe that British rulers were well wishers of India. Within next two years, i.e. in 1945, Education Act of 1944 came into force where recommendations to increase science teaching in Indian schools were incorporated. But the pace of implementation and progress was very slow. Our national leaders fully understood the intention of the British rulers and took suitable measurers for early implementation of educational policies in independent India. In spite of all efforts, it took about six years when a definite directive was issued in 1953 by the Secondary Education Commission to teach 'General Science' as a compulsory subject in high schools. In 1956, first National Seminar on "Teaching of Science in Secondary Schools" was organized at Simla where the participants discussed about different related issues like syllabus, laboratory, equipment, text-books, teaching methods, etc. to analyse the merits and demerits of the existing system. That the policymakers of our government had positive thinking towards improvement of science teaching was evidenced by the following vital steps taken within the next ten years:

- In 1957, National Science Policy was adopted by the Central Government. The main objective of this policy was to inspire qualitative improvement of teaching, training and research for development of a healthy scientific community.
- During 1961-62 period, Indian Parliamentary and Scientific Committee was constituted under the chairmanship of Sri Lal Bahadur Shastri to study the problems and prospects of science education in schools. The terms of reference placed before the committee was to study and analyse the relations between policies and decisions taken by the Central and State Government at the time of implementation, the existing hurdles in respect of infrastructure, trained and qualified manpower and such others. At this stage National Council of Educational Research and Training (NCERT) took its birth as a parent body of National Institutes of Education (NIE) with various departments. Regional Institutes of Education (RIE) at four states like Rajasthan (Ajmer), Madhya Pradesh (Bhopal), Orissa (Bhubaneswar) and Karnataka (Mysore) and also State Institutes of Science Education in different states were constituted. Proposal to introduce 'Science Education' (the subject to deal with teaching of science) as a subject was also considered.
- Recommendations of Kothari Commission (1964-66) where improvement of Science Education from primary to research level was stressed upon has been proved to be a timely step at right direction.
- In 1968, National Policy on Education was framed where specific directives were released to declare Science and Mathematics as compulsory components of syllabi during the first 10 years of school.
- Two more salient features highlighted in the policy were to ensure application of scientific knowledge and

supply of trained manpower to deal with Science teaching.

- Involvement of international bodies like UNESCO and UNICEF in upliftment of standard of Science teaching in Indian schools was a very effective step taken by the government. In 1963, UNESCO Planning Mission rendered academic assistance by suggesting measures to improve teaching of Science and Mathematics in secondary schools. UNICEF assisted Science Education Programme (SEP) introduced in 1970 contributed a lot for overall improvement of Science teaching in classroom situation.

During the last phase of 20th century, educationists and policymakers shifted their focus for educational planning from routine traditional framework to a more dynamic multidimensional pattern to fulfill the needs of 21st century. Nature and flow of that thought was primarily reflected in the National Education Policy of 1986 and its Programme of Action (1992) where in addition to the general issues like National Integration, Social Relevance of Education and Science Education was highlighted. Three international conferences, viz. International Conference on Secondary Education (1993), WTO Conference on GATS (1994) and International Conference on Higher Education (1998) held in New Delhi, Uruguay and Paris in three subsequent years served as platforms where directives and guidelines for educational planning relevant for 21st century were chalked out. Cry for quality education and its percolations at all levels was raised. In the year 2000, when educationists looked back, they found that access has been widened but no significant improvement in other points of concern could be noticed except some routine syllabus revision, diversification at will and inter-disciplinary approach without proper co-relation, co-ordination and scope for application. This observation is true for education in general and Science education also.

## Science Education in Broader Perspective

In general, it is nothing but the teaching-learning process of Science at all levels in schools, colleges and universities. In early sixties, simultaneously with the formation of NCERT, a proposal was initiated to treat 'Science Education' as a subject to deal with different issues of Science teaching like curriculum development, teaching methods, creativity in teaching, evaluation etc. The main objective to promote 'Science education as a subject was to train school teachers from primary to higher secondary stage so that they can teach Science efficiently to the school students. At present, scope for application of 'Science education concept' on college and university teachers is also possible through orientation and refresher courses. With the changing scenario in the global educational arena, Science education is gradually becoming indispensible for Engineering and Technology Education also because thorough knowledge of Science, consolidate the base of Engineering and Technology students.

If anybody looks into the history of Science education in independent India it will be seen that a number of commissions and national/international agencies made several recommendations which were implemented partly or fully for improvement of Science teaching-learning system. Some of such recommendations and the proposing bodies are:

(1) Teaching of Science from primary level (school) to undergraduate level (college) by the University Grants Commission.

(2) Teaching of General Science from Middle School to High School by the Secondary Education Commission.

(3) Teaching Biology, Physics and Chemistry as integral subjects in classes VII and VIII by USNESCO Planning Mission.

(4) Teaching Physics, Chemistry and Biology in Class VI and Physics, Biology, Chemistry and Astronomy in Class VII by Education Commission of 1964-66.

(5) Teaching Science as environmental studies in primary classes and as integrated courses upto class VIII by Ten Year School Curriculum expert group.

(6) Teaching Science and environment related issues in an integrated way by NCERT and State Institutes of Education (SIE).

(7) Yager (1984) as a proponent of STS (Science, Technology and Society) movement suggested that application of Science and Technology knowledge is a necessity for social improvement. School curriculum should be framed accordingly.

(8) Report of the committee headed by Yashpal (1993) suggested that Science textbooks should have analytical reflection of real life situation.

Of the above recommendations at least the last three, i.e. 6, 7 and 8, are influenced by the global bodies like "American Association for the Advancement of Science (AAAS-1985)", "Project 2001, Science for All Americans", "Hands on Science (HOS) Programme", "Nuffield Programmes", etc. Attempts were also made to improve Science education by introducing Hoshangabed Science Curriculum, Eklavya Science Activities and Kishore Bharati Teaching Learning Material at the elementary level.

In addition to implementation of the above recommendations, State Institutes of Science Education (SISE) were established to find out additional ways and means for improvement of Science teaching-learning system. Such institutes were directed to look after the implementation of educational policies and also to take steps for development of National Science Curriculum based on glimpses of international thoughts and ideas suitable for our local target groups. Coordination amongst curriculum developers and teachers was also urged upon. SISE experts were further instructed to frame curricula having inter-disciplinary approach and social relevance and also satisfying needs and interest of the students who are ultimate beneficiaries of the education system. School authorities were directed to uplift their infrastructure towards manpower and laboratory facilities to facilitate improved Science teaching as a pre-requisite to college and university level teaching as well as research.

## Science Education of Today

In spite of all efforts of our policymakers, national leaders and educationists, Science teaching-learning system or Science education as a whole appear a bit gloomy even after sixty years of independence. Starting from Indian school education in Science, undergraduate/postgraduate teaching and research, level of quality in basic Science is not very encouraging in comparison to global standards. Even in the different states of India, uniformity is lacking in all aspects. Quantitative growth has been achieved as evidenced by existing more than a million primary and secondary schools, around 2000 professional institutes, around 2000 training institutes, more than 20,000 general colleges and 400 universities which are ready to accommodate eligible candidates at suitable stages. Infrastructural facilities available for Science teaching is not uniform in the schools where three distinct categories can be identified. The categories are government-aided, government-administered and under total private management. Of these three, the third one, i.e. the private schools provide best facilities for Science teaching-learning system in the form of qualified teachers, well-equipped laboratories, libraries, computer facilities, etc. In addition to all these, professional approach of the school management helps the students to prepare themselves for the tough competition in educational market. Other schools, i.e. government and aided schools somehow manage their systems because of the limitations of varied nature.

Colleges imparting instruction at graduation stage (honours and general pass level) in different basic Science subjects are mostly sponsored by State and/or Central Government. Some of the colleges are under total administrative control of respective State Governments. A few privately managed colleges also exist. Comparatively older colleges of repute do have sufficient infrastructural facilities in the form or laboratories, library, computers, audio-visual aids, etc. which are necessary for quality Science teaching. But the colleges established in and around 1990 are not sufficiently equipped for obvious reasons. The same is true for universities also. Funding is often posed as a major constrain which cannot be denied. Inadequate financial support from the funding agencies force the institutes of higher education not only to restrict upgradation of their laboratories, but also limit the maintenance cost of the existing instruments and technical equipments in use. In addition, the institutes are facing enormous problems to run the practical classes of students in subjects like Chemistry, Zoology, Botany, Environment Science, Microbiology or Biotechnology because of gradual hiking of prices of chemicals, fuels, glass goods and such other consumables. Except the research institutes of repute and some research laboratories of older universities, infrastructure for research in most of the institutes is of very general nature. Modernization and upgradation of these labs are often proposed in the development schemes submitted at the appropriate levels by the concerned persons as a routine work. But nobody knows when the scope of implementation will come.

When our area of discussion is Science education in Indian subcontinent, 'manpower' issue is to be considered simultaneously with non-living infrastructural facilities. Starting from school to the university level, standards of teaching and research mainly depend on the strength of faculty and support staff. The word 'strength' does not qualify a numerical figure only; it stands for 'quality' also. To be more precise, quality of manpower truly influence quality of teaching at any level and quality of research in any area. This is the most important requirement the nation desires to have from the intellectual people for its steady development. Unfortunately, except a few dedicated academicians, most of our Science teachers and researchers think otherwise. To them, taking a number of classes per week or publication of a number of research papers and award of a few Ph.D. degrees will serve the purpose. They do not care to think whether delivery of a few monotonous lectures effectively lead to learning or enrichment of knowledge bank of the students and papers published after working out traditional research problems will be of any use to satisfy national developmental requirements or fulfill societal needs. Casual approach of institutional teachers at any level influences rise of a parallel system of education in the name of private tuition. Standing on a solid platform, this parallel system has gained not only tremendous momentum but also proved its affectivity as an efficient student support system to such an extent that students of schools and colleges attend these coaching centres even when they are supposed to attend their theory and/or practical classes in regular institutes. Leaving apart a few exceptional institutions, success of this parallel education system cannot be denied. At the post graduate level penetration of this private tuition system is insignificant. But amongst the students enrolled in Distance Education Institutes, a sizable number opt for private coaching centres side by side with their DDE academic schedule. The overall picture is not only painful but also alarming.

**Who is Responsible?**

If we throw this question in a gathering of academicians, nobody will come forward to answer the question for obvious reasons. Instead, they may point their fingers to the concerned government or the educational policymakers. In my opinion, neither the entire government nor the concerned ministry of state and/or centre can be held solely responsible for this undesirable poor condition of Science education in India. It is simply a reflection of the outcome of activities of different educational thinkers, planners, policymakers and activists who are responsible members of our academic fraternity. To be more precise, we, the academicians, are mostly responsible for deterioration of teaching and research in Science education. The reasons behind are very clear and transparent: in this rapidly changing knowledge era when 'explosion of knowledge' and 'obsolescence of knowledge' are alternating each other in cyclic manner, we have misplaced our priorities for improvement of Science education. Knowing our deficiencies fully well, we have taken least active interest to rectify those. Science teaching at schools followed more or less the same traditional system. Nature of course structure, content, examination pattern and marks weightage changed from time to time. But the required balance of teaching load at different stages and maintenance of links from one level to the next higher one was not judiciously taken care of. Repetition of topics at different stages, stereotype teaching methods and lack of sufficient practical training have made the teaching-learning system lifeless and monotonous.

Science teaching and research at higher education level would have been more dynamic and improved if suggestions of

Dr. M.N. Saha and Dr. H.J. Bhaba were accepted and implemented for improvement of Science and Technology education. In late fifties and early sixties, the then Prime Minister of India appreciated the suggestions but was unable to consider those during implementation of Science policies. Scientific Advisory Committee to the Cabinet (SACC) played a mechanical role and failed to warn the academicians about the deteriorating university Science education. In spite of the fact that we still have students of outstanding merit and brilliant research workers, our ranking in terms of number of publications, of research papers has fallen down from 8th in 1980 to 13th 1990 and there from to 21st in the new millennium. In terms of "quality" of publication, our ranking came down to 119 as recorded in Science Citation Index. It is true that we have limitations in comparison to other developed countries. But that do not justify our poor performance in the field of higher education. Many of our eminent scientists and academicians have pointed out our drawbacks and lacunae in educational policies. But the persons responsible for implementation of the decisions taken by different bodies ignored their suggestions. India being one of the frontliners amongst the large scientific manpower in the world, have failed to evaluate its own performance in time so that scope for rectification can be availed of.

## Conclusion

Standing on the doorsteps of the 21st century we have no other alternative but to energise ourselves to work as active soldiers of Science education movement. We do not have any deficiency in merit, general capability or skill. Instead we are deficient in strong determination, commitment and farsightedness. After accepting the concept of globalization, we have to go for development of 'quality manpower' who will be entrusted to transfer quality education to the deserving students. As Science forms the backbone of technology, we have to consolidate Science education from the school level so that best technologists emerge out in future from higher education institutes. Our researchers in Science and Technology should remember that demand of 'quality research' is not for Ph.D. award and publication of few papers only.

Output of research must be used as teaching inputs and as raw materials for national development. In this knowledge era, if we fail to recognize and accept the new knowledge from the global scientific arena we will be automatically thrown back beyond the starting point. Let there be no further delay in taking urgent measures to improve Science education at all levels so that its benefits can percolate immediately to different social strata to serve greater interests of humankind around the world.

## REFERENCES

Chatterjee, S.K. (2005), "Aspects of Qualitative Changes in Indian Education: A General Approach", *University News*, 43(17): 11-17.

Chatterjee, S.K. (2008), "Quality Education : An Essential need of 21st Century", *Third Dimension of Higher Education.* Journal of the Dept. of Adult, Continuing Education, Extension Work and Field Outreach. Rabindra Bharati University, Kolkata, 1(1): 83-93.

Kalra, R.M. (2007), *Teaching of Science,* Shipra Publications, Delhi.

Karuppayil, S.M. (2006), "Divorce of Research from Postgraduate Science Education", *University News,* 44(02): 14-18.

Koul, A. (1991), "Science Education through Mass Media", *University News*, 29(44): 19-20.

Nanda, V.K. (1997), *Science Education Today,* Anmol Publications Pvt. Ltd., New Delhi.

Sant, B.R. (2003), "A Journey of Excellence in the Teaching of Science", *University News*, 41(11): 14-16.

Srivastava, P.M. (2005), "Science Education in Indian Universities: Shouldn't Someone be Concerned about It?", *University News*, 43(39): 7-12.

# 25

# The Impact of University—Industry Linkages on English Language Teaching

*Sangeeta Sharma* and *Krishna Mohan*

With the upsurge of linkages with industry, English language teaching (ELT) has undergone a purposeful change in terms of syllabus design, instructional material and techniques of teaching. This change is mainly the outcome of result-oriented tasks which has led to need-based instruction. The constant interaction between the institute and the professional world has led to the interflow of ideas and cross-fertilization of concepts, as a result of which ELT has gradually become academically more meaningful and socially more relevant. In this paper, an attempt is made to identify and analyze the perceptions of contacts with reality that has engendered this evolutionary process.

Though the study of English in India began as a historical accident, even today it continues to be a language of Intellectual Business, Commerce, Law, Political, Science and Technology. In the absence of any Indian language attaining the status of a common link language in the country, the social environment strongly supports the use of English. The constitutional provision about English as an associate official language of the Central Government represents the collective will of the people. In continuing to accord a place of importance to English, we have accepted a reality and ensured a smooth, workable linguistic contact among our people.

**Role of English**

We all know that English served as a powerful instrument of thought and communication during the days of struggle for independence and also as an aid to support the upsurge for social and economic growth. As an example we may mention here Bal Gangadhar's *Mahratta*, Nehru's *National Herald*, and Gandhi's *Harijan* which were used for this purpose. After independence, the importance of English did not diminish, despite sporadic attempts to decry it as a vestige of the British imperialism. Instead, the country made an attempt to respond to the changed situation in a mature way and to evolve a correct perspective on the value of English. Its role in our society has now more or less stabilized after the initial turmoil and there are signs of a fresh and proper attempt to view it as a means of serving our national interests. In fact, recently there have been two interesting developments which deserve mention here. First, there has been a spurt in the growth of the use of English as a vehicle for creative expression by Indian writers. Second, attempts have been made to make out a case for establishing Indian English (also called 'Bharat English' or 'swadeshi English') as recognizable variety of English, this trend was visualized in 1940 itself, when Dr. Amar Nath Jha in his Presidential address at a conference of English teachers observed: "A little courage, some determination, a wholesome respect for our own idiom and we shall before long have a virile, vigorous Indian English." Since then we have marched a long way and taken the initiative to present a systematic description of the distinct features of Indian English (Kachru, 1969, Mehrotra, 1982, Verma, 1979).

Whereas there has been, in general, a proper change in our attitude toward the place of English in our society, its teaching even today continues to be in disarray, largely ineffective and irrelevant, as we shall presently see. In a developing country like ours where the need of the hour is rapid social and economic growth and where there are many heavy demands on existing meager resources, utmost economy in every sphere of activity is essential. No less important is the time factor. Unfortunately, so far as English Language Teaching (ELT) is concerned, there is hardly any conclusive evidence to show that we have been guided, to the extents desirable, by these important considerations.

## New Direction in ELT

English as the spoken and vehicular language has gained importance in the Indian context, more specifically with relation to business and how to conduct business. The transition from regional language to English as the "vehicular" language for trade transactions within and outside the country has been gradual, imperceptible though steady. What is important is the overt recognition of the fact that to create a niche in the global market, English is the required language. Schools and colleges have gradually begun to use it as the medium of instruction. The impact has been felt more so on business schools training students to gain entry in the global market. Bilingual communication skills with emphasis on second language, that is, English, as the preferred and needed choice of communicating messages in a business environment has rapidly gained ground in India.

The current emphasis on language as a social phenomenon does not seem to have exercised any noticeable impact on the shaping of most of the ELT courses. As a result of socio-linguistic studies, the imparting of communicative competence (CC) as the principal objective of $L_2$ teaching programmes is getting global recognition. But the relevance of the results from the comprehensive attempt to examine the relevance of the result from the emergence of this concept and to consider its application to the Indian situation. Another direction in which one can observe new efforts is the development of courses to teach special English to meet the needs of professions. These developments have led to the formulation of the concept of English for Special Purposes (ESP). In fact, the notions of CC and ESP interlock and so their emergence and growth has been simultaneous. These developments demand significant changes in the methods and procedures of syllabus construction, production of teaching material and techniques of teaching.

Das (1977) and Parasher (1979) have shown that the kind of English used by educated. Indians is identifiable in as much as it is generally restricted to certain formal domains (e.g. government and employment) and that English is essential for professional success. Their findings are corroborated by Banerji's study (1984). According to a survey conducted by her, in answer to a question whether the professionals would be able to function effectively, if they were to communicate for professional purposes entirely in a language other than English, out of 207, 136 subjects (65.70%) answered 'no'. This survey also identified 32 communicative tasks (vide Annexure I) in the performance of which English is used by the professionals in varying degrees.

In the early phase of post-independence, English was learned primarily in classrooms making India a multilingual scholastic English country. However, the nature of learning and implementation underwent a radical change in the post-liberalization era. With the growth of international trade, skilled Indian professionals were in constant dialogue with clients overseas. For ease of communication in business transactions, the vehicular language changed in hue and English became the most convenient medium of communication.

When we juxtapose what is actually required with what is being taught, we find a wide gap. The need for teaching the kind of English which can serve as an effective means of attaining professional proficiency has exercised minimal impact upon the English language syllabus planners. The syllabuses of 79 universities which were subjected to in-depth scrutiny (Banerji and Mohan, 1985) reveal an utter lack of awareness of what the society requires. It would not therefore be wrong to say that ELT has largely ignored social considerations and failed to meet the increasing demand by professions for competence in the effective use of English.

This lack of social relevance is a feature which English courses have in common with several other disciplines. The university system has not kept itself in constant touch with the social needs and as a result it is not able to contribute properly to the imparting of the kind of training that is required for the efficient performance of professional tasks.

**BITS Experience**

Realizing the need for making higher education socially relevant, BITS has evolved a strong and flexible system which takes into account the changing requirements of real-life situations. This has been done by forging institutionalized linkages with industry through practice school. Under this system every student, whatever be his discipline, spends seven and a half months in participating in the on-going projects in the world of work. The educational program has thus enlarged and extended the traditional laboratory concept of university training to the use of professional organizations as live laboratories, where a team consisting of student, faculty and professional expert operates the process of education. This involvement makes professional experience as part of learning. Since the student works on projects of interest to professional organizations, the experience in terms of application of knowledge is real and authentic. It also provides a useful exposure to the ethics and work culture of industry by developing mental perception of demands on a professional in real-life environment.

The institute has forged other forms of fruitful contacts with industry. To participate in the human resource development activities of the industries, the institute has evolved several work integrated learning programmes by integrating the working environment of the employees with the academic rigour required by the institute. At the higher degree level, the institute runs ME (collab) and M.Phil (Applied) programs and at the Ph.D. level through the initiation of research activity at off-campus PS and ME (collab) stations. Further, under the Ph.D. aspirants' scheme the institute offers a unique opportunity for experienced personnel in various fields to work for the Ph.D. degree in the settings of their respective professional environments.

These contacts with industry have generated the will and the desire to view the issues of training and employment as interrelated factors and professionalized educational curricula.

The result is that all the programs of the institute are employment-oriented, obviously not on a point to point basis but on the basis of broad education for the product to be mobile and to negotiate for a job from a position of strength.

Its emphasis is on the role of English in modern professional organizations and scientific and technical communication. The teaching of English has been drawn out from the realm of imagination to face the challenges of reality. The courses no longer merely cater to the demands for intellectual sojourn or the desire for basking in the sunshine of aesthetic delight. They instead attempt to impart skills and competence required to function effectively in the highly competitive world of work, which shuns obsolescence and scorns status quo.

There is a judicious mix of courses that constitute the 4-year integrated program. The courses in English, the Humanities and Social Sciences and practice school together with electives constitute the main contents of the program whereas the rest of the part consists of science, applied science and courses of a nature. This lends a professional character to the program and prepares students to function effectively in a world dominated by science and technology.

The linkage with industry has led to the development of courses which prepare students to perform day-to-day communicative tasks in professional organizations. Some of the courses worth mentioning here are technical report writing, technical communication, professional practice, effective public speaking, creative writing, English for professional purposes and applied communication. In designing these courses, the assumption made is that, whatever the profession, it would demand competence in skills such as writing abstracts, summaries, letters, reports, memos, professional papers, proposals, specifications, instruction manuals, handbooks, brochures, as well as issuing notices, drafting agenda for meetings, preparing minutes participating in and conducting meetings and seminars, presenting oral reports, etc. Each of these forms of communication has over the years, developed a set of conventions, and demands unique skills of presentation because there is always a definite purpose to be achieved in well-defined context. However, any formal programme of instruction necessarily demands a selection of items and a course, and however ambitious cannot cover the whole range of language used in all real-life situations relating to all professionals. Therefore, in formulating the courses mentioned earlier, an attempt has been made to select forms most commonly used in the major professions. Experience shows that the confidence gained by the learner in handling simulated communication situations enables him to operate effectively in authentic communicative settings in the world.

The changes in the programme and the contents of courses naturally led to the preparation of suitable teaching materials. The existing textbooks obviously could not fill the bill. Consequently, several writing projects were undertaken and completed within a time frame to sustain the tempo of professionalisation of English courses. The books that have been published so far to meet the unique needs of professions are listed in Annexure II.

The material included in these publications has grown out of interaction with the professional world. Since the interaction is both intense and continuous, the development of material keeps pace with the changing needs and is revised, enlarged and modified at suitable intervals. In this process, however, the academic requirements are not overlooked. A proper use of the material demands sustained intellectual effort and constant practice for acquiring the competence to apply knowledge in appropriate situations.

The classroom instruction too has undergone a change under the impact of university industry linkages. The techniques used have been brought nearer to the processes, procedures and practices of communicative interaction actually employed in the world of work. The task of using language to teach language has thus become more meaningful and result-oriented.

In conclusion, we may point out that the impulse of change towards professionalisation has permeated the entire ELT activity at BITS right from the planning stage to the execution stage. As a result, the value of our institute has greatly increased in the employment market. This is so because, to use Nehru's words, "though we have worked to the sky and strove to reach stars, yet we have kept our feet firmly on the ground".

## ANNEXURE I

### Spoken English

Presenting writing material, oral reporting, making inquiries, giving instructions and directions, dictating, participating in meetings, seminars, etc. Note-taking, establishing social relations, interviewing, negotiating deals, agreements, etc. demonstrating/explaining, making speeches, formal teaching, making announcements.

### Written English

Writing letters, writing reports, writing memos, orders, keeping records, writing notices, circulars, agenda, minutes, etc. filling in forms, writing shorts messages, writing technical proposals, note-making, writing formal invitations, abstraction and summarizing, writing research papers, articles, etc., writing handbooks, manuals, writing publicity materials, writing booklets/brochures, preparing market surveys, editing, writing press releases.

## ANNEXURE II

### List of Books

1. Raman, Meenakshi and Sangeeta Sharma. *Technical Communication—Principles and Practice*. OUP, New Delhi, 2004.
2. Sharnia, Sangeeta and Raghuvir Singh. *Advertising: Planning and Implementation*. Prentice Hall India: New Delhi, 2006.
3. Raman, Meenakshi and Sangeeta Sharma, ed. *International Journal of Communication*. Bahri Publications, Vol. 12, No. 1, New Delhi, 2001.
4. Sharma, Sangeeta and Raghuvir Singh. *International Journal of Communication*. Bahri Publications, Vol. 14, No. 1, New Delhi, 2004.

5. Raman, Meenakshi and Sangeeta Sharma. *Technical Communication—English Skills for Engineers*. Co Author OUP, New Delhi, 2008.
6. Raman, Meenakshi and Sangeeta Sharma. *Technical Communication—Principles and Practice*. For Gujarat Technological University. OUP, New Delhi, 2008.
7. Raman, Meenakshi and Sangeeta Sharma. *Communication Skills for Mumbai University*. OUP, New Delhi, 2009.
8. Sharma, Sangeeta and Binod Mishra. *Communication Skills for Engineers and Scientists*. PHI Learning Pvt. Ltd., New Delhi, 2009.
9. Sharma, Sangeeta et al. *Pester Power Effect of Advertising on Children*. Vanshika Enterprises: Jaipur, 2009.
10. Raman, Meenakshi and Sangeeta Sharma, *Professional Communication*. For UPTU. OUP: New Delhi, 2009.
11. Raman, Meenakshi and Sangeeta Sharma, *Communicative English*. For BPUT. OUP: New Delhi, 2009.
12. Sharma, R.C. and Krishna Mohan. *Business Correspondence and Report Writing*. New Delhi: Tata McGraw-Hill, 1984.
13. Sharma, R.C. *Scientific Contexts*. New Delhi: Tata McGraw-Hill, 1980.
14. Mohan, Krishna and Meera Banerji. *Developing Communication Skills*. New Delhi: Macmillan India Limited, 1990
15. Mohan, Krishna and N.P Singh. *Speaking English Effectively*. New Delhi: Macmillan India Limited, 1995.

## REFERENCES

Allen, J.R.B. and H.G. Widdowson. "Teaching the Communicative use of English", *IRAL*. 12.1.

Banerji, Meera. 1984, "An Approach to syllabus Design for English Language Teaching at the Undergraduate in India", Ph.D. Thesis BITS, Pilani.

Banerji, Meera and Krishna Mohan. 1985, "General English Syllabuses: A Critical Review", *Journal of Higher Education,* 10.3. New Delhi. University Grant Commission.

CIEFL. 1977, *Syllabus Reform in English,* Mimeographed. Hyderabad: CISFL.

Das, Mahajiteswar. 1977, The Needs for English in Orissa: An Investigation into the English Language Requirements and Related Instructional Programmes at the Post-Secondary Level of Education. Ph.D. Thesis. CIEFL. Hyderabad. Unpublished.

Kachru, Braj, B. 1969, "English in South Asia" in *Current Trends in Linguistics. J.,* Vol. 5 Thomas A. Bebeok (Ed.) The Hague: Moutpn.

Mehrotra, R.R. 1982, *Indian English.* Ed. by M. Gorlack. Heidelberg: Groos Veriab.

Mohan, Krishna. 1981, "ESP EST or EPP DO Our Students Need?", *English Teaching Forum,* XIX, 3.

Parashar, S.V. 1979, Certain Aspects of the Functions and Form of Indian English: A School Inquistic Study, Ph.D. Thesis CIEFL, Hyderabad. Unpublished.

Verma, S.K. 1979, "Swadeshi English: Form and Function: Mimeographed", Hyderabad. CIEFL.

26

# Recognizing Challenges and Expanding Horizons of Medical Education in India

*D. Kumar, J.V. Singh* and *P.S. Kharwar*

"It's not enough that we do our best; sometimes we have to do what's required."

—Winston Churchill (1874-1965)

Medical education occupies a crucial position in education as it involves a close and deep study of life itself and its vital processes. It is no more a study of human illness and cure but a comprehensive body of knowledge dealing with health and hence related with productivity and well-being of the citizens. There is a growing awareness of the role of health development as a vital component of socio-economic development. Medical education and training varies considerably across the world. Various teaching methodologies have been utilised in medical education, which is an active area of educational research (Flores-Mateo and Argimon, 2007).

## Medical Education in India

The history of medical education in India dates back to Rig Vedic period, and since this period, the study of medicine is continuing as an utmost important part of Indian education system. With the passage of time its horizon has been expanding with multiple and specialised streams being added now and then. In 1934, the Medical Council of India was formed to monitor the quality of Medical Education. The accreditation process for medical schools focuses largely on the infrastructure and human resources but less on the process and quality of education or outcomes. According to Deshpande (1982), the changing roles of medical colleges and medical education in India have been impressive and in spite of all the criticism, medical education has made enormous strides in this country and elsewhere in the world. At the same time, there is also a growing awareness of shortcomings in medical education and therefore constant need has been experienced to make changes and modify.

### Quantitative Changes

There are several reports of commissions ranging from the Bhore Commission to Mudaliar Commission. The main preoccupation and concern seems to be to make quantitative changes. Medical schools in India produce the largest number of doctors than anywhere in the world (34000 from 299 Medical schools) corresponding to rapid proliferation of medical colleges in the last two decades, especially within private sector. The doctor-population ratio has already exceeded than that required by the country and there is mal-distribution of their services. India has achieved a tenfold increase in the number of medical colleges and the output of doctors, resulting in a large number of specialists and an equally impressive number of super specialists. This has been largely unplanned and has only resulted in a marked increase in output without any thought for finding rewarding careers for them; most of them join the Westward flood. The promotion of medical colleges in the smaller cities in the districts has not made much of an impact on the distribution of medical manpower. The products of these colleges are more hard-hit and the result is brain-drain within the country. The overflow from the cities has always been to the West and now the flow is towards the African and Gulf countries (Deshpande, 1982).

### Changes in Role and Responsibility

The next area of expansion is the scope and range of responsibility of a medical college. These have grown beyond traditional boundaries. The role of a teaching hospital as a static centre to which people come for specialist treatment is no more valid. Preventive and promotive aspects of health have been added in recent years along with physical medicine and rehabilitation. The concept of convalescent homes and homes for aged has, however, not fully matured and leaves a lot to be desired as the number of old people increases. The problem of the aged and retired persons is now engaging worldwide attention (Deshpande, 1982).

The role of patient care in teaching hospitals needs to be emphasised. The teaching medical faculty can set an example of dedicated public service, which can be imbibed by and would have a lasting effect on impressionable undergraduates. The accountability and monitoring of the teaching faculty towards fulfilment of their teaching responsibilities is a sensitive but very important issue. In the West, teachers are not only accountable to the institutes but to the students as well. The students are encouraged to evaluate the performance of their teachers and provide useful feedback to the latter for improvement (Sood and Adkoli, 2000).

## Collaborations and Autonomy

There is growing interaction with social sciences, thanks to the introduction of Psychology and Psychiatry in teaching hospitals. The increasing use of sophisticated equipment has highlighted the need for close collaboration with engineering, electronic and computer sciences. The traditional medical college has grown into a medical centre of great complexity, bringing in tremendous problems of management.

Colleges must actively and openly engage with its membership, with bio-medical industry, and with the public to further drug and device development and to educate on proper and safe use while avoiding "overtly or covertly becoming an extension of a company's marketing efforts". Severe restriction is required in physician involvement in industry-sponsored research and medical education, an outcome that could have devastating consequences for medical education and research. It is also required to critically evaluate this relationship and define policies and procedures that will serve to maintain a positive, ethical, and appropriate relationship (Institute of Medicine of the National Academies, 2009) between them.

Collaboration between the medical schools represents a wonderful opportunity for synergies and efficiencies in international relationships, providing the college with a respected and widely recognized conduit to the international community with a powerful partner in its educational endeavours (Eamonn, 2010).

Desired change is brought about if there is freedom for doing so. This means granting substantial autonomy or even the status of university. If colleges of Pharmacy, Medicine, Dentistry and Nursing are grouped together, they can form a viable university. A department of Life Sciences can be added to give a scientific base for such a venture. Such a step has proved beneficial for fields like agriculture and engineering, who have secured university status for their faculties. If a university is not feasible, provision of autonomy and freedom to run institutions should be granted so that on the spot decisions are possible. Medical institutions have their peculiar problems and they cannot be run as a department of the government (Deshpande, 1982).

## Changes in Curriculum

In spite of changes and expansion in medical education, there is dissatisfaction expressed, both by the people and their representatives, mainly neglect of rural and remote areas. Western model and standards of medical education has made products less useful in our society and perhaps unwittingly promoted brain-drain. So, the changes in the curriculum have to be brought about in a more rational way by assessing our own needs. Every country, and within each country, a geographical region has its own problems. In a way, the socio-economic groups, the rural-urban settings and other parameters differ from country to country and from state to state. The National Health Policy (1983) provided direction for restructuring the curriculum. Undergraduate medical education was to aim at Primary Care Physician, who is capable to provide essential health care services to the rural population.

The medical colleges in India have traditionally followed a curriculum stuffed with a large body of knowledge pertaining to basic science and clinical disciplines. Once qualified, students are expected to synthesise this information and apply it to the care of the patients. With the expanding body of knowledge, there is over-burdening of the student with the content information (Nayar et al., 1995). In 1986, a consortium of Indian Medical Schools was formed which adopted an Inquiry Driven Strategy for Innovation in Medical Education and addressed the key issues of evolving a revised curriculum, defining the departmental objectives, classifying the course content as 'Must Know' and 'Desirable to Know, and compiling a list of essential skills required for a Competent Primary Care Physician. Following MCI guidelines, medical colleges in India have adopted a pattern of one year of basic sciences, one and a half years of para-clinical sciences and two years devoted entirely to clinical subjects. In most of the colleges, the subjects are taught in isolation with little or no attempt to integrate the basic sciences with the clinical disciplines. An integrated curriculum provides a meaningful learning experience as learning takes place in a context (contextual learning). It also promotes a holistic approach to patients and their problems. The MCI has recommended both horizontal (e.g. anatomy, physiology, biochemistry) and vertical integration (e.g. anatomy with surgery) to be introduced throughout the curriculum (MCI, 1992). The Government of India promulgated the "Regulations on Graduate Medical Education" through a gazette notification (MCI, 1997).

### Clinical and Problem-solving Skills

While the graduates generally possess reasonably sound knowledge of medical science, sometime they are found deficient in the performance of clinical skills and problem-solving, which form the core of clinical competence. There is growing level of mistrust among the public for the medical profession as one hears of cases of negligence, misconduct, and unethical practices leading to legal suits. There is increasing public demand for the accountability, transparency and quality assurance among the health professionals. While the commercialisation of medical profession is cited as a common reason for the dilution of quality, doubts have been raised regarding the quality of training. Graduate doctors must be well trained to perform their clinical responsibilities and should be aware of their ethical, moral and legal responsibilities. There are areas in the curriculum, viz. medical ethics, behavioural science, communication skills, managerial skills which do not receive due attention in the existing curriculum as they should do (Verma et al., 1991).

Excellence in medical education is not merely a vertical expansion and achievements. Goal of medical education is imparting knowledge and skills for maximum improvement of health and relief of suffering within available resources. There is thus a clear need to set up innovative models and bring about qualitative changes (Deshpande, 1982). Problem-based learning, problem solving skills, psychomotor skills, attitudinal and communication skills need more emphasis in medical education (Barrows and Tamblyn, 1980).

## Teacher Training

The teacher is the corner-stone for any system of education. Appropriate method of selection and adequate training in the techniques of teaching would go a long way in improving the quality of teaching. Unfortunately, teacher training is perhaps the most vulnerable of issues in medical education (World Federation of Medical Education, 1994). With the phenomenal changes in educational and information technology, the role of teacher has undergone dramatic changes. He is expected to possess skills and abilities to plan the curriculum, make rational use of the media technology and design an assessment strategy. This is possible only through a systematic approach to faculty development. As suggested by MCI, the development of medical education units in all medical colleges will go a long way in the development of teaching skills amongst their faculty (MCI, 1992). In most of our medical colleges, although junior and senior resident doctors are required to undergo teaching experience as part of their academic work, seldom does any formal training accompany this experience. While training forms an essential requirement, it is also necessary to provide academic recognition to the teachers, for their contribution to teaching. Otherwise, teaching will be overtaken by the priorities of research and patient care. It is important to encourage and reward teachers who show a flair for teaching and adopt innovative teaching methods. It is time we brought the modern concepts of pedagogy, educational psychology, etc. nearer to the medical colleges that can be done by establishing a medical education cell. Increasingly, education theory itself is becoming an integral part of postgraduate medical training. Formal qualifications in education are becoming the norm for Medical School Educators, who are becoming increasingly accountable for their students.

### Support to Clinician-educator

Academic clinician-educator is critical to medical education, training, and research. In a context, where the payer and the patient often demand that the attending staff perform all care and where the complexity of the clinical problems are encountered, not to mention the economic pressures of the institution and the medico-legal concerns that continue to hover, often precludes the active involvement of the trainee, teaching becomes an imposition. Personal and professional issues also impact on the sustainability of the clinician-educator. By the time this individual commences in teaching post, he has already spent much of his adult life in education and training and his precarious financial position being further compounded by the sometimes low level of salary in academic medicine. Meanwhile, the apparent riches of private practice beckon and become all the more alluring as the young academic person comes to realize that his much lower salary is not compensated for by a much better quality of life. Institutional attitudes often serve to compound these dilemmas; medical schools have been very slow to recognize and support clinical teaching, development of educational and professional skills, and tools to support training programs and educator (Eamonn, 2010).

### Privatisation of Medical Education

The issue of capitation fees and privatisation of medical education needs to be mentioned here. In spite of the good intentions, the seats in private medical colleges seem to be grabbed by the relatively affluent classes. Private medical colleges have come up throughout the country and measures are required to ensure their proper regulation by the medical council. The menace posed by the growing merchandisation of medical education has to be warded off and efforts should be made to ensure maintenance of standards and check the unplanned growth of substandard medical colleges (Sood and Adkoli, 2000).

### Continuing Medical Education

Indian doctors desperately need Continuing Medical Education (CME) to keep them up to date with the latest drugs, equipment and medical practices and MCI is campaigning for CME as it is in UK and some states of USA. The task of continuing education is receiving attention everywhere. The expansion of knowledge is occurring so rapidly that apart from general practitioners, even specialists working away from teaching institutions get outdated and obsolete. Refresher courses for both these categories have to be organised so that the practice of medicine keeps up with recent advances. Allocation of substantial funds and professional resources will be needed. Despite the lack of legal incentive for doctors to attend regular refresher courses, CME has been catching on in India over the last decade partly due to the efforts of medical associations. Recently, MCI established a code of ethics stating that members should complete 30 hours of CME every five years in order to re-register as doctors, but only about 20 per cent doctors follow this as it is not legally binding. Now the MCI is trying the Indian Parliament to enshrine this principal in law by amending the Indian Medical Council Act of 1956 that governs medical practice across the country. If passed into law, mandatory CME for registered doctors in India could set a precedent for other developing countries (Ketharaj and Jeyakumar, 2009).

**Medical Education Online (Medical e-Learning)**

Increasingly, medical education around the world is being supported by online teaching, usually within Learning Management Systems (LMSs) or Virtual Learning Environment (VLEs). Research areas into online medical education are wide-ranging, and include the roles of the participants (students, teachers, administrators), content generation, especially in a wide range of media, the use of LMSs, VLEs and other systems, and open-source vs. proprietary, methods of interaction; the use online medication education in Problem-based Learning (PBL), practical applications, virtual patients; distance learning, assessment, electronic portfolios (e-Portfolios), mobile learning (M-learning), problems with technology, accessibility, the politics and psychology of e-learning, legal and ethical issues, economics, design issues, standards and specifications (Masters and Ellaway, 2008). Medical education in India has also started incorporating online teaching.

## REFERENCES

Barrows, H.S. and Tamblyn, R.N. (1980), *Problem Based Learning: An Approach to Medical Education,* New York: Springer Publishing Company.

Deshpande, C.K. (1982), "Medical Education in India", *Journal of Postgraduate Medicine,* 28:181-83.

Eamonn, M.M. (2010), "Recognizing Challenges, Expanding Horizons: Doing What is Required". *American College of Gastroenterology.* ACG Education Universe, retrieved on 20 July 2010.

Flores-Mateo, G. Argimon, J.M. (2007), "Evidence-based Practice in Postgraduate Healthcare Education: A Systematic Review", *BMC Health Ser Res,* 7:119.

Institute of Medicine of the National Academies (2009), Conflict of interest in medical research, education, and practice <http://www.iom.edu/CMS/3740/ 47464/ 65721>, retrieved on 20 July 2010.

Ketharaj, M. and Jeyakumar, S. (2009), "Medical Education in India—Problems and Prospects", *University News,* 47(48):20-24.

Medical Council of India (1992), Recommendations of the Workshop on Need-based Curriculum for Undergraduate Medical Education; New Delhi: MCI, 28-30.

Medical Council of India (1997), *Regulation on Graduate Medical Education*, New Delhi: MCI.

Masters, K. and Ellaway, R. (2008), "e-Learning in Medical Education, Guide 32 Part 2: Technology, Management and Design", *Med Teach*, 30(5):474-89.

Nayar, U. Verma, K. and Adkoli, B.V. (Eds.) (1995), Inquiry-driven Strategies for Innovation in Medical Education in India: Curricular Reforms, New Delhi: AIIMS.

Sood, R. Adkoli, B.V. (2000), "Medical Education in India—Problems and Prospects". *Journal, Indian Academy of Clinical Medicine*, 1(3):210-12.

Verma, K.D. Monte, B. Adkoli, B.V. and Nayar, U. (Eds.) (1991), Inquiry-driven Strategies for Innovation in Medical Education in India. New Delhi: AIIMS.

World Federation of Medical Education (1994), *Proceedings of the World Summit on Medical Education*, 28 (suppl. 1).

27

# NKC on Management Education

*Dinesh D. Harsolekar*

Formation of the National Knowledge Commission (NKC) was probably the most important initiative taken by the government to improve the education system of our country. The tenure of NKC was fixed for three years, i.e. from October 2005 to October 2008. Thus, its tenure is going to end in October 2008. (Whether it will be extended or not depends on the political situation.) At the time when the tenure of NKC is getting over this article tries to take the stock of what NKC has suggested for management education. Till date NKC has submitted two reports to the nation giving widespread suggestions on the various issues concerning education. After NKC submitted its first report in 2006, it received significant attention of the academia. Some called it a panacea of all ills, whereas others dubbed it as old wine in a new bottle. Some balanced reactions were in between these two extremes (*University News*, Vol. 45, No. 48).

All said and done, NKC must be given full marks for giving a new perspective and adopting a very comprehensive approach while giving recommendations. Whether these recommendations will see the light of the day or not, again unfortunately, depends on the whims and fancies of our great politicians. It is also possible that the recommendations which give political mileage would be accepted and others which seek to change the education system radically would be ignored. Education system in our country is damaged so badly that if we try to repair it, it becomes more complicated and creates new problems. That means, it has gone beyond repairing. And when something goes beyond repairing we are left with only one choice—replacement of the system with a new one. From this viewpoint one can say that many of the recommendations given by NKC are certainly unconventional and show out-of-the-box thinking. One statement made by NKC in its report is extremely important—'Higher education in India is over-regulated but under-governed'. This statement has been made for two main reasons. One, there are too many regulators and two, the system is based on priori controls and not on practical regulatory provisions.

In its second report, submitted in the beginning of 2008 NKC has included recommendations, inter alia, on management education. Earlier, these recommendations were sent to the Prime Minister in the form of a letter. Through these recommendations, NKC is apparently trying to overhaul the system of management education in our country. There are eleven excellent recommendations in the report. The areas in which recommendations have been given are, regulatory framework, grading, accreditation, wider accessibility, social context, faculty development, mentoring of MEEs by a leading MEE, focus on leadership, innovation and entrepreneurship, autonomy, governance and finally, non-traditional management education. It is not possible to analyze all of them in one article. Therefore, this attempt is only to take an overview with a focus on the most important issue, i.e. regulation of management education.

In its first report, NKC has suggested to set up a single regulatory authority called, Independent Regulatory Authority for Higher Education (IRAHE), for all the higher educational institutions in the country. It has suggested the process of forming this body and appointing its chairman. According to NKC, this body should be solely responsible to grant licenses to all the new institutions of higher education in the country, including Management Educational Entities (MEEs). NKC has used the term MEEs, to cover all types of institutions engaged in management education. In its second report while giving recommendations on management education, NKC has further suggested having an autonomous Standing Committee (SC) on management education working under IRAHE. The main job of IRAHE would be granting licenses to start new institutions, whereas the job of SC would be to do due diligence for granting licenses, give licenses to agencies to take care of accreditation, nominate independent rating agencies to assess and categorize MEEs, collate and communicate information on MEEs, set up information exchange, conduct demand forecasting of managerial manpower and develop and maintain a low cost e-monitoring system.

The suggestions given by NKC in many areas are excellent but as far as the regulatory framework is concerned, NKC has failed to take into consideration the political implications, the span of control of the regulator and most importantly it has not taken an integrated approach while suggesting a new regulatory system. Let us examine these points.

Because of the lack of transparency in functioning of the present regulators NKC has suggested that the IRAHE should be at an arm's length from the government and independent of all the stakeholders including the concerned ministries of the government. Many academicians have raised questions on this. What is the guarantee that IRAHE will not have the same fate as that of the present regulators? If it is possible to function at an arm's length from the government then why the present regulators are not made to work that way? Looking at the Indian political and governmental system there is tremendous substance in these questions.

NKC has spoken about the multiplicity of regulators. It is indeed a serious problem. But what kind of multiplicity NKC is talking about? At the central level there is just one agency for each stream of professional education and this multiplicity is not creating any problem or confusion. In fact, by suggesting the formation of IRAHE, SC, rating agencies and accreditation agencies, the NKC itself is suggesting to create many agencies at the central level. The problem lies somewhere else. NKC has not given a thought (at least it appears) to an important arrangement in the Constitution that education is on the Concurrent List. This means, the centre and states, both will have a say in the education system of the country and both can pass legislations. This provision has been grossly misused by the politicians to have control over professional education. If we look at the school education, non-professional higher education and universities, we will find that the centre and states, both are running these institutions but they are running them independently. The same institution is not regulated by the centre as well as a state. Unfortunately, this is what precisely is happening in case of professional education. The same management institute, medical college or an engineering college is regulated by a central regulator as well as many state level regulators. A management institution is regulated by as many as four state level regulators in addition to AICTE. This multiplicity of regulation is the real problem. In fact, if this two level regulatory system would not have existed, many of the present problems would not have occurred. (Of course, our politicians, babus and some orthodox academicians will have their arguments in favour of this system.) If the intention of NKC is to substitute all these (central and state level) agencies with IRAHE then the political implications cannot be ignored. Similarly, if private universities, which have come into existence through state Acts, and deemed universities are also brought under IRAHE then it will also be difficult politically.

While suggesting a system for management education an important management approach has been ignored, i.e. integrated approach. If we are looking at putting management education on proper tracks then an integrated approach is a must wherein licensing (granting approvals), admissions, academics, examination and accreditation are brought under one regulator. Further, NKC has not suggested anything about the most important problem, i.e. admission process. May be, NKC considers this as the responsibility of SC once it comes into existence. But that assumption is not correct and to maintain uniformity in all the streams of professional education NKC must have suggested a broad policy on admissions. A large number of admission tests conducted in our country with different rules is a root cause of many ills and evils of management education.

A wide variety in the nomenclature of degrees and diplomas is the peculiar problem of management education in our country which does not exist in any other stream of education. This variety is quite confusing for the students and probably, NKC has left this issue also for the SC to resolve.

With the objective of keeping the span of control of the regulator limited and by adopting an integrated approach, two alternative models have been suggested here to put management education in order.

An important flaw in the present regulatory system is that it does not distinguish between genuine players and fly-by-night operators. Same rules are applied to both the categories. Also, it is biased in favour of government institutions. This kind of bias does not exist in the other regulatory systems (banking, insurance, etc.) of our socio-economic life. The suggested models are capable of correcting these flaws.

### Model-I

There should be two types of management institutions on the lines of school and university education—institutions regulated only by the state bodies (every state should have only one regulator) and institutions regulated only by a central body. Institutions should be given the choice of joining any one of these two regulatory regimes. Institutions coming under state regulation should be given an additional choice of going for national accreditation. Affiliating universities play the most important role in management of the institutions coming under state purview. However, these days universities, unfortunately, have been reduced to the status of only testing centres (conducting examinations) and the entire regulation has gone to different bodies. Therefore, the State Governments must ensure that the universities are given back their status by giving them all the powers to regulate management institutions (approvals, admissions, fees, curriculum design, examinations and granting degrees). Some states have set up technical universities for management and technical education. This is a good move but these universities should also be given the complete charge of regulating the affiliated institutions.

Alternatively, complete regulation (everything but accreditation) of all the management institutes, baring Central Government institutions, should remain only with the state bodies and accreditation should be at the central level. Under either of the alternatives, the universities would play pivotal role for regulating the institutions coming under state regime. This model would not create any political issues. However, if the governments have lost confidence in the capabilities of universities in the field of professional education then it is better that the professional education is taken away completely from the State Governments. The option then is to go for the second model.

Even for the success of the first model some of the arrangements of the second model must be adopted.

### Model-II

The second model suggested here is on the lines of the system suggested by NKC but still substantially different. This will bring a radical change in the system and help India appear on the world map of management education very fast. If radical changes are to be brought in any system then the most important pre-requisite is to amend the legal framework because the outdated legal provisions create all the obstacles in bringing radical changes. This model will be possible only if government is willing to amend the UGC Act, AICTE Act, various state universities Acts and even the Constitution. Under this model, states and universities will have no role in the regulation of management education. They can own the institutions but regulation would remain with the central body. This model, however, may be difficult to implement for political reasons. But as presumed by NKC if the Central Government is determined to bring standardization in management education throughout the country then the model is strongly recommended. All the powers of State Governments to start private universities, granting permission to new institutes, etc. will have to be withdrawn and all the institutions, including IIMs, will have to be brought under the central regulator. The most important point one must bear in mind is that such a system can succeed only if each and every institution in the country, without any exception, is brought under one regulatory system. The suggested model is as under—

- There should be only one regulatory body for management education in the entire country, called All India Council for Management Education (AICME). Incidentally, this is a very old demand of management educators and has been discussed on many platforms.
- AICME should be set up under the Act of Parliament and its constitution should be on the lines (not exactly like) of ICAI, ICSI, ICWAI, etc. All the management institutes (MIs) should be members of AICME and should elect the office bearers. Except one government nominee on the board, there should be no government interference.
- All management institutions (government, private and foreign institutes operating in India), including IIMs, should be brought under AICME and uniform rules should be made applicable to all of them.
- All the MIs should be given autonomy from the day one of their existence and legislation should authorize AICME to permit MIs to grant degrees. There should be only one degree, i.e. MBA. This will clear all the confusion because of the variety of degrees and diplomas granted by various MIs and universities.
- All the aspects of regulation, viz. approvals (license), admissions, accreditation, academics, fee, accounts and finance, etc. should remain with AICME though the processes can be outsourced.
- Government should provide only initial funding to set up AICME. Subsequently, it should be financially self-supported.
- Industry representation on AICME should not be restricted only to attending meetings. They should participate in the strategic and operating functions too.
- The regulatory model adopted by AICME should be based on the principles of self-governance and not based on impractical controls.

- For granting license or approval an X amount of endowment fund and availability of an independent building should be the only requirement. In the absence of an own building (institutes can be permitted to operate from a rented premises for a certain period), the amount of the fund should be X+. All other academic and physical infrastructure should be the subject matter of accreditation. While giving a license the word 'approved' or 'recognized' should not be used. The MI would be just 'registered' with AICME. This would motivate institutes to go for accreditation as early as possible.
- AICME should regulate the quality of input (admissions) and output (a comprehensive test at the end of the course) as part of the continuation of the 'registration' and the quality of processes should be checked as part of the accreditation.
- There is no need of authorized rating agencies. A number of business publications are doing the rating of B-schools every year and it should be left that way.
- Accreditation should be voluntary. The norms should be decided by AICME but the process should be outsourced to a company like CRIS1L or CARE.
- Accreditation should be a two step process, Level I and Level II. Level I accreditation should focus on physical and academic infrastructure, student-faculty ratio, governance and transparency, academic standards, curriculum, exams and results, teaching/learning processes, etc. Level II accreditation should look into research, publication, industry interaction, placements, international and other tie-ups, faculty and student exchange programs, community services, national and international conferences, faculty development, etc.
- The two levels of accreditation should be linked to certain controls/restrictions/concessions, etc. (For example, institutes having both the levels of accreditation can themselves decide their student intake without any permission from AICME; their students need

not appear for the course end comprehensive test.) This will have two major benefits; first, premier institutes (like IIMs and few others) will not be subject to too many checks and enjoy total freedom/autonomy because they will have both the levels of accreditation. Second, other institutes will be motivated to go for accreditation despite being voluntary.

- The entire process of licensing and accreditation should be open and transparent and all the reports should be made available for public scrutiny.
- There should be only one admission test for the entire country and all the admissions should be regulated by AICME, however, the process can be outsourced. At the time of admissions, the students should be informed as to which MIs are only 'registered', which have Level I accreditation and which have Level II accreditation along with a brief explanation about the meaning of the three stages. Students taking admission to MIs which are only 'registered' would take admission on the basis of their own information and assessment of the institute.
- There should be no direct control or regulation on fee structure. There are indirect ways to ensure that the fee structure remains at the realistic levels. This will give a lot of relief to the MIs. Government funding should be directly to the needy students and not to the MIs or AICME.
- Finally, there should be a performance audit of AICME, at least, once in three years.

This system of 'registration'; two levels of accreditation; single admission test for the whole country and information to the students will certainly be able to single out the fly-by-night operators and at the same time will give chance to the genuine players to breathe freely without any harassment.

As said earlier, Model-I is a politically correct model and will bring in some positive changes in management education but will not achieve all the desired objectives. Model-II is a politically incorrect model but will radically reform the discipline of management education and will solve most of the problems. Therefore, if the government is serious about education then it must act going beyond political interest.

## REFERENCES

Harsolekar, Dinesh D., "Self-governance in Professional Institutions", *University News*, Vol. 44, No. 04, January 23-29, 2006.

Various articles from *University News;* Vol. 45, No. 48.

# 28

# Strategies for Knowledge and Skill Development in Environment Education: Need for Paradigm Shift in Pedagogy and Curriculum Development Process

*Santanu Das* and *Debasish Paul*

Since its evolution environment has remained both a matter of awe and concern to man. The frontier attitude of the industrialized society towards nature has not only endangered the survival of all other life forms but has also threatened the very existence of human life. The realization of such potential danger has necessitated the dissemination of knowledge and skill vis-a-vis environment protection at all stages of learning. Therefore, learners of all stages of learning need to be sensitized with a missionary zeal. With a view to sensitize these learners mere capsule form of information stuffed curriculum on environment shall be of no use. Traditional curriculum practiced at all levels of learning has shown little concern for the development of psycho-motor (skill learning) domain of human behavior.

At this backdrop it has become imperative to follow a pragmatic approach in designing a curriculum and pedagogy for all stages of formal and non-formal learning as these stages embody students representing diverse socio-economic strata of the society. This may ensure transformation of students into committed citizens for averting global environment crises.

The genesis of Environment Education in India can be found in the movement of Basic Education launched by Mahatma Gandhi in 1937 that was an early sustainable educational endeavour relating education to local environmental needs. 'Nature has enough to fulfill everybody's need but not everybody's greed', is a prudent statement of Mahatma Gandhi's thoughts on environment and sustainable development. The report of the Education Commission (1964-66) glorified Basic Education scheme as it relates education to the life, needs and aspiration of the nation. Environmental education has therefore remained one of the priority areas of concern in all curriculum and pedagogic development programmes.

### Need for Environment Education

Environment Education assumes great significance as humanity increasingly realizes, after a long journey from Stockholm to Rio de Janeiro to Johannesburg, that a development paradigm that largely ignores the environment has disastrous consequences. Human centered approach to development has endangered the natural systems that support life on earth. The industrial world operated with the frontier mentality has so far caused much harm to the life support systems on earth. The various earth summits held till date throughout the world has given prime importance to nature-centered development popularly termed as 'sustainable development'. Many of us might have noticed a popular caption "Save oil Save nation", found decorated on the rear portion of an oil tanker that used to enthrall everyone. The caption itself symbolizes the spirit of sustainability. At the advent of new information age, education is occupying a centre stage in dealing with all environmental problems. Thus, education is expected to play a pivotal role in all developmental processes, which ought to be eco-friendly in nature. It has to help raise awareness and build the capacity of communities to elaborate a vision and participate in the pursuit of environmentally and socially sustainability. Truly meaningful Environmental Education today genuinely needs a paradigm shift in education to promote the pursuit of sustainable development. Education helps raising awareness and builds the capacity of communities to elaborate a vision; and participate in the augmentation of sustainable development not only in development process but also in the attainment of sustainable attitudes.

Focal Points of Environment Education: Curriculum and Pedagogy for Environment Education should stress on developing the following:

- Concern for reality by exposing students to the real-life world, natural and social environment in which they live.
- Enable students to analyse, evaluate and draw inferences about problems and issues related to environment.
- Enable students to understand environment issues and take positive environmental actions.
- Develop skills of environmental actions among students in order to facilitate the journey of mankind towards sustainable development.

Environmental education is a lifelong process and it has to be an academic response to social change i.e. transformation from frontier society to sustainable society. Therefore, the contents of curriculum of Environment Education need to synthesize knowledge with skill. However, the strategies for knowledge and skill development to curriculum planning must be rested on following premises:

- Learning about the environment
- Leaning through the environment
- Leaning for the environment.

The new generation of learners should embody the ideals of democracy and spiritual values judicially blended with the spirit of science. In this context, following are the key components in curriculum planning process:

- Placing premium on learning rather than teaching.
- Building capacity among students at each stage of learning for critical thinking and problem solving.
- Locale specificity in the context of a global vision.

- Multidisciplinary and interdisciplinary approaches to curriculum planning.
- Participatory involvement of various stakeholders of education.
- Lifelong and continuing nature of learning
- Generation of new knowledge particularly at higher stages of learning.
- Inculcating desirable skills and competencies.
- Empowerment, not indoctrination as the highest form of learning.
- Responsive to natural and social change.
- Accessibility to multi-source of knowledge and issues to skill component.

Curriculum construction indeed needs a paradigm shift i.e. gradual shift from the tradition bound narrowly conceived book-centered informative tool to a highly dynamic tool which even Professor Nelson A. Foell, University of Georgia, USA, has viewed as an academic device highly responsive to social change. Nowadays, it has compelled the mankind to admit the fact that environment changes shall determine the future pattern and the structure of the society. Social institutions and systems and even human relations need to be built upon by the philosophy of sustainability. On the contrary, the journey of human civilizations towards the future shall be extremely miserable. The curriculum transaction of environmental education at each stage of learning needs to be relied upon the following three major parameters:

- Active orientation towards the development of skills rather than imparting information only.
- Knowledge should be concretely shaped into both soft and hard skills.
- Development of positive attitudes, values and appreciation towards the nature.

A curriculum of environmental education may adopt three major approaches—

- *Disciplinary*—An independent study of the subject having a syllabus of its own with specified content areas.

- *Interdisciplinary*—It is an integration of contents and issues across various disciplines and curriculum.
- *Multidisciplinary*—Content of environmental education is integrated separately into the other disciplines.

The objectives of environmental education are as follows:

- *Awareness:* to help students acquire an awareness of and sensitivity to the total environment and its allied problems.
- *Knowledge:* to help students to gain a variety of experiences and acquire a basic understanding of the environment and its associated problems.
- *Attitudes:* to help students to acquire a set of values and feeling of concern for the environment and the motivation for actively participating in environmental improvement and protection.
- *Skills:* to help students acquire the skills for identifying and solving environmental problems.
- *Participation:* to provide students with an opportunity to actively involve all levels in working towards the resolution at of environmental problems.
- *Empowerment:* to empower students with environment ethics as they become citizens of sustainable society in future.

The approaches towards the realization of these objectives have to be wholesome and inclusive in nature. A model towards this end is presented below.

### Paradigm Shift: A Clarion Call to Curriculum Planners and Pedagogues

Paradigm shift in pedagogy curriculum development process may bring changes in attitudes, values, skills and responsible participation in local decision making process in relation to the protection of environment. Curriculum designed on the principles of environmental science could only pave the way for scientific study of environment which in turn would establish environment ethics in society. It has been observed that the curriculum and pedagogy in most developing countries tends to be dominated by external examination system and generally students study under the pressure of examinations. Therefore both curriculum and pedagogy should have to come out of the confinement of the school environment. These two aspects of teaching learning process should extend itself to the active involvement of parents, family and the entire community. Environmental education, therefore should become a way of life of the all the stakeholders in the school as well as the community. Curriculum and Pedagogy must, therefore, be based on—

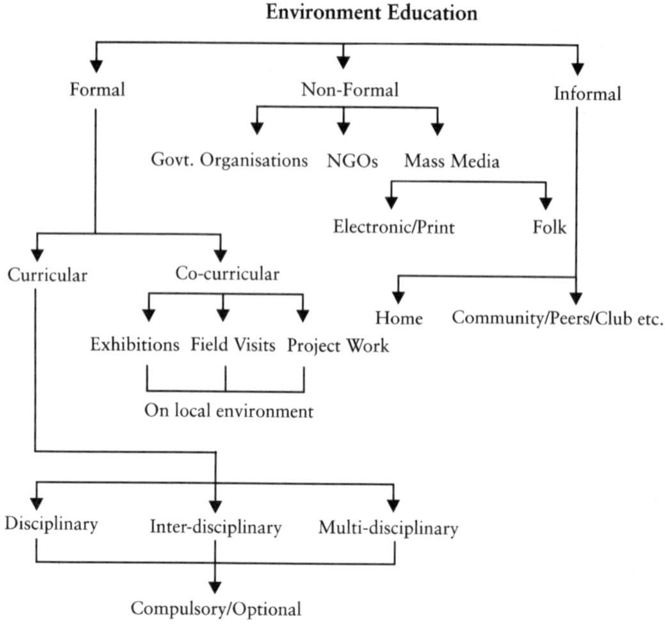


**Fig. 1:** Model on Approaches to Environment Education

- *Principle of Local Contextuality, i.e. Locale Specific*: Curriculum development process and pedagogy of environmental education must be locale specific. The centralized authority may provide basic framework for environmental education. But selection of learning experiences and appropriate skills as well as teaching-learning strategies must be contextualized through locally available resources in relation to environmental concern of a particular locality. This principle hints at community involvement in the process of developing responsible behavior skills in dealing with environmental hazards.

- *Principle of Indigenous Social Perception of Environment:* Indigenous knowledge and skills are constructed on natural background. These are ecologically viable. Therefore social perception of indigenous people and their knowledge and skills regarding natural phenomena must be taken into consideration while designing a curriculum with appropriate pedagogic orientation.
- *Principle of Cultural Tradition:* Cultural traditions of a particular region are the products of nature of that region. These are intrinsically related to environment. Nevertheless the curriculum design and pedagogy should find their necessary ingredients in traditional cultural patterns.
- *Principle of Multi-disciplinarity or Inter-disciplinarity:* Curriculum for environment education must follow either multi-disciplinary or inter-disciplinary approach. Students from each frontier of knowledge need to be sensitized with environment concerns. And pedagogy must follow that particular approach to curriculum construction.
- *Principle of Experiential Learning:* 'Experience' must be treated gateway to all knowledge and skills especially related to environment problems. For example global climatic changes have no longer remained a subject matter of environment scientist only. Therefore experiences gathered amidst the changing environment scenario throughout the world should find their fullest manifestations in curriculum designing process as well as pedagogic realization.

**Identified Components of Knowledge and Skill for Environment Education**

- Building awareness is a key component to environmental education. Awareness involves making the students conscious about the physical, social and aesthetic aspects of environment
- Exposure to real life situations needs integration of knowledge and skill. Real life situations are location—specific. For example, students need exposure to real life situations particularly related to the harmful consequences of deforestation, agricultural pollution, unplanned *Jhum* Cultivation (shifting cultivation), killing and poaching of endangered species and identifying and conserving the local flora and fauna especially medicinal plants.
- Knowledge in relation to the sustainable use of conservation of resources without over exploitation of resources.
- Development of healthy practices (skill) in relation to the disposal of bio-degradable and nonbiodegradable waste products.
- Knowledge about the habitat where the stakeholders (particularly students) live. For example, knowledge regarding local plants and animals, quality of surface water, availability of medicinal plants, existence of wild life species, frequency of flood occurrences and landslides in the surrounding region etc.
- Skill for participation in aforestation programmes.
- Knowledge and skill in relation to the application of indigenous technologies such as indigenous healing practices, medicines and agricultural practices etc. Moreover knowledge and skill should be developed for the prevention of rich indigenous knowledge from being bio-pirated.
- Development of knowledge and skill in relation to the use of eco-friendly products.

- Knowledge and skill in relation to the causes of pollution as well as measures for prevention to all forms of pollution such as avoidance of using pesticides, noise making devices such as horns, minimizing the level of air pollution and above all sustainable use of non-biodegradable products such as plastics, polythene etc.
- Leadership skills for arranging mass movement vis-a-vis environmental protection should receive paramount priority. For example, programmes can be initiated for saving trees and other forms of plants and animal life and participation in environmental conservation and protection activities.
- Developing responsible behaviour skills in dealing with environmental hazards.
- Knowledge about taxonomy of local flora and fauna, relief features, climatic and soil conditions etc.
- Knowledge and skill in relation to the use of renewable sources of energy.
- Knowledge and skill in relation to the sustainable use of non-replenishable sources of energy such as petroleum products, coal etc.
- Knowledge regarding environment legislations.
- Knowledge and skill regarding the use of harmful chemical substances which has disastrous consequences upon the human health as well as other natural systems.
- Knowledge regarding the evil impacts of *jhum* cultivation (shifting cultivation), deforestation and overgrazing, increasing rate of urbanization and other problems associated with development projects.
- Last but not the least, knowledge regarding environment phenomena such as ozone layer depletion, acid rain and the causes and impact of global warming (green house effect).

**Desired Learning Outcomes of Curriculum**

A student at each stage of learning should be able to:

- recognize common objects, plants and animals in the immediate surrounding;
- acquire skills of observations, collection of information, classification, description and self expression concerning various phenomena of the environment;
- understand eco-systems and their interrelations;
- develop awareness about the utilization, overexploitation of natural resources;
- develop ability to identify, analyze and reflect upon different environmental concerns;
- acquire skills to collect, analyze and interpret data and information relating to environmental education;
- develop skills for effectively tackling problems related to the local environment;
- participate in activities and programmes for protecting, preserving and conserving environment;
- appreciate and respect legal provisions for protection of animals and plants;
- understand facts and concepts concerning various aspects of the environment;
- recognize dependence of human life on environment;
- identify local and region specific environmental problems;
- understand the role of individuals, society and the government in protection, preservation and conservation of environment;
- develop awareness about rules, regulations and legal provision for protection, preservation and conservation for the environment;
- develop skills for making judicious use of resources;

- adopt proper ways for management and disposal of waste;
- value attitude of sustainability onto environmental concerns;
- develop skill of practicing sustainability while using non-biodegradable products and nonrenewable sources of energy;
- sensitize and empower oneself with environment ethics of sustainable society.

## Curriculum Transaction Modalities/ Methodologies

- Interactive mode of teaching.
- Demonstration method of teaching.
- Comparative method of teaching.
- Discovery approach.
- Action research method.
- Field visit methods- Field activities like identifying local flora and fauna, measurement of carbon emission and noise pollution etc.
- Community based approach.
- Project method, seminars, symposiums, debate etc.
- Problem solving approach.
- Survey method, Case study and participatory observation.
- Role Playing, simulation approach and brain storming strategies etc.

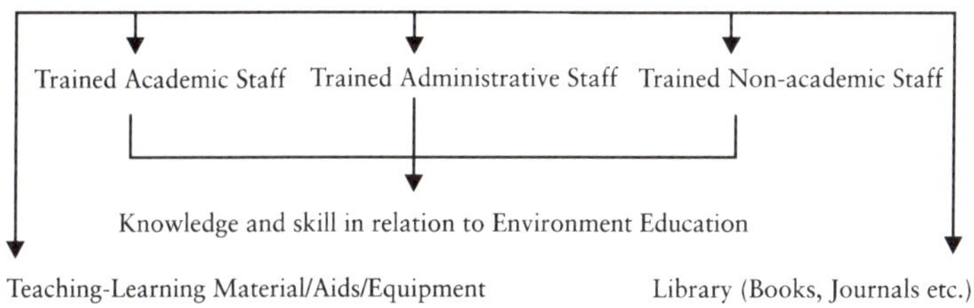


**Fig. 2:** Support system for on-campus curriculum implementation strategy

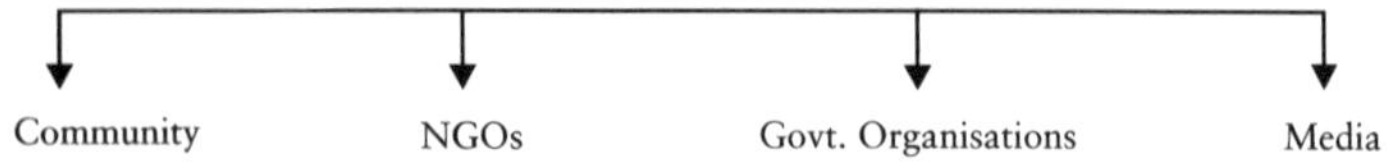


**Fig. 3:** Support system for off-campus curriculum implementation strategy

## Support System for Curriculum Implementation Strategy

Curriculum for environmental education can be implemented through a comprehensive support system strategy both in off-campus and in on-campus educational system (Figs. 2 & 3).

## Environment Education: North-east Perspective

North East Region is a nature's paradise. Mighty rivers, high mountain ranges and plateaus, rich biodiversity, vast wetlands, largest river island, oxbow lakes and other natural resources feature her physiography and climatic regimes with grandeur of uniqueness and exclusivity. Like other parts of the world, global climatic changes have aversively affected this region too. Man made giant technologiest construction of big drums and other unsustainable development projects and industrial units are viewed as huge threats for ecological degradation. It is a matter of hope that the so called ecologically unfit development exercises have not jeopardized this region yet. An eco-friendly curriculum and pedagogy is relevant today for North East region like other parts of India as she harbours numerous ethnic communities bearing inherent sustainable attitude towards nature since time immemorial. Curriculum planning process and pedagogic reorientation should certainly help the learners to value for the protection, conservation and preservation of immensely rich natural resources of this region.

People of this region therefore, need to be sensitized with the potential threats of ecological degradation. Most prominent ecologically high risk threats of this region are—

- Threat to the existence of *Majuli* (the largest river island of the world);

- Diminishing trend of bio-diversity i.e. potential threats to rich flora and fauna in their natural habitats as well as National Parks, Wild life Sanctuaries and Biosphere reserves.
- Threat to wetlands (swamps, oxbow lakes)
- Threat of deforestation that results in frequent occurrence of floods and landslides.
- Unplanned and unsustainable practices of *Jhum* cultivation (shifting cultivation).
- Threat to the existence of aquatic flora and fauna of the rivers and wetlands owing to water and soil pollution etc.

At this backdrop the environmental education has paramount implications in pedagogy and curriculum development with a view to protecting rich natural resources of this region. Curriculum and pedagogy are two most important devices which can equip the learners of this region with necessary knowledge and skills for protecting, conserving and solving environmental problems.

## Conclusion

It is a matter of profound grief that in India, the philosophy of Basic Education of Mahatma Gandhi has not been empathetically valued at all. Through basic education, Gandhiji stressed upon an eco-friendly or "basic needs model centred" education which can put limit to the unlimited wants woven with unsustainable attitude of human beings. In fact he was the champion of appropriate technology that could have paved the way for rapid economic transformation in rural India. As an ardent follower of the ideals of the holy Gita, Gandhiji believed that incessant search for material comforts and their multiplication is an evil and unhealthy indication. His Basic Education remodeled on his thoughts on environment make interconnections between environment, economic development, sustainability and peace. This is equally true of today's eco-unfriendly world where the survival of humanity would have not been possible owing to this present rate of unsustainable industrialization attuned with the policy of profit maximization. Therefore, the chief aim of education should be pivoted around his philosophy of establishing a "basic-needs-model" of social order for future generations. In a nutshell, the need of the hour is a paradigm shift in curriculum development process that will enable our students equip with the knowledge and skill on environmental education in establishing the social order once dreamt by the Father of our Nation. Perhaps that will be a real tribute to his great soul.

## REFERENCES

Bhosle, Smriti (2006), "Environmental Education in School", *University News* (special issue on Environmental Concerns), Vol. 44, No. 12, March 20-26, 2006.

Human Environment (AHE-1) Management of Environment-I and II, Block-5 and Block-6, IGNOU Publications.

Moolakkattu, John S. (2009), Mahatma and the Environment—The Message of Green Swaraj (2009, cover story). *Terra Green-Earth Matters*, Vol. 2, Issue-7, October, 2009. The Energy and Resources Institute (TERI) Publications, New Delhi-110003.

Mrunalini, T. (2007), *Curriculum Development,* Neelkamal Publications Pvt. Ltd. New Delhi/ Hyderabad.

National Curriculum Framework (2005), Position Paper, National Focus Group on Habitat and Learning, NCERT Publications, New Delhi.

Sungoh, S.M. (2007), "Environmental Education and Sustainability: An Environmental Concern In Higher Education", *University News* (special issue on Environmental issues and Global Warming), Vol. 45 No. 44, October 29- November 04, 2007.

Vernal, Louis (2006), "Pedagogy in Environment Education", *University News* (special issue on Environmental Concerns), Vol. 44, No. 12, March 20-26, 2006.

# 29

# Improving Research Programme in Education Departments

*Mohd. Akhtar Siddiqui*

The main purpose of a university, as rightly emphasised by Kothari Education Commission, is to deepen man's understanding of the universe and of himself, body, mind and spirit and to disseminate this understanding throughout society and to apply it in the service of mankind. This purpose is achieved when different departments and colleges constituting a university accomplish their functions of teaching and advancement of knowledge by considering them as complementary dimensions of their work. With the passage of time these twin functions have increased in range, depth and complexity. In the meanwhile, universities have also assumed many new functions in the changing contexts and fresh needs of the society. However, the function of advancement of knowledge is not receiving desired attention due to the deterioration in research environment in most of the universities. It is often argued that the increasing burden of large number of students seeking post-school education is responsible for deviation of attention from research. At the same time, universities in themselves have also been found least sensitive to the changing needs of modern society. Massive expansion in demand for higher education has made it extremely difficult for universities to find sufficient number of such teachers who would have received good quality education and are willing to join teaching profession. Unattractive remuneration offered by universities has further contributed in deterring good talent from joining university teaching, especially in the wake of better pay packages and career promotion avenues offered to them by alternative sectors of employment. As a result, one finds a large mass of the teachers inducted in colleges and universities of mediocre quality which often prefers to keep itself confined to the teaching task that too in a routinised manner. These teachers keep themselves away from research activity on the pretext of their preoccupation in teaching as well as due to their low level of competence in research. At the same time, institutional environment in university departments also fails to push them to engage themselves in research activity. Undoubtedly, teaching is and will remain an important function of a university and a crucial responsibility of the faculty as it helps develop the vision of the youth by extending their intellectual horizons and prepares them to face the challenges of life. However, to keep teaching and training activity in each of its departments constantly relevant and useful in the present and future contexts and in order to provide leadership to society in all spheres of life, it is essential that the university faculty regularly discovers such new knowledge that helps the society to continue to grow and develop and its members receive avenues of better living (MHRD, 1992). Deficiencies in the pursuit of research gradually weakens teaching and training activities and, indeed, it renders these activities largely frozen in time, irrelevant and least useful for the society. Today, the ability to create new knowledge and the capacity to apply it for development has almost become the barometer of affluence. It has rightly been said that the intrinsic strength and the affluence of a nation can be attributed to the strong knowledge base created by independent and original contribution to knowledge (Basa, 2003).

Research in the discipline of education occupies a special significance for it helps in improving and strengthening all aspects of the education system including curriculum, its transaction, teacher preparation and performance, development of teaching learning material, learning achievement, institutional management, etc. on the one hand, and on the other, in formulating appropriate policies and plans for educational development at all levels and for all people. Although the volume of educational research in India has substantially increased during the last few decades, its quality has gradually deteriorated due to several reasons. In departments of education generally primary attention and importance is assigned to initial teacher preparation and in-service teacher education programmes which are of highly compressed nature and are full of various activities. This keeps the entire faculty round the year awfully occupied in teaching, training and supervising student teachers thus leaving very limited time for them to conduct research or guide students in research pursuits. As a result, sketchy supervision and guidance of research activity right from the stage of finalisation of the research proposal through various stages of research study leads to poor accomplishment of the research work. It happens even in those cases where initially the researchers are found quite motivated and enthusiastic about research. However, besides preoccupation of faculty in teaching and training, there are other reasons that impact quality of research in these departments. Sometimes the researchers do not choose their own areas of research rather they work on the topics suggested by their guides that brings down the level of their stimulation and involvement which otherwise could have been there in case they had got a chance and freedom to work in the areas of their interest (Venkataiah, 2001). Similarly, many research scholars with a tacit concurrence of their guides prefer to choose such areas of research which are a mere extension or minor variation of an already accomplished piece of research for, this often allows the researchers to devote less time and effort to complete their work. They do so either due to their regular engagement in their livelihood pursuit and non-availability of ample time for research or due to their preference for a quick research work which can earn them a degree in a short time. It is also partly due to the fact that these prospective researches are not adequately equipped to sense, understand and articulate a research problem. Obviously, in all such circumstances, research work comes out to be of unsatisfactory quality, repetitive in nature and has very little to add to the existing corpus of knowledge or has nothing new to offer to solve educational problems faced by the society. Sometimes lack of ability to guide students in new and creative areas of research also makes guides to approve reproductive kind of research work. The university regulations in several cases also provide enough room for pursuing research without much rigour by not compelling the scholars to be present on the campus on full time basis at least for first couple of years after their enrolment. In most institutions, Ph.D. research programmes in education do not have any course work in research methodology to be completed by every scholar before embarking on actual research work. Only a few universities offer M.Phil. programme in education or research methodology coursework as a compulsory component of Ph.D. programme. Sharing of research work related experiences, difficulties and problems with experts other than the guide and with peers may also contribute to improvement in quality of research. This opportunity is found missing in many institutions. Peer sharing also provides good learning opportunity especially for newly enrolled scholars. It also facilitates mid-course learning, correction and clarification in research work. Hence, there is a need to lay down such conditions whereby all the enrolled scholars would be required to share their scheme of work and the accomplished part thereof with other fellow researchers and faculty members at short intervals at a colloquium platform for mutual learning and further guidance.

Research in education in Indian universities is predominantly confined to the themes of teacher, teaching learning process, curriculum, teaching learning material development and educational administration. There are many such areas in foundations of education which directly impinge upon the educational process and need to be explored and studied in the context of diverse conditions existing in India. However, this aspect of the educational phenomenon has often evaded the attention of educational researchers. In this regard, a pioneering attempt was made at Jamia Millia Islamia some time ago by establishing a unique Department of Foundations of Education which was devoted to the much needed planned and dedicated focus on research and development in foundation areas in the Indian context. This exercise needs to be replicated in other universities also for its own academic worth.

It has also been observed that some research supervisors are always available to guide educational research in any area worth the name. This is partly encouraged by the flexibility or ambiguity contained in the university regulations regarding research programme. It is not difficult to understand the implications of this practice for quality of research undertaken. In this case, researchers are deprived of the opportunity of acquiring the desired level of research competence that they could have otherwise attained while pursuing research under the supervision of competent guides. Increasing rush for acquiring research degree in education these days, which may be true in case of other disciplines also, is often advanced as an important reason for this practice in departments of education. Among research supervisors, a section also prefers to guide those degree seeking scholars who are ready to work in a convenient area. Such students are neither interested in serious and rigorous work nor their guides are so concerned about quality for their own lack of professional ability and commitment.

The research supervisors themselves in many cases do not remain active researchers soon after joining their job or completing their own initial research. They do not keep themselves regularly abreast of the developments and researches in their area of specialization which finally reflects in the work produced by their research students. Supervisors need to develop themselves in a particular area or aspect or set of aspects of the educational phenomenon as their field of specialization for purposes of conducting and guiding research effectively. Professional responsibility demands their active engagement in research as this would enable them to grow academically, broaden their vision in the area of their specialization and deepen their understanding of the discipline.

Its impact would surely mirror in their research scholars' enhanced competence at every stage of research. They would be able to develop a deeper understanding of the problem and phenomena of education and arrive at meaningful results through rigorous probing into the situation.

In order to improve the quality of educational research, therefore, it is necessary that attempts are made at the level of both the research guides and research scholars to take up the educational research professionally and its supervision to be done with a sense of mission. It is also important to clearly identify the areas in which educational problems need to be studied on priority. The research scholars should be given full liberty to explore and choose an area of concern in education of their interest and to uncover the truth systematically. In the interest of quality educational research, the part-time research by research scholars along with their full-time employment needs to be discouraged as far as possible and enrolment for research be preferred on full-time basis so that scholars are able to devote themselves completely to their research work and are really able to gain meaningfully from this exercise. Entry into research programmes also needs to be regulated through such screening mechanism, other than the oral interview as is the current practice, that students with an understanding and aptitude for research in the educational phenomenon may only be admitted. This step alone will lead to marked improvement in research quality. University of Delhi has recently taken a conscious decision in this direction. This needs to be followed in other institutions also.

Good quality research can also be ensured by making the research students undergo a detailed orientation and training at the beginning of their study as it often happens compulsorily in universities in the USA and other countries. A part of this training should essentially be in workshop mode and a sizable section of it must be devoted to development of ICT related skills of research scholars. When the research students get on to the task of actual research then, in the course of completing their study, they must also be required to publish a given number of research papers emanating from their study in reputed and referred journals, both print and electronic ones. In order to be more effective, the supervisors also need to update their own skill of guiding research through their self study and own research work and by publishing their research work from time to time. The quality of doctoral research in education and original contribution to knowledge in the discipline would substantially enhance if these conditions are strictly enforced in departments of education with a sense of professional commitment. One very important requirement for carrying out quality research work in today's scenario where knowledge is expanding at amazingly phenomenal pace is that the researcher must have a ready access to the literature, emerging ideas and new knowledge in his field of study which is regularly disseminated through books, journals, e-journals and Internet. In most of the departments of education, the researchers often feel handicapped due to non-availability of latest relevant material especially standard journals that may help them improve the quality and relevance of their work (POA, 1992). In the present era of IT boom, the libraries in universities and colleges need to be digitally networked with each other at national as well as international levels. Through a central arrangement like INFLIBNET, UGC may help in building up this network and can subscribe to hundreds of journals of education and other related disciplines published world over for the benefit of colleges and departments of education. The NPE, 1986 has already provided for implementing this idea of networking of libraries for improving quality of higher education. In view of rising prices of books and journals, the library funding also needs to be substantially enhanced so that standard stuff may be acquired by libraries regularly.

The departments of education in universities also need to take a decision voluntarily that enrolment of research scholars will be encouraged for those studies which relate to educational needs and problems of the society and which will lead to their creative and original contribution to the corpus of knowledge in the field of education and associated disciplines and will also help in developing a better understanding of the content, delivery and distribution of education.

## REFERENCES

Basa, D.K. (2003), "Quality Assessment in Ph.D.", *University News*, Vol. 41, No. 37, Sept., 15-21, 2003, pp. 12-15.

Govt. of India (1990), *Towards an Enlightened and Humane Society*, New Delhi, Govt. of India, pp. 218-27.

MHRD (1992), NPE-1986 (New Delhi: Govt. of India).

MHRD (1986), POA-1986 (New Delhi: Govt. of India).

MHRD (1992), POA-1992 (New Delhi: Govt. of India), pp. 84-89.

NCERT (1996), Report of Education Commission (1964-66), New Delhi: NCERT, pp. 497-99, 585-88.

Udgaonkar, B.M. (1993), "Scientific Research: Autonomous Research Institutions and Universities" in Suma Chitnis and Philip. Altbach (Eds.) *Higher Education Reform in India*, New Delhi: Sage, pp. 245-76.

Venkataiah, N. (2001), *Educational Research in Indian Universities* (New Delhi: APH Publishing Corp), pp. 1-10.

# 30

# Internationalising Courses of Political Theory in the Undergraduate Curriculum

*Mohammed Viquaruddin*

## The State of Political Theory

Judging from a general survey of syllabi of introductory political theory courses, the critical training we as a discipline are offering our students in political theory is almost exclusively Western. Standard courses in political theory commonly include readings in the Greek tragedies, Plato, Aristotle, sometimes Augustine, less often Aquinas, usually Machiavelli, Hobbes, Locke, Rousseau, Rawls, occasionally Marx, sometime Hume, Nietzsche, Foucault, etc. In general, these courses could appropriately be renamed Political Thought in the Western Tradition. These courses are what we were taught, and what we teach our students, and we have a lot of students.

Between 1991 and 2001, and 2007 thousands of degrees were awarded to majors in political science, and a sizably larger number of non-majors enroll in political science classes. In our current world context, it is critical that Indian and other world college graduates, particularly in political science, understand more that the nature and history of neo-liberal capitalism that is generally taught in political science courses in India. Such limited training is inadequate. This generation of students, and their instructors, should have the ability to understand the cultures and contexts with which the world market places us all in contact. It is incumbent upon the discipline to cultivate transcultural competence in our students and instructors so that we are to decipher political speech across cultural boundaries.

Not only should additional materials be taught, but these materials should be taught with a far more international approach than they are currently in the classrooms? The following sections offer some possibilities that correspond to the period organisation of most political theory courses.

**The Ancient**

Political theory instructors can place assigned readings in international perspective, beginning with the earliest canonical texts. Eduard Meyer (1995), for instance, addresses the visit of Herodotus to Egypt, underscoring how understanding Egyptian thought is critical to understanding that of the Greeks. While Plato's *Timaevs and Critias* explicitly mention Plato's visit to Egypt, the importance of the Egyptians to Greek civilization is rarely, if ever, mentioned in traditional political theory courses. Furthermore, the extensive debates on the influence of Egyptian culture on Greek thought since the publication of *Black Athena* typically go unmentioned as well, despite the availability of numerous articles that outline these debates. Classroom examinations of debates surrounding the comparative and influential relationship of Greek to Egyptian thought would contextualise canonical texts in a broader global context. Moreover, at the very least, a substantive explanation is in order in introductory courses of why political theory courses begin with the Greeks, rather that the Egyptians, or sub-Sharan African thought. An internationalist approach to classical material in political theory may also consider scholarship on African oral traditions in relation to the oral traditions on which the tragedies are based, as well as in relation to the Socratic oral tradition. Segun Gbadegesin argues in *African Philosophy* that "communal wisdom derives from ongoing critical debate and rational inquiry among individuals, which is only popularly formulated later and remembered perhaps unquestioningly, as oral tradition" (Presby Gail-M, 2001). Gbadegesin's analysis reverses the customary view of oral traditions as deficient in critical rationality. His revaluation of those traditions can enrich classroom discussions of folklore as expressed in the tragedies, and the nature of philosophical political thought.

Introducing into the classroom treatments of oral traditions in African thought, including those of Gbadegesin, Teodros Kiros, Gail Presby, and Claide Sumner, would enrich our study of the nature of the Socratic tradition and inform us of how, if at all, knowledge created by the Socratic method differs from that created by the critical method, which produces folklore (Presby Gail-M, 2001). Such considerations would encourage students development of critical skills, as well as their intellectual sensitivity to cultural difference, while also raising the possibility of indigenous African political philosophy, something our current disciplinary curricula generally do not do.

Looking now forward, rather than to historical precursors of the foundational canonical texts in the discipline, an examination of the Islamic world would provide a richer internationalist orientation to introductory political theory courses. The short introductory chapter, for example, of Majid Fahry's *A History of Islamic Philosophy* (2004), "The Legacy of Greece, Alexandria, and the Orient", has been recommended by the Lebanese scholar, Lloyd Precious. Including such pieces, which are short enough to be incorporated into syllabi, adds the important voice of nonscholarship to rest of the world (Fahry, 2004).

## Modern Political Thought

### *Machiavelli*

From an internationalist perspective, an introductory political theory course that includes Machiavelli, can also include Dallmayr's work on the political notion of peace in Confucian thought, which contrasts the Western emphasis of peace. Dallmary's work also directs the reader to primary sources.

*Hobbes and Locke*

Likewise, a course that covers Hobbesian materialism can also include a treatment of Mahatma Gandhi's critique of materialism through the incorporation of such pieces as Anthony Parel's "Mahatma Gandhi's Critique of Modernity" (2003) and/or selections from Gandhi's political tract *Hind Swaraj* (1939). Gandhi's work, informed by the traditional Hindu idea of the importance of the spirituals development of individuals to statecraft argues that corporative soul force is superior to brute force. In addition, informed by the Hindu notion that political economy must be subsumed under conception of the moral good of the community, Gandhi's work levels a critique against Western political economy (Shah, 2003). Both Hobbes and Locke could be placed in conversation with Hindu traditions of political thought.

**Three or Four Concepts of Liberty**

Similarly, in addition to such classic readings as Isaiah Berlin's "Two Conceptions of Liberty", Hobbes, Locke, and Mill's emphasis of rights can be contrasted to the Confucian emphasis of goods and benefits to the community, which continue to influence Chinese politics, and contrasted Hindu and Confucian emphases of communal responsibility for moral and spiritual development and direction, in secular as well as religious Eastern thought (Ware, 2003).

**Non-Western Adoptions of Western Thought**

Obvious modifications to syllabi would include Eastern and colonial adaptations of Western thought such as Franz Fanon's adaptation of the ideas of Jean-Paul Sartre and G.W.F. Hegel and Mao Zedong's conception of communism. But these texts should be understood as products of interactions between cultures, rather than mere appropriations of Western thought, for example, some understanding of Confucian thought and culture would illuminate the form communism takes in China. Indeed, Mao's politics of charisma were supported by the emperor tradition that preceded him, just as Gandhi's liberalism was informed by Hinduism (Keith, 2003).

Rodgers, Daniel T. (1998), *Atlantic Crossings: Social Politics in a Progressive Age*. Cambridge, Harvard University Press.

Shah, K.J. (2003), "Of *Artha* and *Arthsastra*". In *Comparative Political Philosophy: Studies Under the Upas Tree*, eds., Anthony J. Parel and Ronald C. Keith, Lanham, MD: Lexington Books, pp. 141-62.

Ware, Robert (2003), "What Good is Democracy? The alternatives in China and the West". In *Comparative Political Philosophy: Studies Under the Upas Tree*, eds., Anthony J. Parel and Ronald C. Keith, Lanham, MD: Lexington Books, pp. 113-40.

# 31

# Library and Information Science Curriculum in Indian Universities: A Rethinking

*M.A. Prodhani*

Human knowledge is growing on hyper media exponentially. Here measurement of knowledge does not depend upon the totality of printed publications available world over. It is the Internet which actually accounts the growth of knowledge. Knowledge grows in every nanosecond, exceeding the exponential growth value as considered in case of printed publications. The exponential growth of knowledge now is not applicable for measuring the growth of knowledge. This has brought major changes in our existing communication of data and information. All areas of human knowledge have been influenced immensely.

In this new environment, the traditional method of teaching, learning and research have to be moulded in such a manner that they may cope up with the new environment without much trouble and travail. In order to do so, our universities have to think seriously and accordingly, the syllabi in subjects should be modified in such a manner so that the teaching materials and the mental make up of the teachers should have a gradual adaptation with new and advance knowledge for new situation. The UGC after every ten years revises the syllabi of all subjects taught in different universities in India. This period of revising the syllabi should be reduced to five years as it is being done in developed countries in the world.

In the field of library and information science, the syllabi of B.L.I.Sc and M.L.I.Sc courses have been revised and implemented. The present study has reflected some of the important issues which need to be considered for addition in the syllabi of both the courses in L.I.Sc. in near future.

## L.I.Sc. Syllabus in Indian Universities

Present knowledge base of Library and Information Science professionals and teaching community in the field of information and communication technology in India is not in a comparable state with Library and Information Science professionals in the developed countries. This has resulted very less application of ICT in Indian libraries, information centres, etc. and also its incorporation in the syllabus of library and information science course. The root cause of this miserable status is due to the extent of knowledge base of L.I.Sc. teachers in ICT in Indian universities.

There was a big spade work in revising the syllabi of B.L.I.Sc. and M.L.I.Sc. courses in the past. But no fruitful result is observed in the present syllabus. There are many reasons, and some of them are briefly reflected below.

If we study in detail, the academic background of all the teachers in L.I.Sc. courses in Indian universities, we will find that almost all of them are having the following qualifications:

(i) M.A./M.Com/M.Sc.

(ii) M.L.I.Sc.

In addition to the above required qualifications, some of them are having M.Phil and PhD degrees. Almost none of them has Associateship in information science from INSDOC, New Delhi and DRTC, Bangalore. The courses taught in these two training institutions equip the students with sufficient knowledge, which really copes up with the present development in the field of ICT. Unfortunately, in most of the L.I.Sc. departments in the Indian universities, the products from INSDOC and DRTC have been rarely found.

With the background of traditional M.L.I.Sc. degree, it is difficult for them to introduce exhaustive ICT papers in the syllabus. Moreover, with this background they face problem in teaching the ICT papers to the students. In such a situation, the fate of the syllabus for inclusion of ICT papers is in bleak.

Meanwhile, B.L.I.Sc. and M.L.I.Sc. syllabi of some of the important universities in India have been viewed on the Internet. It is found that only two papers—one theory and one practical—on ICT have been included. On examining the contents of these papers, it is found that they cannot satisfy the requirements of the present development of ICT.

Though the contents of M.L.I.Sc. papers cover quite a considerable number of topics on ICT, yet they do not include many basic topics which are very important for the students in handling the digital objects on the Internet.

### Inclusion of Topics in M.L.I.Sc. Course

To accommodate all the topics as mentioned below, it is necessary to include at least one more ICT paper in M.L.I.Sc. syllabus. It is possible to include one ICT paper entitled "Advance Information and Communication Technology" (Theory and Practical) in the revised L.I.Sc. syllabus for M.L.I.Sc. course.

(i) Auto classification and auto cataloguing for organizing digital resources on the Internet.

(ii) Handling of metadata by using Dublin Core metadata elements and other schemes such as EAD (Encoded Archival Description), TEI (Text Editing Initiative) header, VRA (Virtual Resources Association) Core, METS (Metadata Encoding and Transmission Standard), etc.

(iii) Library automation software such as SOUL, LIBSYS, TLMS, TECHLIB, etc. with practical.

(iv) Digital library software both commercial and open source software.

(a) VTLS (http:www.vtls.com), ACADO (http://www.transversalnet.com)

(b) Greenstone (http://www.greenstone.org), DSpace (http://www.dspace.org), E-Print http://www.ncsi.iisc. ernet.in/indest-ncsl-ir), etc.

(v) At least two languages: C++, Visual Basic.

(vi) For web designing: HTML, XML, Java Script, etc.

(vii) Complete idea about National and International Digital Preservation Projects.

(viii) Knowledge on operating systems: Windows XP, Windows Vista, Linux, etc.

In case of classification and cataloguing papers for organizing traditional materials, it is necessary to focus them towards organization of digital and digitized materials.

## New Approach in Teaching Techniques in ICT Environment

### *Development of Class Room with ICT Flavour*

Classroom in any level of education in India is normally, furnished with one chair and one table for teacher, one black board and seating arrangements for the students, including sufficient lights and fans.

In ICT environment, the classroom should be additionally equipped with one desktop/laptop computer with broadband Internet connectivity and one UPS with more than half an hour back up time (in case of desktop computer only). The computer is to be connected with LCD. One big screen should be hanged in an appropriate location so that it is clearly visible for all students in the class. The L.I.Sc. department should have well-equipped computer laboratory with broadband Internet connectivity for both B.L.I.Sc and M.L.I.Sc students.

### *Teacher Equipped with Current Knowledge on the Subject*

Teacher should have updated tacit and explicit knowledge with current information available on the Internet. While searching and selecting information on the web, he should take care of the authenticity, currency and relevancy of information. The topic on which the teacher is to deliver lecture in the class be restructured so that he can provide explanation of any concept by a click of the mouse on the Internet. All the required explanation, concepts, sources, etc. should be kept ready on the computer at the task bar in a minimized form in sequence. Relevant to the topic he should provide very authentic and current sources of information on the web, so that for further study, the students should be highly benefited. There are many online books and journals in open source system on the Internet. Teachers should have access to quite a good number of journals and books, and their links. As a reference material he should dictate or give a print out of all the links to the students. They should be motivated and encouraged to visit all the links on the Internet in the computer laboratory, which is well-equipped with broadband Internet connectivity.

Each student should get one terminal for his/her work on the Internet. They should be trained in the beginning with the logical Internet search techniques. There are many search engines for searching information on the Internet. At least five search engines under the categories: (i) Directory, (ii) Meta-crawler and (iii) Indexer should be taught in the beginning. At this stage they should know all the techniques of evaluating Internet resources as the resources available on the Internet are not authentic, updated and current in many cases.

### *Teaching Method for the Teacher in ICT Environment*

The normal time schedule for a class is 45 minutes. This is divided into two parts. The first part is for 15 minutes and the second part is for 30 minutes. In the first part, the teacher should have a discussion of topic taught in the last class. Importance should be given on the resources on the Internet as mentioned in the class. If any confusion comes to the mind of the students, they should be given clarification during this period. In the next part of 30 minutes duration, he should teach the new topic or in continuation of the first topic as taught in the previous class. In this class also he will have to follow the same procedure as in the first class. And this way he/she will have to continue for the whole year as per schedule.

## Benefits for the Teachers and the Taught

The new approach to the teaching method in ICT environment will provide benefits to both teachers and the students immensely. Firstly, the teachers will be well-equipped with all the current information on the subject he teaches in the class. Because of the online class environment, he will have all the relevant resources on his finger tips. He will now be able to show the sources online and have discussion with the students on the topic relevant to the syllabus.

Secondly, the students will have tremendous exposure to the online knowledge resources for study and preparation for the subject taught in the class. Simultaneously, the students will have vast exposure to the usage of Internet resources in all areas of human knowledge.

## Conclusions

Library and information science course must expose students and the practicing library and information professionals to various components of information technology, keeping in mind that these must supplement and complement the curriculum of library science and instruction patterns. Regular redesigning of the syllabus must be made to include the development of information technology. In the process of restructuring of the courses, an integrated approach must be followed to avoid overlapping and ensure quality control.

Main thrust of curriculum should aim to shifting emphasis from teaching to learning which has to be important element in the new approach to education. This will necessitate re-organizing the curriculum packages, possibly in modular form. Curriculum should be so designed that it would make the education more meaningful to the needs and aspirations of its beneficiaries as well as to make it socially relevant.

Syllabus of L.I.Sc. course may be revised in every five years as it is being done in the universities of developed countries. They are very aware of the rapid societal changes due to tremendous development in ICT sector worldwide. These changes have great impact on around development of human society world over. To keep pace with this development, it is high time to ponder on it and accordingly, our educational system should take shape in a manner so that the products after acquiring university degrees can face the challenges of real dynamic world.

## REFERENCES

Alise: Educating Library and Information Professionals for a New Century (www.alise.org/nondiscuss/kaliper_final.pdf).

Kumar, R. and Roy, S. (2007), "The Role of Teachers in Digital Era", *University News*, 45(36), September 03-09, pp. 8-11.

Laurillard, D. (1993), *Rethinking University Teaching: A Frame work for the Efficient use of Educational Teaching*, London, Routledge.

Prodhani, M.A. and Gautam, J.N.: New Direction towards Improvement of Library and Information Science Curriculum in Indian Universities, Paper presented in International Conference held in New Delhi from 11-17 October 1998, organized by FID, The Hague.

# 32

# Professional Ethics in Librarianship

*T.R. Deivanai* and *J. Selvam*

The field of ethics, also called moral philosophy, involves systematizing, defending and recommending concepts of right and wrong behaviour. Being ethical is also not the same as following the law. The law often incorporates ethical standards to which most citizens subscribe. But laws, like feelings, can deviate from what is ethical.

Ethics refers to well-based standards of right and wrong that prescribe what humans ought to do, usually in terms of rights, obligations, benefits to society, and fairness. As mentioned above, feelings, laws and social norms can deviate from what is ethical. So it is necessary to constantly examine one's standards to ensure that they are reasonable and well-founded. Ethics also means, then the continuous efforts of studying our own moral beliefs and our moral conduct.

In any society, most people accept standards that are, in fact, ethical. But standards of behavior in society can deviate from what is ethical. An entire society can become ethically corrupt.

The library as an institution exists for the benefits of a particular social group. It may be the citizens of a community, members and students of an educational institution or some larger or more specialized groups—the library is a resource learning center and it is a service-oriented organization.

Hence, those who enter the library profession assume an obligation to maintain ethical standards of behavior in relation to the governing authority under which they work for the library as an institution and fellow workers, the staff, to other members of the library profession and to society in general. The ethical structure of the librarian is:

**Framework of Librarianship**

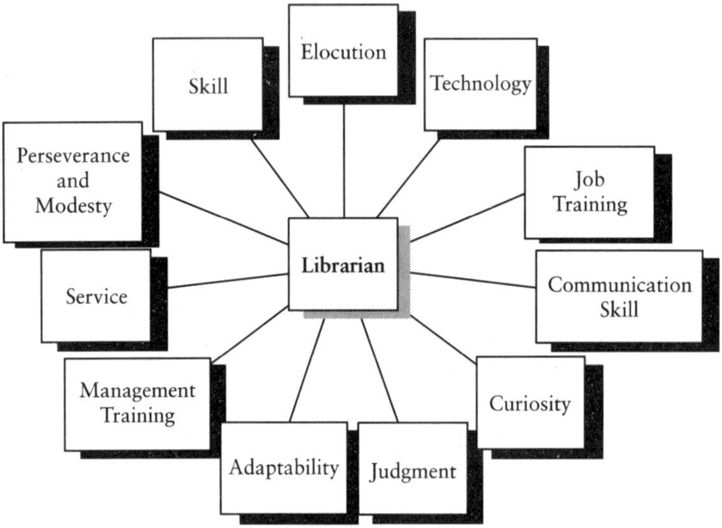


## Characteristics of the Profession

### *Sound Theory*

Librarianship for long was based on rules-of-thumb and practices were involved or improved on trial and error basis. Establishment of library associations gave opportunities for professionals to meet and discuss matters of mutual interest work of documentation brought in scientists from diverse professions into the library and documentation profession. This helped the profession to understand the users better and to evolve new systems and services to meet their demands.

The demands of the users started changing fast. With the result there has been a great thrust on library, documentation and information professionals to understand user needs better, understand the technology, adapt and refine them from time to time to provide pin-pointed information.

### Professional Ethics

A set of moral principles and code of conduct is a necessary guide to professional behavior. The code of ethics are dedication, devotion, determination and commitment of the profession.

### General Social Ethics

- Understand the users need
- Social obligations of the library
- Social behavior
- Equality before services
- Moral responsibilities.

### Task before the Profession

- Technical knowledge
- Manipulative tasks
- Supervision training.

### Seven Lamps of Conduct

- Service before self
- Unbiased
- Split-mind
- Sympathetic behavior
- Tact industry
- Scholarship.

### Area of Specialisation

In this profession, specialist skills reflect the type of information unit; the functions of the documentary chain which it covers; and its subject fields.

The major specializations are archival administration; library administration; information management; documentation services, etc. particularly in the field of information and documentation (I&D).

Another area of specialisation is teaching and research in large information system (LIS). Lately with the development of large information systems and networks, some of the retired professionals have started offering consultancy service and liaison service.

## Code

Library and information profession is a service profession. Library and information professionals should gather information, organize into easily accessible collections, provide mechanisms that help productive utilization of the same by all the eligible clientele.

- Library and information professionals must familiarise themselves with all available information sources that are of interests of their clientele either on demand or in anticipation. They may be in the form of books, technical papers, and other non-print records and even sometimes specialist in any field of knowledge.
- Library and information professionals must be governed by the democratic principle of giving every user his/her opportunity to access to information resources and make special efforts to keep their interest growing towards further developments.
- Library and information professionals must keep service orientation in their professional work. Personal philosophies and attitudes should not interfere with those of the institutional organisations.
- Library and information professionals should aim at the development of their own professional organisation and take pride in the ethos, activities and services. They should encourage younger generation of professionals with their own exemplary services.

## Conclusion

Library and information professionals should cultivate their field of knowledge in a professional way. They should contribute to the field by research, teaching and dissemination through literature.

## REFERENCES

Aggarwal, B.S. (Eds.) (2005), *Education for Librarianship*, ABD Publishers, Jaipur, Rajasthan.

Kumar, P.S.G. (Eds.) (2002), *A student's Manual of Library and Information Science*, B.R. Publishing Corporation, Delhi.

Panda, B.D. (Eds.) (1993), *Library Administration and Management*, Anmol Publication Pvt. Ltd., Delhi.

Panwar, B.S. and Vyas, S.D (Eds.) (1986), *Library Management*, B.R. Publishing Corporation, Delhi.

Tripathi, S.M., and Lal, C. (Eds.) (2000), *Descriptive Questions in Library and Information Science*, Ess Ess Publication, Delhi.

# Contributors

**Saroj Sobti Farwaha** and **Vandana Malik**, Lecturer, Ganesh Dass, DAV College of Education for Women, Karnal.

**Misri Lal Verma**, Associate Professor, Sociology, Vikramajit Singh Sanatandharm College, Kanpur, Uttar Pradesh.

**Pratima Katiyar (Verma)**, Associate Professor, Education, Dayanand Women's Training College, Kanpur, Uttar Pradesh.

**A.P. Sudheer** and **G. Varaprasad**, Lecturer in Mechanical Engineering, National Institute of Technology, Calicut, Kerala.

**Mahendra Sodha**, Disha Academy of Research and Education (DARE), Disha, Katchna Road, Shankar Nagar, Raipur, Chhattisgarh.

**Mohd Muzammil**, Professor of Economics, Lucknow University, Lucknow, Uttar Pradesh.

**P.V. Gupta**, Former Director IIET (TU), Patiala and REC (NIT), Kurukshetra, Haryana.

**S. Chaturvedi,** Director, Institute of Information Technology and Management, D-29, Institutional Area, Janakpuri, New Delhi.

**R.B.S. Verma,** Department of Social Work, University of Lucknow, Uttar Pradesh.

**Tapan Kumar Basantia**, Lecturer, Department of Education, Assam University, Silchar, Assam.

**M.S. Kurhade**, Senate Member of University of Mumbai, President of Association of Non-Government College, Mumbai; Principal, Sanskar Sarjan Education Society's, D.T.S.S. College, Kurar, Malad (E), Mumbai, Maharashtra.

**Dinesh Kumar Paliwal**, Deputy Educational Adviser, Department of Higher *Education*, Ministry of Human Resource Development, Shastri Bhawan, New Delhi.

**Bucherla Murahari**, *Maulana* Azad National Urdu University, Hyderabad.

**V. Vijaya Kumar,** Dean, Faculty of Computer Science and Engineering, GIET, Rajahmondry, Andhra Pradesh.

**Sohanvir S. Chaudhary**, Vice Chairman, National Council for Teacher Education, Hans Bhawan, 1, Bahadurshah Zafar Marg, New Delhi.

**S. Parthiban**, Lecturer in Education, St. Joseph College of Education, Marthandan, Tamil Nadu.

**B. William Dharma Raja**, Senior Lecturer, Department of Education, Manonmanjam Sundaranar University, Tirunelveli, Tamil Nadu.

**Sreekala E.**, Assistant Professor, Department of Education, Pondicherry University, Pondicherry.

**Z. Zayapragassarazan,** Senior Grade Lecturer, Department of Education, Pope John Paul II College of Education, Pondicherry.

**E. Ramganesh**, Reader, Department of Educational Technology Bharathidasan University, Tiruchirappalli, Tamil Nadu.

**Mahabir Singh Dhankhar,** Controller of Examinations, Deenbandhu Chhotu Ram University of Science & Technology, Murthal (Sonepat), Haryana.

**S.K. Singh,** Professor, Faculty of Law, University of Lucknow, Lucknow, Uttar Pradesh.

**Sambit K. Padhi**, Lecturer in Education, Guru Ghasidas University, Bilaspur, Chhattisgarh.

**A.K. Singh**, Professor and Head, Department of Agricultural Extensions, Banaras Hindu University, Varanasi, Uttar Pradesh.

**Surya Rathore**, Associate Professor (Agril. Communication), G.B. Pant University of Agriculture and Technology, Pantnagar, Uttarakhand.

**Deepa Sikand Kauts,** Senior Lecturer, MGN College of Education, Adarsh Nagar, Jalandhar, Punjab.

**Minakshi Vig Aggarwal**, Lecturer, SMDRSD College of Education, Pathankot, Punjab.

**Subimal Kumar Chatterjee**, Professor, Institute of Science Education, the University of Burdwan, Golapbag, Burdwan, West Bengal.

**Sangeeta Sharma**, Group Leader, Languages, Birla Institute of Technology and Science, Pilani, Rajasthan.

**Krishna Mohan**, Erstwhile Professor of English and Group Leader, Languages, Birla Institute of Technology and Science, Pilani, Rajasthan.

**D. Kumar**, Senior Divisional Medical Officer, North Eastern Railway, Kanpur, Uttar Pradesh.

**J.V. Singh**, Dean, Medicine and Head, Department of Community Medicine, C.S. Medical University, Lucknow, Uttar Pradesh.

**P.S. Kharwar**, Lecturer in Education, Ramabai Govt. Girls P.G. College, Akbarpur, Ambedkar Nagar, Uttar Pradesh.

**Dinesh D. Harsolekar**, Director, IES Management College and Research Centre, Mumbai, Maharashtra.

**Santanu Das,** Senior Lecturer, Department of Education, Maibang Degree College, Maibang, N.C. Hills, Assam.

**Debasish Paul,** Senior Lecturer and Head, Department of Education, Kamalanagar College, Chawngte, Mizoram.

**Mohd. Akhtar Siddiqui,** Chairperson, National Council for Teacher Education, Wing 2, Hans Bhavan, Bahadur Shah Zafar Marg, New Delhi.

**Mohammed Viquaruddin,** Developing World Member of American Political Science Association (APSA), 64, Dilras Colony, Asif Baugh, Near Ghati, Aurangabad, Maharashtra.

**M.A. Prodhani,** Deputy Librarian, Hamdard University, Hamdard Nagar, New Delhi.

**T.R. Deivanai,** Lecturer, Department of Library and Information Science, AVVM Sri Pushpam College (Autonomous), Poondi Thanjavur, Tamil Nadu.

**J. Selvam,** Lecturer, Department of Library and Information Science, AVVM Sri Pushpam College (Autonomous), Poondi Thanjavur, Tamil Nadu.